THE IDEAL PROBLEM SOLVER

THE IDEAL PROBLEM SOLVER

A Guide for Improving Thinking, Learning, and Creativity

Second Edition

John D. Bransford
Barry S. Stein

W. H. Freeman and Company
New York

Library of Congress Cataloging-in-Publication Data

Bransford, John.
    The ideal problem solver : a guide for improving thinking,
learning, and creativity / John D. Bransford, Barry S. Stein. — 2nd
ed.
       p.   cm.
    Includes bibliographical references and indexes.
    ISBN 0-7167-2204-6 (cloth). — ISBN 0-7167-2205-4 (pbk.)
    1. Problem solving. 2. Thought and thinking. 3. Creative
ability. 4. Learning, Psychology of.   I. Stein, Barry S.
  II. Title.
BF449.73 1993
153.4'3—dc20   92-36163
                                              CIP

Copyright 1984, 1993 by W. H. Freeman and Company

Printed in the United States of America

1 2 3 4 5 6 7 8 9 0 VB 9 9 8 7 6 5 4 3

To
J. Ashley Bransford
and her outstanding namesakes:
Ann Bransford and Jimmie Brown.

And to
Michael, Norma, and Eli Stein

CONTENTS

PREFACE

This book is not simply for people who love the intellectual challenge of solving problems. It is also for people who dislike problem solving or who feel intimidated by problems. And it is for people who want to help others solve problems. For example, many parents may find this book useful for helping their children perform better in school. Business leaders who recognize the importance of skills that enable their employees to identify and solve potential problems may also find this book useful. In addition, we believe that this book can provide a helpful tool for educators and researchers. For example, we have tried to illustrate how knowledge acquisition and knowledge production activities such as classroom teaching and scientific research are instances of problem solving. By becoming more aware of the processes used to solve problems, people can improve their learning and their abilities to use knowledge to solve new problems that they face.

We do not claim that this book will dramatically increase your IQ, make you wealthy, or free you from all personal problems. However, based on our work with high school, college, and even graduate students, and with teachers, administrators, and business leaders, we are confident that you will find something of value that you can use for the rest of your life. It has been our experience that different people find different parts of the book valuable, probably because people have different strengths and weaknesses with respect to problem solving. Nevertheless, we have not yet met anyone who felt that they learned nothing from this book.

We believe that this second edition of *The IDEAL Problem Solver* represents a significant advance over the first edition. In talking and working with people who have used the first edition, we have had the opportunity to focus on the final component of IDEAL: *looking* at the effects of our earlier efforts and *learning* from them.

We thank the hundreds of people who have given us feedback. Some have shown us how they have creatively applied the IDEAL framework to problems such as enhancing their professional growth, improving their grades, and interacting with their children. They have used IDEAL in creative ways that we never imagined and that have taught us a great deal. Others have helped us see the need to clarify the IDEAL framework.

In this edition we have modified the framework to make it easier to understand and apply. For example, we have modified both the "define problems" and the "act on strategies" components of the original IDEAL framework. The changes take into account the fact that the way we define our problem-solving goals affects our perception of problems and constrains the types of strategies we explore. They also reflect the importance of anticipating the outcome of particular strategies before they are fully implemented. The new edition includes many new examples and exercises that will make it easier to understand and apply the IDEAL framework. Finally, we have added a new chapter that explores strategies for improving how schools and organizations prepare people to think and solve problems.

This edition has benefited from the efforts of hundreds of dedicated researchers in human thinking and problem solving. Thanks to them, we now have a better understanding of the nature of problem solving than we had before. We have tried to keep this book as "user oriented" as possible, and hence we do not spend a great deal of time discussing the scholarly literature on problem solving. Nevertheless, this literature has had a profound effect on our thinking, and we are grateful to all of the people who contribute to it.

It is impossible to thank everyone for the contributions they have made to this book. However, some people have had such a long-term, fundamental impact on our thinking that they deserve special mention. These include Jeff Franks, Jim Jenkins, Bob Shaw, and Walter Weimer. Rick Barclay, Marcia Johnson, and Nancy McCarrell have also made significant contributions to our development. Others who have made major contributions include Ruth Arbitman-Smith, Ann Brown, Joe Campione, Keith Clayton, Reuven Feuerstein, Carl Haywood, and Mildred Hoffman. Nevertheless, none of these people should be held responsible for any of our mistakes.

Some of the people who have played especially strong roles in guiding our thinking for this edition are Linda Barron, Bill Corbin, Jim Dickinson, Linda Giesbrecht-Bettoli, Laura Goin, Elizabeth Goldman, Susan Goldman, Bob Harwood, Ted Hasselbring, Richard Johnson, Charles Kinzer, Alison Moore, Jim Pellegrino, John Pigg, Victoria Risko, Deborah Rowe, Diana Miller Sharp, Robert Sherwood, Richard Troelstrup, Jim

Van Haneghan, Nancy Vye, Susan Warren, Susan Williams, and Mike Young.

We are also grateful for the opportunity to work closely with many people who completed their graduate training at Vanderbilt—people who taught us a great deal. These include Lea Adams, Pam Auble, Sue Burns, David Chattin, Vic Delclos, Jon Doner, Joan Littlefield, Karen Mezynski, Don Morris, Greg Perfetto, and Nancy Vye. Reviews of this book by Bunny Bransford, Wesley Henry, Joy Henshall, Richard Mayer, Thomas Mosley, and Robert Sternberg have also been very helpful. In addition, we are grateful to the many students at Tennessee Technological University and Vanderbilt University who have participated in our courses on problem solving and provided us with feedback.

We are especially grateful to members of our families who have been instrumental in helping us prepare this second edition. We thank Bunny Bransford, Jason Bransford, Ashley Bransford, Camille Bransford, Ada Haynes, and Michael Stein for all their help. Without them, we could not have improved and completed this edition.

Finally, we thank Faapio Poe for her excellent assistance in helping us prepare the second edition manuscript and Diana Siemens and Gina Goldstein for their helpful editorial suggestions.

A number of people have asked whether we, as authors of *The IDEAL Problem Solver,* are ourselves ideal problem solvers. If you think of an ideal problem solver as someone who always knows or can immediately derive the answer to every problem, then the answer is no, we are not ideal problem solvers. As you read this book, however, you will see that our ideal problem solver is someone who continually attempts to improve by paying attention to his or her processes and by learning from any mistakes that are made. It is this *commitment* toward becoming an ideal problem solver—toward continuing to learn each day—that we endorse and try to live by. We find that it is an exciting commitment because we learn something new almost every day.

It is our hope that you too will find it valuable to think about your own problem-solving processes and that, by analyzing them, you will enjoy the continual challenge of discovering ways that they can be improved. And as you make discoveries and observations, we would love to hear from you. Your ideas will help us continue to learn.

John D. Bransford
Barry S. Stein
January 1993

THE IDEAL PROBLEM SOLVER

CHAPTER 1

THE IMPORTANCE OF PROBLEM SOLVING

The date was October 16, 1962. The president and special members of the Executive Committee of the National Security Council met in an emergency session. Information had just been obtained that the Soviet Union was in the process of building missile-launching bases in Cuba. The missiles were capable of carrying nuclear warheads that could destroy most major cities in the Western Hemisphere. During six days of secret meetings, these men had to develop a plan that would remove or destroy the missile bases before they became operational.

Several different plans were considered and evaluated. One plan called for an air strike that would quickly destroy all the missile installations. Another called for a naval blockade that might then be followed by an air strike or invasion if the missile bases were not voluntarily removed. After the blockade plan was selected, the president made a televised speech in which he conveyed details of the crisis to the nation and explained the immediate course of action that would be taken.

Many historians consider the Cuban missile crisis the closest the world has come to an all-out nuclear war. Had these men selected a different course of action for the problem they confronted, the world as we know it might have changed drastically. In any case, we, the people of the world, would have had to live with the solution they formulated, for better or for worse. Such historical events dramatically illustrate the significance of problem-solving skills.[1]

It is instructive to stop and think about the many ways in which our lives are influenced by attempts to solve problems. We studied problem solving for some time before we began to appreciate the following point, which now seems obvious: Our lives are influenced tremendously by the solutions to problems that were proposed and implemented by people who preceded us in history. Solutions to problems such as the Cuban missile crisis and polio stand out as prime examples. However, many more solutions proposed by others have had an even greater impact on our daily lives. For example, you may not think of such things as stop signs, traffic signals, or rules about which side of the road to drive on as solutions to problems, but they are. Many of them were originated by William Eno, often called the father of traffic safety. Eno, who was born in New York City in 1858, became concerned about the problem of massive traffic jams (involving horse-drawn vehicles) caused by the absence of traffic regulations. Eno published an article entitled "Reform in Our Street Traffic Urgently Needed" and thereby focused people's attention on an important problem. He also proposed solutions for this problem, such as stop signs, one-way streets, and pedestrian safety islands—ideas we take for granted today.

Laws and rules represent only a small part of our everyday lives that are affected by other people's solutions to problems. Such artifacts as furniture, clothing, tools, and appliances are also the result of attempts to solve problems. Even our language and number systems are inventions that allow people to solve problems. Imagine the difficulties we would experience if we did not have a language for expressing our ideas, or if we had only a spoken language but no system for producing and interpreting written language. Number systems are equally important. These inventions make it possible to solve a variety of problems that otherwise might be impossible or at least very difficult to solve.

Many of our solutions create new problems of their own. Cars increase the probability of pollution; advances in physics can increase the potential for menacing weapons; medical breakthroughs often raise new ethical dilemmas about life and death; new inventions like computers place new demands on people's ability to learn. It seems that we will always need effective thinkers and problem solvers. Indeed, researchers such as Lauren Resnick[2] and Ray Nickerson[3] argue that now more than ever, increasingly rapid changes in society require citizens who can think, reason, and solve problems on their own. In modern factories, for example, managers want employees who can spot problems that have gone unrecognized and do something about them. Many companies are attempting to improve their operations by helping their employees to develop more effective problem-solving skills.

New Views about Thinking and Problem Solving

How do you rate yourself as a problem solver? We find that people's answers to this question depend on their beliefs about the nature of thinking and problem solving. We will discuss several important ideas about problem solving in the following paragraphs.

Is Problem-Solving Ability Determined by Intelligence?

Many people tend to equate the ability to solve problems with the general concept of intelligence. If they have received poor or average scores on intelligence tests, they feel that they are poor or average problem solvers as well.

During the past decade, researchers have developed a number of important new ideas about the nature of intelligence and its relationship to problem solving. An excellent example stems from the work of Ulrich Neisser[4] who argued for the need to differentiate "academic intelligence" from "practical intelligence." Typical intelligence tests tend to predict how well people do in academic settings. High scores on such tests, however, are no guarantee of successful everyday problem solving. You may have met someone who is very proficient academically but does quite poorly at ordinary problem-solving tasks.

Theorists such as Richard Wagner and Robert Sternberg[5] have begun to explore in detail the concept of academic versus practical intelligence. They find that typical intelligence tests do very poorly at predicting real-world success, such as success in business. They have constructed tests of practical intelligence that do a much better job of predicting people's everyday success. Howard Gardner's[6] work on multiple intelligences also indicates the need to stop thinking about problem-solving ability as equivalent to scores on standard intelligence tests.

One danger of believing that typical measures of intelligence can predict success in thinking and problem solving is that these beliefs can lead to self-fulfilling prophecies. For example, research by Carol Dweck[7] indicates that people may avoid tasks in which they initially experience failure if they believe that intelligence is a fixed entity that someone either has or doesn't have. David Schwartz,[8] a business consultant, voices a similar concern about self-fulfilling prophecies. He notes that one of the major barriers that holds people back in business is their belief that they are "not smart enough." Schwartz argues quite strongly that factors other than intelligence test scores are much more important in determining success.

The Importance of Specific Knowledge

In addition to identifying the need to expand our traditional ideas about the nature of intelligence, research conducted during the past two decades shows that problem-solving abilities often depend on specialized knowledge in a discipline. Our ability to solve problems is not simply equivalent to a set of general problem-solving skills. One implication of this conclusion is that the same individual may be both good and poor at problem solving, depending on the nature of the problem. A brain surgeon may be brilliant in the operating room but be unable to solve a plumbing problem.

Imagine the problem of looking at a chessboard that shows a game after 20 moves and predicting who is going to win and why. We made a videotape of two people attempting this task. One of them, James, was very good at predicting the winner and explaining his answer. The other, Rob, did quite poorly and could not analyze the situation in depth. People who see the videotape remark that it is easy to believe that one is simply smarter than the other. But in fact, both are successful individuals. Something else is going on.

Now imagine another task. You are shown the code for a computer program and are also shown that it does not do what it was supposed to do. The problem is to find the bug (error) in the program so that it can be fixed. We have a videotape of the same two individuals trying to solve this problem, and once again, one does well and the other doesn't. This time, however, it is Rob who does well and James who does poorly.

You can probably guess the reason for the differences in James's and Rob's performance. James has spent literally thousands of hours playing chess; Rob has spent only ten. Conversely, Rob has spent hundreds of hours debugging computer programs written by his students, whereas James's programming experience is much more limited. Overall, the ability of James and Rob to solve problems is strongly affected by the amount of experience they have had in particular areas.

Micheline Chi, Robert Glaser, and Marshall Farr note that researchers in cognitive science have shown clearly that the ability to solve problems is strongly affected by the amount and organization of people's knowledge about an area (for example, chess, biology, sports, computers, physics, card games such as bridge).[9] Similarly, the ability to solve intellectual puzzles is strongly affected by people's experience with these kinds of problems. For example, if you work with puzzles like the ones shown below, you gradually learn that there are tricks of the trade that can help you find solutions with relative ease (see Appendix A for answers). The same is true with the kinds of problems that are frequently found on intelligence tests (for example, verbal analogies such as "doctor is to hospital as mechanic is to ————").

Solve the three puzzles below.

GSGE   ECNALG   BAN   ANA
GESG
SGEG

These observations are important because they illustrate the powerful effects that experience can have on problem solving, as well as the limitations of such expertise for solving problems in other domains. The beneficial effects of specialized knowledge are constrained by the problem domain (for example, playing chess, computer progamming). The beneficial effects of specialized knowledge are also constrained by the goals we have in a particular problem domain. For example, in the previous discussion we noted that James was very good at predicting the winners of chess games; we doubt, however, that his specialized knowledge of chess would allow him to do any better than Rob if the goal were to determine whether the chess game was played by right- or left-handed players or to determine the age of the chess pieces. The interaction of these three variables (specialized knowledge, problem domain, and specific goals) in thinking and problem-solving tasks is illustrated in Figure 1. The tetrahedral model of thinking (adapted from Jim Jenkins[10]) also shows that the ability to use specialized knowledge to solve problems can be influenced by general thinking and problem-solving skills. We will discuss these general skills in Chapter 2, when we explore a model for improving thinking and problem solving.

Routine Versus Nonroutine Problems

When thinking about problem-solving abilities (either your own or others'), it is important to distinguish between routine and nonroutine problems. A routine problem is one that is familiar to an individual because it is similar to a problem that he or she has solved before. In

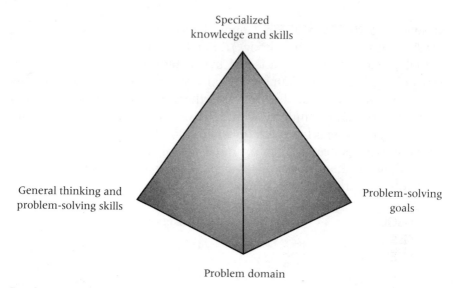

Specialized
knowledge and skills

General thinking and
problem-solving skills

Problem-solving
goals

Problem domain

Figure 1 Tetrahedral model of problem solving. Adapted from Jenkins (1979).

contrast, a nonroutine problem is novel and requires new thinking. *The important point is that any given problem may be relatively routine for one person and nonroutine for another.* In general, it is much easier to solve problems that are routine than ones that are not.

Consider James and Rob, whom we discussed earlier. In chess, certain board configurations and patterns of moves and countermoves are classics that are routine to chess experts like James but not to relative novices like Rob. Similarly, anyone who has taught computer programming knows that there are routine patterns of bugs in student programs that are very likely to occur. Familiarity with these basic patterns makes it much easier to spot bugs and correct them.

An article in the magazine *Dogfancy*[11] illustrates the advantages of dealing with routine problems. In the article, a dog owner writes that he installed a dog door for his two dogs. One uses it all the time. The younger one (five years old) uses it to go out but will never use it to come back in. What can he do?

The dog expert, Bardi McLennan, began by asking whether the door offers the dog the same angle of entrance from each side. She then stated, "One of my dogs alerted me to this one. When I placed a large flat stone as a step outside the door, he was able to go through in both directions in the same body posture." Note that the pet owner's problem reminded McLennan of a similar problem that she herself had encountered and solved. As Roger Schank notes, these "remindings" of similar problems often occur to experts and hence make their problem solving routine.[12]

McLennan realized that the angle of entrance might not be the only feature that was responsible for the dog owner's problem. Therefore, she also discussed other possible causes, such as that sunlight might be reflected off the door from the outside and this might keep the dog from entering, or that the flap of the door might have hit the younger dog in the face when it was following the older dog in from outside, making it wary of the entrance. Overall, McLennan's discussion of the possible causes of the problem, plus her suggested solutions, seemed to come from her great deal of experience with dogs over her career. It is a good bet that this experience makes many of the problems she is asked to solve seem relatively routine.

Whenever you assess people's problem-solving abilities (including your own), it is important to ask whether the problem is relatively routine or nonroutine for the particular problem solver. We say "relatively" routine or nonroutine because most problems will fall somewhere in between. The important point is that even people who are experts in a particular area often have to deal with nonroutine problems. Furthermore, they will not deal as efficiently with nonroutine problems as they will with problems that are routine for them. Problem-solving books like this one are designed to help people learn to deal with nonroutine problems. Anyone who is involved in cutting-edge work needs skills for dealing with the nonroutine.

Our Definition of Problem

Throughout this book, we will deal with problems that are probably nonroutine for you. In fact, most theorists' definitions of "problem" assume that it is nonroutine. The definition that we will use is this: "A problem exists when there is a discrepancy between an initial state and a goal state, and there is no ready-made solution for the problem solver." The initial state is where you are as you begin the problem; the goal state is where you want to end up when you solve it. The lack of a ready-made solution is illustrated by the maze shown in Figure 2.

◼ Some Common Approaches to Problems

A framework for dealing with nonroutine problems is discussed in the next chapter. For now, we emphasize the need to begin to pay attention

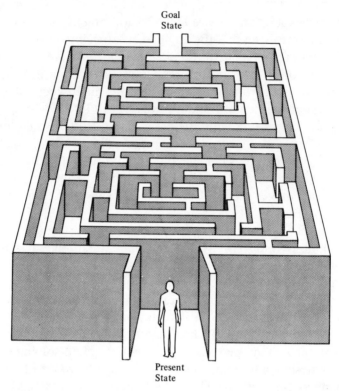

Goal
State

Present
State

Figure 2 A problem exists when an obstacle separates the present state from the goal state.

to your own approach to problem solving, especially when you are dealing with nonroutine problems where answers do not come to mind immediately. When people begin to analyze their approaches to problems, many discover that they often employ a "let me out of here" approach when a problem seems difficult. At times like these there is a natural tendency to attempt to get out of the situation and do something else that is associated with a higher probability of success.

Over time, the let-me-out-of-here approach can result in self-fulfilling prophecies. For example, people who initially have difficulty solving math problems may come to believe that they have no math ability; they may then avoid situations in which they must deal with math problems. Since these people receive little practice with math because they avoid it, their initial hypothesis about not being able to solve math problems is quite likely to come true. In general, it seems clear that people who avoid dealing with problems place limitations on themselves that are not necessarily there to begin with.

In our classes on problem solving we often present the following problem. Imagine that the right front turn signal on your car stops working. Try to figure out why it won't work. For many people, the reaction to this problem is "I don't know anything about cars." Therefore, they assume that they cannot solve the problem. Once they are encouraged to think about the problem, however, they discover that they know more than they realized. For example, a turn signal presumably requires a bulb, just as a lamp does. Similarly, both a lamp and a turn signal undoubtedly require some power supply. The first step in diagnosing trouble with a turn signal, therefore, might be to ask whether the problem is caused by the bulb or the power supply. As a test, we could replace the bulb on the right (the broken side) with the one from the left turn signal. If the good bulb still does not work, we could then consider possible problems with the power supply—for example, a fuse may have blown. The important point is that most people can do a relatively good job of figuring out why something like a turn signal is not working, if they think about the problem.

Negative reactions not only keep us from solving problems that we could solve but also can keep us from exploring new areas. For example, while participating in a weekend workshop on sports psychology, a friend of ours became aware of ways he was limiting himself unnecessarily. Part of the workshop was spent competing with others in such events as Indian wrestling, leg wrestling, and arm wrestling. A major goal of these activities was to help people explore their feelings about winning and losing. Since our friend was quite muscular, he won most of these events. Nevertheless, he felt sure that he was a humble winner; that is, he was confident that his ego would not have been shattered had he lost.

Later in the workshop the activities turned from more muscle-oriented events (such as arm wrestling) to more coordination-oriented events. In particular, participants in the workshop were asked to learn a new type of intricate dance. As the dance instruction proceeded, our friend, who had always believed that he couldn't dance, found that he was making many more errors than were others in the group (for example, he kept turning the wrong way).

Our friend's most important discovery was that he had a strong reaction to his dilemma: "This workshop has gotten ridiculous; I'm going to leave." He almost did leave but was persuaded by the instructor to stay (the instructor was watching for such reactions and knew how to deal with them). The instructor then recruited some volunteers to work with our friend (and with several other individuals in a similar predicament) until they had mastered the dance. According to our friend, this was a very significant experience. It made him realize that he had been avoiding a number of situations because they were difficult at first. As a result of his experience, our friend resolved to increase his "courage span" when dealing with uncomfortable situations. Wertime[13] provides an excellent discussion of the concept of courage spans.

■ Mental Escapes

Actually walking away from important problems is a relatively extreme negative approach to problem solving. In other cases, people may mentally walk away without physically removing themselves. For example, people often think that they are diligently trying to complete tasks, yet when prompted to stop and think about it, they realize that they have not been attending to the problem to be solved.

Consider the activity of studying a text or one's notes to prepare for a test. Most people have had the experience of going through the motions of reading and suddenly realizing that nothing has registered; their attention was directed somewhere other than toward the material to be learned. Similar difficulties can arise when listening to lectures. We begin to think about something else and only later realize we missed what was said.

John Holt[14] notes that attention can be an important factor in classroom learning:

> *During many of the recitation classes, when the class supposedly is working as a unit, most of the children paid very little attention to what was going on. Those who most needed to pay attention, usually paid the least. The kids who knew the answer to whatever question you were asking wanted to make sure that you knew they knew, so their hands were always waving. . . . But most of the time, when explaining, questioning, or discussing what was going on, the majority of children paid very little attention or none at all.*

Holt's observations suggest that differences in attention have important effects on the degree to which people learn. He also suggests that most of us have imperfect control of our attention.

> *Watching older kids study, or try to study, I saw after a while that they were not sufficiently self-aware to know when their minds had wandered*

LEAVES OF GRASS BOOKSTORE

630 So. Main St. Willits, CA 95490   (707) 459-374

Monday-Saturday 10:00-5:30 Sunday 12:00-5:00

Complete General Bookstore

Special Order any book in print, Mail Order, VISA/MC

TOYS ✦ CARDS ✦ TOPO & TRAVEL MAPS ✦ MUSIC ✦ BO

his is what you shall do: ove the earth and sun and he animals, despise riches, ive alms to everyone that sks, stand up for the stupid nd crazy, devote your income and labor to others, ate tyrants, argue not concerning God, have patience nd indulgence towards people, take off your hat to nothing known or unknown, re-examine all you have been told at church or school or in any book, dismiss whatever insults your own soul, and your ver flesh shall be a great po

Preface to the f
tion of *Leave
by Walt
(1

off the subject. . . . Most of us have very imperfect control over our attention. Our minds slip away from duty before we realize that they are gone.

Lack of attention to a task is not simply a result of laziness or lack of interest. Attention can also be affected by fear and anxiety. For example, it can be very difficult to focus attentively on a problem while we are concerned with competing thoughts about personal problems or about fears that we may fail.

Difficulties caused by competing thoughts can be illustrated by considering a problem we presented to a number of college students. We asked them to note their thoughts and feelings from the moment they read the following problem. You might try this, too.

> Two train stations are 50 miles apart. At 1 P.M. on Sunday a train pulls out from each of the stations, and the trains start toward one another. Just as the trains pull out from the stations a hawk flies into the air in front of the first train and flies ahead to the front of the second train. When the hawk reaches the second train, it turns around and flies toward the first train. The hawk continues in this way until the trains meet. Assume that both trains travel at a speed of 25 miles per hour and that the hawk flies at a constant speed of 100 miles per hour. How many miles will the hawk have flown when the trains meet?

For many of the students, initial reactions to the problem included such thoughts as "Oh no, this is a mathematical word problem—I hate those things"; "Boy, am I going to look stupid"; and "I hope I don't have to turn in my answer." Furthermore, these negative thoughts occurred often throughout the five minutes allotted to the task. Such thoughts make it difficult to concentrate on problems, and indeed, despite the fact that the preceding problem requires no sophisticated math skills, a large number of the students got it wrong. (Try to solve it if you haven't done so already. The answer is presented in Appendix A.)

Fears of failure and of looking stupid are not the only feelings that can interfere with attention. All of us sometimes need to perform tasks (study for a test or prepare for a presentation at the office) that we really don't want to perform. When this happens, it is not uncommon to find ourselves thinking, "I can't stand this" or "If only I didn't have to do this." As the psychologist Albert Ellis notes, such thoughts often involve whining.[15] In essence, we are acting like babies and whining about things "not being fair." We can continue to do this if we choose, says Ellis. However, it is usually much more efficient to simply accept the fact that life is not always a bowl of cherries, stop whining, and get on with the task.

The Purpose and Structure of This Book

It seems clear that simply telling people to avoid any negative thoughts while trying to solve problems is unlikely to produce large gains in problem-solving success. People need to know *what to do* as well as *what not to do*. Thanks to research that has been conducted during the past 20 years or so, we now know a great deal about the processes used in successful problem solving.[16] This information is often available only in piecemeal fashion and only in relatively technical scientific books and journals; furthermore, it is usually presented in a way that can be quite difficult to understand. Our goal is to make the existing information about problem solving both comprehensible and useful. We also furnish extensive references to the scientific research that provides the basis for our discussion.

The book is divided into two parts. In Part 1 we present a model for analyzing the processes that underlie effective problem solving, and we discuss various ways that this model can be used to help people access and apply knowledge and skills that they have already learned. For example, one purpose of the model is to increase people's awareness of various aspects of the problem-solving process so that they can analyze their own approaches to problems. We especially emphasize the importance of viewing problems from a variety of perspectives so that creative solutions are more likely to be discovered. The model presented in Chapter 2 is used throughout the rest of the book.

Chapters 3 and 4 emphasize ways to enhance creativity and the importance of being able to criticize ideas. Chapter 3 discusses how the IDEAL model can be used to enhance your creativity. People's abilities to formulate creative solutions to problems are often hampered by implicit assumptions; hence, it is important to analyze these assumptions and consider alternatives. We discuss strategies for making implicit assumptions explicit and for generating a wide range of novel ideas.

In Chapter 4 we discuss strategies for spotting flaws in arguments that others, or we ourselves, might make. These strategies are important because—whether the domain is advertising, personal conversation, or science—we are all bombarded by a host of supposedly factual and logical arguments that, when analyzed carefully, are found to be full of holes.

Chapter 5 focuses on effective communication. A variety of strategies can help us communicate our ideas more effectively. We emphasize that different strategies are necessary, depending on *with whom* we are communicating, *how* we are communicating (orally or in writing, for example), and *what* we are trying to accomplish.

Throughout the discussion in Part 1 it becomes obvious that the improvement of problem-solving skills requires that people be able to learn effectively. Just as we must learn to use physical tools (hammers or computers) to solve certain kinds of problems, we must also learn to use conceptual tools (strategies for remembering, concepts and theories that facilitate the comprehension of patterns, and so on). In Part 2 we discuss ways to learn new information. Chapter 6 discusses ways to improve memory. We emphasize that different types of strategies are necessary for different goals or purposes. For example, some strategies are sufficient for short-term memory but not for long-term memory. Even for long-term memory, strategies must be varied depending on the nature of the problem. Thus, the problem of devising strategies for remembering people's names when you see them is different from the problem of studying for an essay test.

Chapter 7 discusses the strategies needed to comprehend new information. We emphasize that such strategies are different from those required to simply memorize information. We also show why the strategies necessary for adequate comprehension are generally more difficult than those needed for merely memorization. Nevertheless, the extra effort is worthwhile because information that is comprehended can serve as a conceptual tool for solving subsequent problems we may confront.

In Chapter 8 we discuss some reasons that formal educational environments do not always promote the acquisition of knowledge and skills that can be transferred easily to problem solving. We then consider some new approaches to instruction that are designed to help people learn in ways that allow them to apply new information more readily to problem-solving tasks.

■ Notes

1. For more information on the Cuban missile crisis, see R. A. Divine, *The Cuban Missile Crisis.* Chicago: Quadrangle Books, 1971.
2. L. Resnick, *Education and Learning to Think.* Washington, D.C.: National Academy Press, 1987.
3. R. S. Nickerson, On improving thinking through instruction. *Review of Research in Education,* 15 (1988):3–57.
4. U. Neisser, General, academic, and artificial intelligence. In L. Res-

nick (ed.), *The Nature of Intelligence*. Hillsdale, N.J.: Lawrence Erlbaum Associates, 1976.

5. R. K. Wagner and R. J. Sternberg, Tacit knowledge and intelligence in the everyday world. In R. J. Sternberg and R. K. Wagner (eds.), *Practical Intelligence: Nature and Origins of Competence in the Everyday World*. New York: Cambridge University Press, 1986.

6. H. Gardner, *Frames of Mind*. New York: Basic Books, 1983.

7. C. S. Dweck, Motivation. In A. Lesgold and R. Glaser (eds.), *Foundations for a Psychology of Education*. Hillsdale, N.J.: Lawrebce Erlbaum Associates, 1989.

8. D. Schwartz, *The Magic of Thinking Big*. New York: Cornerstone Library, 1981.

9. M. T. H. Chi, R. Glaser, and M. Farr, *The Nature of Expertise*. Hillsdale, N.J.: Lawrence Erlbaum Associates, 1988. See also K. A. Ericsson and J. Smith (eds.), *Toward a General Theory of Expertise: Prospects and Limits*. New York: Cambridge University Press, 1991.

10. J. J. Jenkins, Four points to remember: A tetrahedral model of memory experiments. In L. S. Cermak and F. I. M. Craik (eds.), *Levels of Processing and Human Memory*. Hillsdale, N.J.: Lawrence Erlbaum Associates, 1979.

11. B. McLennan, Prevent problems by considering the dog's viewpoint. *Dogfancy* (August 1991):68.

12. R. C. Schank, Case-based teaching: For experiences in educational software design. *Interactive Learning Environments* 1, no. 4 (1991): 231–253.

13. R. Wertime, Students' problems and "courage spans." In J. Lockhead and J. Clements (eds.), *Cognitive Process Instruction*. Philadelphia: The Franklin Institute Press, 1979.

14. J. Holt, *How Children Fail*. New York: Dell, 1964.

15. A. Ellis, Rational-emotive therapy. In R. Corsini (ed.), *Current Psychotherapies*. Itasca, Ill.: Peacock, 1973, pp. 167–206.

16. A classic on problem solving is A. Newell and H. Simon, *Human Problem Solving*. Englewood Cliffs, N.J.: Prentice-Hall, 1972.

▋ Suggested Readings

Practically Oriented Readings

Tobias, S. 1978. *Overcoming Math Anxiety*. New York: W. W. Norton.

Williams, R. L., and J. D. Long. 1975. *Toward a Self-Managed Life Style*. New York: Houghton Mifflin.

Theoretically Oriented Readings

Diener, C. I., and C. S. Dweck. 1978. An analysis of learned helplessness: Continuous changes in performance, strategy and achievement cognitions following failure. *Journal of Personality and Social Psychology* 36:451–462.

Mayer, R. E. 1992. *Thinking, Problem Solving, Cognition* (2d ed.). New York: W. H. Freeman.

A FRAMEWORK FOR USING KNOWLEDGE MORE EFFECTIVELY

A MODEL FOR IMPROVING PROBLEM-SOLVING SKILLS

In Chapter 1 we noted that people often have difficulty solving problems even though they may have the knowledge necessary to do so. Our goal in this chapter is to provide a model that can be used to improve thinking and problem solving. The model is based on contemporary research and pioneering work in the field of problem solving by such people as Max Wertheimer,[1] George Polya,[2] and Alan Newell and Herbert Simon.[3] We have tried to integrate these ideas into a framework that is easy to understand and apply to realistic problems. The components of the model are represented by the acronym IDEAL. Each letter in IDEAL stands for an aspect of thinking that is important for problem solving.

■ The IDEAL Approach to Problem Solving

The IDEAL approach to problem solving is based on many powerful ideas, yet it is not ideal in the sense of being perfect or the best system that could possibly be created. Nevertheless, it can be very helpful to those who want to improve their problem-solving skills.

The IDEAL approach is designed to help you identify and understand different parts or components of problem solving; each letter in the word stands for an important component of the problem-solving process

I	=	Identify problems and opportunities
D	=	Define goals
E	=	Explore possible strategies
A	=	Anticipate outcomes and Act
L	=	Look back and Learn

Figure 3

(see Figure 3). The IDEAL framework is most useful when it is applied flexibly. For example, you may *identify* an important problem or opportunity, *define* your goals, *explore* strategies, *anticipate* possible outcomes, and realize the need to redefine your goals before actually acting on strategies. In short, you won't always want to go through the IDEAL components in a fixed order. This will become clearer as you gain experience using IDEAL.

I = Identify Problems and Opportunities

The first component of the IDEAL approach is to **identify** potential problems and treat them as opportunities to do something creative. When problems are treated as opportunities, the result is often a solution or invention that otherwise would have eluded you. In fact, it can be beneficial to actively attempt to identify problems that have gone unnoticed. Most books on problem solving begin with the assumption that you have already experienced problems rather than stress the importance of actively attempting to locate them. As we shall see, however, people who identify important problems and treat them as opportunities are often among the most successful in their fields.

The importance of actively identifying problems that provide opportunities for improvement is nicely illustrated by Edwin Bliss. Bliss discusses the experiences of Marks and Spencer, a prosperous retail chain in Britain.[4] Members of that organization discovered a problem that had gone undetected for many years: too much unnecessary paperwork. The company had a procedure for filling out cards on merchandise sold to keep track of inventory; nearly a million such cards were filled out each year. Similarly, each employee was required to fill out a daily time card indicating the number of hours worked; again, this amounted to approximately a million cards a year. After some thought, company representatives realized that all this paperwork was unnecessary and that more efficient procedures existed for inventory control. By treating the discovery of this problem as an opportunity for creative action, the business was made much more efficient. Within a year after the paperwork problem was discovered, 26 million cards and sheets of paper (120 tons' worth) had been eliminated.

Ladislao Biro and his brother Georg provide another illustration of seeing problems as opportunities.[5] They were proofreaders and spent a great deal of time checking for errors. To communicate these errors to others, they needed to write things down, and it was important to write in ink because pencil often fades. However, the only way to write in ink was to use a fountain pen, which was messy and time-consuming. Although you are probably not familiar with the names of these men, you are undoubtedly familiar with their invention, the ballpoint pen. The company they created is now part of a corporation known as BIC.

A common reason for people's failure to identify problems and view them as opportunities is that they do not stop to think about the possibility of improving a situation. Instead, they tend to take inconveniences and unpleasant situations for granted and accept them as facts of life. Our earlier discussion of traffic congestion caused by the lack of traffic rules illustrates this. People in the 1850s presumably did not like traffic congestion, but most did not take the time to ask whether it might not represent an opportunity for creative thinking. Until this was done, no one attempted to consider systematically how the problem might be solved.

A friend of ours recently discovered an example from his everyday life of taking something for granted rather than adopting a problem-solving approach: the task of frying bacon. For years he had never questioned the fact that he often got splattered with grease. He simply accepted this as a fact of life.

One day, while looking through a mail-order catalog, our friend discovered the object illustrated in Figure 4. This device does an excellent job of protecting cooks from hot, splattering bacon grease. What impressed our friend most was not the invention itself, which represented a relatively straightforward solution to the grease problem. Instead, he was impressed that someone had identified the problem in the first place and viewed it as an opportunity. Our friend had never thought explicitly about the fact that splattering grease signified the existence of a problem that, once identified, might be solved.

Figure 4   An invention for reducing grease splatters.

Mail-order catalogs provide fascinating testimony of the importance of identifying problems and turning them into opportunities. The objects illustrated in Figure 5 represent just a few of our favorite inventions.[6] Note that *the first step taken by the inventors of these objects was to identify the problems that the objects were designed to solve.* Ideally, an inventor wants to identify problems shared by a large number of people. This increases the probability that the inventions will sell. (Ask yourself whether you have faced the problems that the inventions in Figure 5 are designed to solve.)

■ Failure to Identify the Possibility of Future Problems

The preceding discussion emphasized situations in which people tended to accept unpleasant situations and as a result failed to ask whether they pointed to the existence of a problem that might be solved. Other examples of the importance of identifying problems are situations in which one fails to realize that actions or policies may lead to problems later on. For example, during the 1980s the United States relaxed the regulation of the banking industry, making it easier for banks to make speculative loans. Few people realized the magnitude of the problem that would ensue as real estate values declined. The U.S. taxpayers have already paid about $100 billion to rescue failed banks, and some estimate the total cost will be closer to $500 billion. On a more everyday level, people who carefully balance their checkbooks after each transaction are less likely to experience the trauma (and expense) of an overdrawn account.

Consider the following example of the importance of predicting problems that may arise in the future. Imagine that your phone rings at

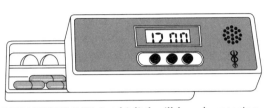

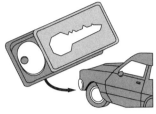

MEDICINE CLOCK. Set this little pill-box alarm to ring every ½, 1, 2, 4, 8, or 12 hours, and it plays a little song to remind you to take your medicine.

DON'T LOCK YOURSELF OUT OF HOUSE, CAR! Magnetic cases hide spare keys safely.

A QUICK TWIST opens the most stubborn jars and bottles!

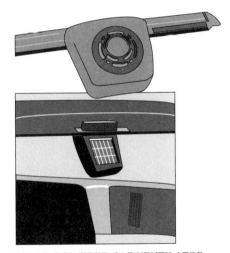

SOLAR-POWERED CAR VENTILATOR. Reduces heat build-up without leaving windows open.

Figure 5　Inventions designed to solve some common problems.

3 A.M. and a man asks, "Is this Home Pac Pizza?" What should you do? If you simply say, "No, you have the wrong number," you will have failed to anticipate the problem the caller will face as soon as he hangs up: knowing whether the number itself was wrong or he had merely mis-dialed.

Several years ago, after moving and receiving a new phone number, one of us began to receive calls at all hours of the night. The callers all asked about pizza deliveries, so there seemed to be some explanation for the calls. As it turned out, the new number provided by the phone company had previously been the number of an all-night pizza place.

When the calls first started coming in, we would say, "No, you have the wrong number" and try to go back to sleep as quickly as possible. Without fail, the phone would ring again 30 seconds later and the same caller would be on the line. Since the number of the pizza place was in the current phone book, the callers assumed they had misdialed the first time around.

Once we identified the problem with the way we answered the phone, we changed our strategy, saying, "The number has been changed." The moral of the story is that it pays to look for potential problems. If problems are not identified, solutions to them are unlikely to be proposed.

D = Define Goals

The second aspect of the IDEAL approach to problem solving is to carefully **define** your goals in the problem situation. This is different from identifying the problem. For example, a group of people could identify the *existence* of a general problem and agree that it represents an opportunity but still disagree about what their *goals* should be. Different goals often reflect differences in how people understand a problem.

Consider the problem of disposing of waste generated by individuals and businesses. Although there is general agreement that we are running out of space in our landfills, there are many different ways to define our goals in this situation. One possible goal would be to find alternative ways of disposing of trash other than landfills. Another would be to reduce the amount of trash generated in the first place. Different goals can lead people to *explore* very different strategies for solving a problem. If our goal is to find alternative ways of disposing of trash, we might consider such ideas as incineration or sending the trash to some remote location. On the other hand, if our goal is to reduce the trash being generated, we might consider recycling or encouraging companies to package goods in reusable containers. Of course, you often may want to pursue multiple goals.

The difference between identifying problems that represent opportunities and defining one's goals can be clarified further by considering the example of the frying bacon. A number of people might *identify* the splattering grease as a problem representing an opportunity. Nevertheless, the way they define their goals could differ. One possible goal would be to reduce the heat that causes grease to splatter. Here the emphasis is on the importance of heat, and the solution to the problem would focus on ways to reduce this factor. One solution is to turn down the heat on the stove (assuming that one is cooking over a stove). If the heat source is not variable (if one is cooking over a campfire, for example), the solution could be to increase the distance between the frying pan and the fire.

Another way to define your goal could be to make people less susceptible to burns from bacon grease. This emphasizes people's vulnerability to burns, and the solutions would focus on ways to make them less vulnerable. A long-sleeved, heat-resistant glove would be a good solution given this definition of the problem.

A third goal would be to reduce the distance the hot grease travels. This goal leads one to consider that hot grease splatters and can travel relatively long distances; the solution would therefore focus on ways to decrease the grease's journey. The invention illustrated in Figure 4 is one solution that might be expected to stem from such a problem definition.

James Adams provides an excellent example of how our problem-solving goals can affect the strategies we consider.[7] He describes the experiences of a group of engineers who were attempting to design a mechanical tomato picker that could harvest tomatoes in large quantities without bruising them.

The engineers initially defined their goal as *optimizing the design of mechanical pickers so that tomatoes do not get bruised and damaged*. As you can imagine, this led them to consider various strategies for modifying the machine, such as slowing it down to reduce the impact or padding its arms. Although all of these solution strategies were plausible, none was considered a breakthrough.

It wasn't until people considered alternative ways of defining the goal—such as *creating a tomato that is less likely to be bruised*—that they were able to explore a more productive solution like breeding tomatoes that would be less likely to be damaged by mechanical pickers. By exploring strategies to modify the tomato, the problem was eventually solved. Growers and packers can now supply grocery stories with large quantities of inexpensive, unbruised tomatoes.

We have found that people often fail to consider alternative goals when they attempt to solve a problem. Instead, they jump immediately to the exploration of strategies. For example, when one of us was working with a team of engineers who were exploring strategies to protect people in automobile crashes, most of those involved immediately started exploring such strategies as better shoulder harnesses and energy-absorbing barriers that could be placed between the driver and the steering wheel. These strategies were all related to the goal of preventing people from smashing into the steering wheel and dashboard. When people realized there were alternative goals for solving this problem, such as preventing crashes or reducing the damage caused to humans hitting the dashboard, they began to search for information that was relevant to strategies such as braking systems that are automatically activated when a crash is imminent or soft, shock-absorbing steering wheels and dashboard components.

The Importance of Conceptual Inventions

People do not simply invent objects (such as a splatter screen to protect against hot grease) that help them solve various problems. They also invent or create concepts and ideas, and these frequently reflect the goals people have in particular problem situations. The creation of units of measurement, such as *miles per gallon, passenger-miles per gallon,* and *miles per tankful,* are cases in point.

Imagine that you are a consultant for a company that wants to purchase a fleet of vehicles to be used to transport executives to and from work. Your task is to find the most fuel-efficient way to reach the company's goal. One goal could be to find the type of vehicle that gets the most *miles per gallon.* This particular goal may focus your attention on the most fuel-efficient *vehicle* that can be used to transport an executive to and from work.

Another way to define your goal might be to find a vehicle that can transport the largest number of executives who live close to one another to and from work. In this case, you might evaluate different types of vehicles in terms of *passenger-miles per gallon* rather than merely miles per gallon. Emphasizing passenger-miles might suggest that it would be more economical to purchase vans or even a bus.

Several years ago, when gasoline was scarce because of a severe oil shortage, many car makers focused on the concept of *miles per tankful.* For people who had to travel long distances with no assurance of finding a gas station, the unit of miles per tankful was more relevant than miles per gallon. The goal in that situation was not to find a vehicle that would permit people to go the most miles on the fewest gallons, but to find a vehicle that would allow people to go the greatest distance without having to stop for gas.

E = Explore Possible Strategies

The third component of the IDEAL approach to problem solving is to **explore** alternative approaches to solving a problem. This often involves a reanalysis of your goals plus a consideration of options or strategies that might be employed to achieve those goals.

In Chapter 1 we discussed some approaches to problems that people often do not realize they are taking. These approaches include physical escapes from problem situations (the let-me-out-of-here approach), as well as mental escapes in which one avoids problems by thinking of something else. However, even when people explicitly try to solve problems they often fail to use appropriate strategies. This is in part because many people seem to be unaware of the importance of taking strategic approaches to problems. In other cases people may be aware of the *general* importance of strategies yet not have learned the *specific* strategies needed for the problem they are trying to solve.

One way to think about strategies is in terms of their generality. Some strategies for problem solving are very general and apply to almost any problem you might consider. Others are very specific and apply only in a small set of circumstances. We begin by discussing some relatively general strategies and then consider the issue of specific strategies that are appropriate to particular types of problems.

■ The Importance of Systematic Analysis

Consider first the general process of analyzing problems systematically. When we watch others solve problems we cannot observe what goes on in their heads. It is therefore easy to assume that their answers just came to them and that, if answers don't just come to us, there is nothing we can do.

Of course, there are times when answers do seem simply to pop into one's mind. If you are asked, "What's two times two?" for example, you automatically say, "Four"; the answer is overlearned. However, consider the following problem.

What day follows the day before yesterday if two days from now will be Sunday?

Arthur Whimbey and Jack Lochhead have asked people who were good at problems like these to think aloud as they solved them.[8] In no case did people simply read the problem and then have the answer pop into their minds. Instead, these experienced problem solvers took a very careful, systematic approach. In particular, they usually broke complex problems into simpler ones that could each be solved more easily. Given the problem just presented, for example, effective problem solvers might ask themselves:

1. What is today if two days from now will be Sunday? (Friday)
2. If today is Friday, what is the day before yesterday? (Wednesday)
3. What day follows Wednesday? (Thursday)

The problem becomes quite simple when broken into its component parts. Furthermore, human beings seem to *need* to break complex problems into component parts in order to succeed.

Proceeding systematically is also necessary for effective reading comprehension. Arthur and Linda Whimbey provide information relevant to this point.[9] They presented the following passage to college students who had comprehension difficulties.

> If a serious literary critic were to write a favorable, full-length review of How Could I Tell Mother She Frightened My Boyfriends Away, Grace Plumbuster's new story, his startled readers would assume that he had gone mad, or that Grace Plumbuster was his editor's wife.

The Whimbeys note that the college students who were poor comprehenders failed to take a systematic approach to the problem. They state:

> This was the first sentence of a reading comprehension article, and I had to stop for a moment and reread a portion of it in order to understand its meaning completely. Not so for the low-aptitude student I was testing. He was halfway down the page by the time I had the details of the first sentence sorted out. I asked him if he understood the sentence, and he answered "No, not really." So I suggested he give it another try.

The Whimbeys go on to note that good readers are much more systematic in their efforts to comprehend information.

> *To the poor reader, however, the pattern of gradual, sequential construction of exact meaning is totally foreign. One-shot thinking (Bereiter and Englemann's term) is the basis on which the poor reader makes interpretations and draws conclusions.*

The Importance of Using External Representations

For many problems it is easy to consider all the relevant information without experiencing a strain on short-term memory capacity. As the problems we work on increase in complexity, however, it becomes more and more difficult to keep track of all this information. Indeed, in some situations the problem solver's goal may be to find a good way of keeping track of it. Assume, for example, that you are confronted with the task of operating a large corporation or even managing a small business inventory. People responsible for such tasks often rely on computers, charts, and graphs to help them represent all the information needed to make purchasing and management decisions. Without these aids, they could not cope with the deluge of information.

Of course, one does not have to operate a business to run into this difficulty. Experienced problem solvers often keep track of information by creating external representations. Rather than trying to keep all the information in their heads, they move it into the outside world—they put it on paper, for example, so they can think more freely about the problem they are trying to solve.

As an illustration, try the following problem.[10]

> There are three separate, equal-sized boxes. Inside each box are two separate, small boxes, and inside each of the small boxes are four even smaller boxes. How many boxes are there altogether?

Many people quickly realize the need to represent the problem by drawing, but many others do not. We know college students who attempted to do this problem in their heads and had difficulty with it. This was especially true of younger students with whom we have worked (fourth and fifth graders). Performance improved considerably when the students were prompted to draw a representation of the problem (although there is still one aspect of the problem that is easy to overlook, even after it is drawn out; the answer to this problem appears in Appendix A).

Here is another problem that requires an externalization of memory (though that's not all it requires).

A man had four chains, each three links long. He wanted to join the four chains into a single, closed chain. Having a link opened cost 2 cents and having a link closed cost 3 cents. The man had his chains joined into a closed chain for 15 cents. How did he do it?

By actually drawing the four chains, you don't have to use your memory to keep imagining them (the answer to the problem appears in Appendix A).

There are many other ways of externalizing memory to keep track of information. Additional examples, such as the use of graphs and Venn diagrams, are discussed later. For the moment, the important point is that problems can often be represented in a variety of ways, yet some representations are more likely to lead to efficient solutions than others. For example, if you are asked, "What is two-thirds of one-half?" you might represent it on paper as $2/3 \times 1/2$. A simpler way to think of the problem is "What is one-half of two-thirds?"

It is important to recognize that the most effective way to represent information will depend on the nature of the problem and how we define our goals. John Hayes[11] and Diane Halpern[12] note that some problems are better solved if one uses a verbal representation, whereas others are better represented visually or perhaps mathematically. In some situations the most effective methods for representing information may differ from those that we typically use. For example, Ruth Day[13] has found that people often fail to use representations that would make it easier to achieve their goals. Effective problem solvers explore a variety of representations. We will explore alternative ways of representing information later when we consider strategies that can facilitate learning.

Some Additional General Strategies

In addition to working systematically, breaking a problem into parts, and using external representations, good problem solvers rely on other general strategies to help them achieve their goals. Working a problem backward is one such strategy. In many situations a problem can be worked backward more easily than it can be worked forward. For example, imagine that you have to meet someone for lunch at a restaurant across town and you do not want to be late. It is much easier to solve the problem of determining when to leave by working backward: If you wanted to arrive at noon and you determined that it would take 30 minutes to get to the restaurant, you could solve the problem easily by working backward in time (12 A.M. – 30 minutes = 11:30 A.M. departure). Generally speaking, working backward is a good strategy to use whenever the goal state of a problem is clear and the beginning state is unclear.

Consider the following problem (see Appendix A for the answer).

> It is 4 P.M. and you have just learned that you are expected for an important company meeting in Chicago at 8 the next morning. There are two flights open. One is a dinner flight that leaves at 6 P.M. and arrives in Chicago at 6 A.M. the next day. The other flight departs at 7:30 P.M. and arrives in Chicago at 7:30 A.M. the next day. When you arrive in Chicago you will need to wait 20 minutes for your luggage and it will take 20 minutes by taxi to get to your meeting. Which flight should you take, and will you need to buy dinner?

Another general strategy that good problem solvers often use is to work out a complex or abstract problem by focusing on a simpler, specific situation.[14] Building scale models or performing experiments that simulate certain characteristics of a real-world environment are good examples of this strategy. Consider the following problem (see Appendix A for the answer).

> You are the director for an upcoming racquetball tournament, and 103 people have entered the open single-elimination tournament (after losing once, the player is eliminated). If you need a score card for each match, how many cards will you need if each player shows up? (*Hint:* Work out the problem for a very simple case first.)

The Importance of Specialized Concepts and Strategies

So far, our discussion of the *explore* phase of IDEAL has emphasized such strategies as breaking a problem into parts, working backward, and using a specific case. These are *general* strategies that are important for problem solving. However, studies of effective problem solvers reveal that they have much more than a repertoire of general strategies; they also have a great deal of specialized knowledge that allows them to understand when, how, and why to apply a host of specific strategies. It is very difficult to solve problems without knowledge of these specifics.[15]

Consider the following problem, which was presented to college students by Bob Sherwood and his colleagues.[16]

> In the movie *Raiders of the Lost Ark*, Indiana Jones successfully removed a golden idol from a booby-trapped platform by substituting something that weighed approximately the same—a bag of sand. Assuming the golden idol was solid gold and that it and the bag of sand were approximately the same size, is it reasonable to assume that the idol and the bag of sand weighed approximately the same?

To solve this problem, you clearly need to do more than break the problem into parts. You also need some way to estimate the weight of a bag of sand and a golden idol of approximately the same volume. Since the objects are not available, you cannot weigh them directly. How else might you proceed?

People who have learned and understood the concept of density are able to generate a strategy for solving this problem. They know that different types of materials have different densities and that density tables can be found in some science texts. By consulting these tables, it is easy to determine that the density of a solid-gold object is approximately 19.4 grams per cubic centimeter, whereas the density of sand is approximately 2 grams per cubic centimeter. This means that a golden idol of the size depicted in the movie would weigh approximately 60 pounds. In contrast, the bag of sand would weigh only about 6 pounds.

Note that the strategy of consulting a density table to solve the Indiana Jones problem requires knowing about the concept of density. Without it, it is very difficult to know how to proceed. There is often no substitute for specialized knowledge when solving certain types of problems. For example, by learning concepts in algebra and geometry (concepts that have been refined over the centuries), it becomes possible to solve a variety of problems that otherwise would be extremely difficult if not impossible to solve. Similarly, concepts in physics enable people to solve such problems as how to put a satellite into orbit at a particular distance from the earth, and concepts in biology help us to alleviate various infectious diseases. All areas of study, including biology, psychology, economics, physics, and chemistry, among many others, involve core concepts and theories that people have found helpful in defining and solving important problems. These concepts actually *simplify* the process of problem solving.

For a simple illustration of the power of concepts, consider the drawings in Figure 6. By prompting people to make use of concepts they

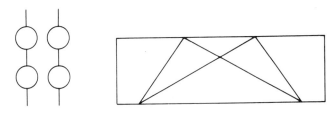

Figure 6   Some perceptual patterns.

have already learned, one can help them see these drawings in a new way. The first can be viewed as a bear climbing up the opposite side of a tree and the second as the Eiffel Tower viewed from the inside of an armored car. Note how one understands the drawings differently when they are viewed from these perspectives. The philosopher N. R. Hanson argues that the creation of new scientific theories fulfills an analogous function: It enables people to conceptualize events in new and previously unappreciated ways.[17]

That concepts provide tools that have powerful effects on problem solving has important implications. The most important is that *people who want to develop effective problem-solving skills must become effective at learning about relevant conceptual tools.* Our discussion in Part 2 focuses on the problem of developing more effective learning skills.

A = Anticipate Outcomes and Act

So far we have emphasized the importance of *identifying* problems and opportunities to be creative, *defining* goals, and *exploring* plans or strategies for solutions. Once a strategy is selected, it is important to **anticipate** possible outcomes and then **act** on that strategy. Anticipating possible outcomes can save you from actions you may regret later on.

Several years ago the Coca Cola Company introduced a new cola and stopped producing the old one. The result was not what the company either expected or wanted. Millions of people wanted the old product, and the company had to cope with a great deal of negative reaction and publicity. Eventually the old product was reintroduced as Classic Coke.

Could the Coca Cola Company have avoided its costly error? Hindsight is better than foresight, of course, but it seems possible that the company could have anticipated the negative consequences of its strategy. For example, it could have asked people how they would feel if the drink they had been purchasing all their lives were no longer available.

An article in the *Wall Street Journal*[18] discusses the importance of anticipating the consequences of one's strategies. Entitled "Building a Better Mousetrap Doesn't Ensure Success," the article discusses the plight of several companies that have attempted to deal with a problem faced by thousands of stores across the country: the theft of shopping carts. Since the carts cost around $90 each, a store can lose a considerable amount of money in a year.

Different companies have come up with different solutions for the shopping cart problem. Several of them involve locking up carts when they are not in use. For example, customers may have to pay to unlock a cart and get their money back when they return the cart to its original location.

Imagine that you are a grocery store owner trying to decide whether to invest in an antitheft shopping cart system. There are a number of steps you might take to anticipate the effects of implementing such as system. First you might estimate the number of carts that you lose per year, calculate the cost, and decide that the locked-cart system would pay for itself within a year. Then you might test the invention that locks up the carts and find that it works very reliably. Finally, you might recall having seen similar types of devices in airports and conclude that since the invention worked there it should work for your store as well.

Ideally, there are additional steps that you would take before purchasing a locked-cart system. One concern should be customer perception—you need to anticipate their reactions to locked carts. A negative reaction could be caused by inconvenience. If the cart system requires customers to have correct change, what will they do when they don't have it? If the store is busy, many customers will not want to spend time standing in line at a change machine.

Another, potentially more serious, reaction to a locked-cart system is that many customers will react negatively if a store suddenly appears not to trust them. The consequences could be severe. Note that people are probably much less likely to feel the same way about locked-cart systems in airports. Airports are visited by masses of people, and many other types of security measures have already been put in place to protect the public. Also, airports usually have a monopoly on air travel so that customers cannot always seek other alternatives. Therefore, the fact that a system works in an airport may not mean that it will work well someplace else.

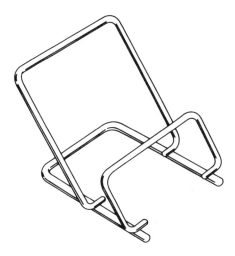

Figure 7 A book holder.

The Importance of Acting on Strategies to Evaluate Outcomes

In many situations we have to take a more active role in testing our strategies before we can anticipate possible outcomes. For instance, building and testing prototypes can often help you anticipate the outcomes of particular strategies. Imagine that you have built a prototype of a cookbook holder like the one shown in Figure 7 and are trying to decide whether to manufacture it in large quantities. It is designed to let people read a cookbook while their hands are busy preparing food. Does it have flaws? Can it be improved? By actively using it in various settings, you may be able to discover features that would improve your prototype considerably. It can also be useful to include in your thinking a worst-case scenario—the worst thing that might happen given your strategy or invention. This often leads to ideas for alternative strategies or designs. An alternative design for a cookbook holder—a design that is quite useful in certain settings—is illustrated in Appendix A.

For another example of anticipating outcomes, consider the familiar task of attempting to do well on an upcoming exam. Assume that you have defined your goal (for example, to learn the first three chapters in the book) and have explored some possible study strategies. One might be to read each chapter twice and make sure you understand everything you read. Will that strategy be sufficient to achieve your goal of doing well on the test?

Most students know that they have to anticipate the consequences of using a particular study strategy in light of the test requirements. If the test will involve a presentation of one or two paragraphs from the text with the requirement that students explain the meaning of the paragraphs in their own words, the study strategy noted above (to read each chapter twice) may be adequate. On the other hand, if the test requires students to recall key concepts from the text and discuss them in order of importance, that same study strategy will probably be insufficient. (See Chapter 7 for more discussion of this issue.) Unless students anticipate the effects of adopting particular study strategies by acting on them, they cannot make adjustments that will ensure success. In our example, the best way to anticipate probable effects is to actually perform various tasks such as recalling key concepts from the book chapters. If you are not successful, you will know ahead of time that you need to change your approach.

The previous discussion shows that it is often necessary to act on our strategies before we can anticipate possible outcomes. We have experienced case after case in which people (including ourselves) believe that an initial idea makes great sense and then are unpleasantly surprised by obvious flaws that become apparent after the idea is put into practice. Ideally, many of these flaws can be discovered during the *act* and *anticipate* outcomes phase of problem solving rather than later on, when real damage can be done.

L = Look and Learn

The final component of the IDEAL framework is to **look** at the actual effects of your strategy and **learn** from the experience. The suggestion to look and learn from problem-solving experiences seems so obvious that you may wonder why we bother to mention it. The reason is that, as obvious as it seems, it often isn't done. We have been surprised many times by the degree to which students fail to look and learn from their attempts at problem solving. Consider tests, for example. These represent problems that students attempt to solve by selecting appropriate study strategies. Most students look at the effects of their attempts at problem solving in terms of their grade on each test, but this provides only very general information. To learn from their experience they need to examine their performance in more detail. For example, it can be beneficial to examine the exact questions missed and to understand why one missed them. Strategies for debugging—looking at and learning from your approach to studying—are discussed in more detail in Chapter 7.

The cannonball problem presented below provides another illustration of the importance of the *look* and *learn* phase of problem solving. Do not try to solve the entire cannonball problem right away. Instead, focus on the first step toward a solution that comes to mind. Here is the problem.

> There are 12 cannonballs. They all look alike, but one is the oddball. The oddball is either heavier or lighter than the other balls. You are supplied with a balance scale that can hold as many cannonballs as you like on each side. The problem is, in four weighings (four uses of the scale), find the oddball.

Try only the first step in this problem—that is, the first weighing—and then consider what you have found out. We have given this problem to more than 300 college students. The first strategy considered by over 90 percent of them is to place six cannonballs on each side of the scale to determine the side that contains the oddball. Once students actively attempt this strategy and look at the possible effects, they discover a dilemma: They still do not know which side the oddball is on.

After the initial weighing, most students understand the problem in a different way. They now understand that the difficulty of the problem lies in the fact that the oddball can be *either lighter or heavier;* hence, the six-six weighing does not tell them which side the oddball is on. Note that without *actively* trying out their initial strategy and *looking* at the effects, the definition of oddball would not be adequately understood. (You may now want to continue to try to solve the oddball problem. The answer is in Appendix A.)

In addition to looking at the effects of one's actions or decisions, it is important to learn from the experience. Ideally, one learns something general so that subsequent attempts at problem solving can be improved. For example, imagine that you have created a new advertisement for a product and had attempted to anticipate its effects by using a focus group of businessmen and women. When the ad actually airs on television, you discover a very negative reaction to it by various groups of people, especially those who are out of work and unable to find a job. As a result, you will have learned something about how better to select people to participate in any future focus groups that you decide to use.

The IDEAL Cycle

The purpose of the preceding discussion was to illustrate five components of the problem-solving process: **identify, define, explore, anticipate and act**, and **look** at the effects. Each of these components has important effects on how well a problem can be solved.

In our discussion, different types of problems were used to illustrate different components. For example, the splattering bacon grease problem was used to illustrate the importance of identifying opportunities as well as defining goals; the Classic Coke example was used to illustrate the *anticipate* and *look* components. It is important to note that solving any problem actually involves all five components of the IDEAL framework. In addition, the solution usually involves a number of passes through the IDEAL cycle.

Consider the problem of comprehending a passage. Assume that an effective reader encounters the statement, "The haystack was important because the cloth ripped." Unlike a less effective reader, who may simply be going through the motions of reading while actually daydreaming, the effective reader will realize that a problem exists (that is, he or she will *identify* the existence of a problem). Furthermore, the effective reader will view the identification of the problems as being good rather than bad. It represents an opportunity to clarify what is not understood.

After the problem has been *identified*, the reader must carefully *define* his or her goals. For example, the reader may assume that the sentence is incomprehensible because of a lack of information. Perhaps his or her attention had lapsed, causing crucial information in the text to be missed. The goal might then be to find the information that would render the statement comprehensible. This goal will lead to *exploring* such strategies as going back and rereading the preceding text for information that would help to illuminate the confusing statement. The student reader therefore *anticipate* the effects of using this strategy and *act* on it by actually rereading. He or she can then *look* and *learn* from these activities by evaluating whether they helped to solve the problem of what the sentence means.

Assume that the act of rereading does not solve the reader's comprehension problem. To the extent that he or she realizes this, a problem has again been *identified*. The reader must then *define* new goals, *explore* possible strategies, and so forth. In short, the reader has reentered the

IDEAL cycle and will remain there until the problem is solved or he or she gives up.

Different ways of reentering the IDEAL cycle can result in strategies that are more or less creative. The creative person will often redefine his or her goals and try to use strategies that differ considerably from those used previously. For example, the creative problem solver may reexperience the failure to comprehend the haystack sentence and redefine the goal as *attempting to use his or her own knowledge to make sense of the sentence.* This redefinition of goals suggests a new strategy. Rather than rereading, the optimal strategy is to generate a context that allows the sentence to make sense (if you find yourself trying to discover such a context, the word "parachute" should help). Strategies for enhancing creativity are discussed in more detail in Chapter 3.

■ Blocks to Creative Problem Solving

As you gain experience working with the IDEAL framework, you will notice that it often involves dealing with failure or frustration. If you *identify* a problem with your own ideas or statements, for example, it can be difficult to admit it. Similarly, as you *define* new goals (and hence reject earlier ones) or *act* on strategies and find a need to *explore* alternative plans, you may find yourself reacting negatively. This is natural; all of us would rather be right about everything than wrong on occasion. Nevertheless, the IDEAL problem solver views these kinds of experiences as opportunities rather than failures. The major opportunity they provide is to learn something new. And the earlier in the IDEAL cycle you can find the need to change direction, the better it is for you.

Scientists often must attempt to think about problems from new perspectives. According to the popular portrayal, scientists are supposed to be totally objective and seek only the truth. In actuality, scientists are much more human than this suggests. Their humanity has both positive and negative implications. On the positive side, scientists generally make better parents, friends, and spouses than one would expect from a cold-hearted individual. On the negative side, scientists may have difficulty abandoning sets of assumptions that are near and dear to their hearts.

The physicist David Bohm discusses the emotional impact of receiving criticism that questions one's initial approach to the definition of a problem. He describes a scientist's reaction to alternative assumptions proposed by another scientist.[18]

His first reaction is often of violent disturbance, as views that are very dear are questioned or thrown to the ground. Nevertheless, if he will "stay with it" rather than escape into anger and unjustified rejection of contrary ideas, he will discover that this disturbance is very beneficial. For now he becomes aware of the assumptive character of a great many previously unquestioned features of his own thinking. This does not mean that he will reject these assumptions in favor of those of other people. Rather, what is needed is the conscious criticism of one's own metaphysics, leading to changes where appropriate and ultimately, to the continual creation of new and different kinds.

Of course, scientists are not the only people who have difficulty redefining their goals because of emotional attachment to a set of assumptions. Nearly all people experience such difficulties at one point or another. When this happens, we fail to critically evaluate our assumptions. The IDEAL approach provides an important reminder of the value of questioning assumptions and defining our goals in new ways.

■ Summary

Our goal in this chapter was to provide a model that can be used to improve problem solving. The model, represented by the acronym IDEAL, emphasizes five components of the problem-solving process: *identify, define, explore, anticipate/act,* and *look/learn.* Each of these components is involved in any attempt to solve a problem; furthermore, people often need to move through the IDEAL cycle flexibly and repeat the cycle several times to arrive at a satisfactory solution. Creative problem solvers are especially likely to view a problem from a variety of perspectives; that is, to define their goals in a number of different ways.

In the remaining chapters we will apply the IDEAL model to situations in which people must solve such problems as spotting flaws in arguments and communicating effectively. In Part 2 we will examine problems such as remembering sets of facts, comprehending new information, and learning in ways that facilitate future problem-solving tasks. Since the IDEAL model provides the organizing structure for the rest of this book, it is important that you understand it and are able to use it in a variety of ways. To help you reach this goal, we include at the end of this and other chapters a number of exercises designed to provide practice in thinking within the IDEAL framework. The exercises are meant to be fun as well as instructive. Some involve problem solving while others involve quotations, statements of fact, and so forth. The exercises illustrate how the IDEAL framework can be used to think about a variety of situations. The best way to work with these exercises is first to read the problem or statement, then to think about it for a while, and finally to turn to the answers at the back of the book (Appendix B) to see how we thought about the problem from the IDEAL perspective. Our thoughts will not be the only correct ones, and they may be less interesting than your own. Nevertheless, by seeing how we use the IDEAL approach to think about experiences, you should learn to see the world from this perspective and evaluate whether or not it may be useful for you.

■ Exercises

Try to solve the two following problems as quickly as possible.

1. *Quickly, now:* How many members of each species did Adam take with him on the ark? (Note that the question is how many *members* of each species rather than how many species.) Do not look up the answer until you have also tried the problem below.

2. Spend approximately five seconds studying the phrases presented below and then, without looking back at them, write down what you saw. Please begin now.

Are the inventions shown below simply gimmicks, or do they address real needs?

3. Talking scale that remembers your weight:

4. Sound-activated light switch:

5. Solar watch cap:

Three actual inventions are shown below. Try to define the problems they were designed to solve.

6. Unusual shovel:

7.

8.

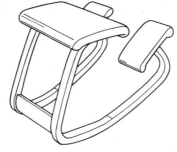

9. What kind of problem were these inventions designed to solve?

   ? . , !

10. Can you make sense of the following?

    That that is is not that that is not is that it it is

11. One morning, exactly at sunrise, a Buddhist monk began to climb a tall mountain. The narrow path, no more than a foot or two wide, spiraled around the mountain to a glittering temple at the summit. The monk ascended the path at varying rates of speed, stopping many times along the way to rest and to eat the dried fruit he carried with him. He reached the temple shortly before sunset. After several days of fasting and meditation, he began his journey back along the same path,

starting at sunrise and again walking at variable speeds with many pauses along the way. His average speed descending was, of course, greater than his average climbing speed. Prove that there is a spot along the path that the monk will occupy on both trips at precisely the same time of day.

12. A social psychologist was interested in the custom of hand-shaking. He noticed that some people are more inclined than others to shake hands when they are introduced. One evening when he and his wife had joined four other couples at a party, he took advantage of the occasion to collect data. He asked each of the other nine people at the party how many people they had shaken hands with during the introductions. He received a different answer, from zero through eight, from each of the nine people. You can assume that husbands and wives don't shake hands with each other during introductions, and of course, people don't shake hands with themselves. Given this information, find out how often the psychologist's wife shook hands.[20]

13. There are two large jars. One jar is filled with a large number of blue beads, and the other is filled with the same number of red beads. Five beads from the red-bead jar are scooped out and dumped into the blue-bead jar. Someone then puts a hand in the blue-bead jar, scoops out five beads without knowing what color they are, and dumps them into the red-bead jar. Are there the same number of red beads in the red-bead jar as there are blue beads in the blue-bead jar?

14. Imagine you have a piece of tissue paper, such as a Kleenex tissue. If you fold the paper in half it doubles in thickness; if you fold it in half again it is four layers thick. Imagine that it is possible to fold the paper a total of 50 times, and assume that the sheet of paper was originally 0.001 inch thick. How thick would the folded paper be after 50 folds?

15. Suppose that each of the fish illustrated below eats two fish in front of it each day. That is, fish 1 eats two like fish 2, each fish 2 eats two like fish 3, each fish 3 eats two like fish 4, and so forth. How many of fish 7 will be eaten to supply fish 1 with enough food for one day?

16. On the facing page is a design[21] for a robot (imaginary) manufactured to wash outside windows in high-rise buildings. It has suction-cup feet (to help it climb), a bucket head (to hold water), large sponges for hands (since the windows are large), a padded stomach (so it won't scratch the building), a battery (for power), and a parachute (in case it falls). Do you think the design is adequate?

17. A man has 25 cigar butts and uses 5 butts to make a new cigar (he rerolls the butts). How many cigars can he smoke after he has made them?

18. A scientist who is experimenting with a new type of mushroom notices that the number of mushrooms she has in her greenhouse doubles every day. She started with 12 mushrooms on the first day. If the greenhouse will be completely full on day 29, when will it be exactly half full of mushrooms?

19. On New Year's Eve, a small hospital in Cookeville, Tennessee, reported ten separate births. Only nine women had entered the hospital that year and there were no multiple births. How could this be?

20. If a hen and a half lays an egg and a half in a day and a half, how many hens will it take to lay six eggs in six days?

21. Imagine a game in which 15 coins are placed on a table. Each of two players alternates taking coins from the table. On each turn a player can take from 1 to 5 coins from the table. The player who takes the last coin wins the game. Is there a strategy that can be used to always win this game?[22]

22. You are visiting a strange land where there are only truth-tellers and liars. Liars always lie and truthtellers always tell the truth. You ask the first person you meet whether he is a truthteller or a liar. The person mumbles something that you cannot understand, but someone nearby says, "He says he is a truthteller. He is a truthteller and so am I." Can you trust the directions that these two may give you?

23. A man pays $1 to get into a gambling casino. He loses half of his remaining money there and has to pay $1 to leave. He goes to a second casino and pays $1 to get in. He loses half of his remaining money there and has to pay $1 to leave. He goes to a third casino and pays $1 to get in. He loses half of his remaining money there and pays another $1 to get out. He is now broke. How much money did the man start with?[23]

■ Notes

1. M. Wertheimer, *Productive Thinking*. New York: Harper & Row, 1959.
2. G. Polya, *How to Solve It*. Garden City, N.Y.: Doubleday Anchor, 1957.
3. A. Newell and H. A. Simon, *Human Problem Solving*. Englewood Cliffs, N.J.: Prentice-Hall, 1972.
4. E. C. Bliss, *Getting Things Done*. New York: Bantam Books, 1976.
5. This example is from E. de Bono (ed.), *Eureka, An Illustrated History of Inventions from the Wheel to the Computer; A London Sunday Times Encyclopedia*. New York: Holt, Rinehart & Winston, 1974.
6. Additional examples of inventions can be found in de Bono (see note 5).
7. J. L. Adams, *Conceptual Blockbusting: A Guide to Better Ideas* (3d ed.). Reading, Mass.: Addison-Wesley, 1986.
8. A. Whimbey and J. Lochhead, *Problem Solving and Comprehension* (3d ed.) Hillsdale, N.J.: Lawrence Erlbaum Associates, 1985.
9. A. Whimbey, with L. S. Whimbey, *Intelligence Can Be Taught*. New York: Dutton, 1975.
10. From Whimbey and Lockhead (see note 8).
11. J. R. Hayes, *The Complete Problem Solver* (2d ed.). Hillsdale, N.J.: Lawrence Erlbaum Associates, 1989.
12. D. Halpern, *Thought and Knowledge: An Introduction to Critical Thinking* (2d ed.). Hillsdale, N.J.: Lawrence Erlbaum Associates, 1989.
13. R. S. Day, Alternative representations. In G. H. Bower (ed.), *The Psychology of Learning and Motivation*, Vol. 22. New York: Academic Press, 1988, pp. 261–305.
14. Additional examples of general problem-solving strategies can be found in J. R. Hayes, *The Complete Problem Solver* (2d edition). Hillsdale, N.J.: Lawrence Erlbaum Associates, 1989; B. F. Anderson, *The Complete Thinker*. Englewood Cliffs, N.J.: Prentice-Hall, 1980; G. Polya, *How to Solve It*. Garden City, N.Y.: Doubleday Anchor, 1957; W. A. Wickelgren, *How to Solve Problems*. San Francisco: W. H. Freeman, 1974.
15. For an excellent discussion of general versus specific strategies and skills, see A. Newell, One final word. In D. T. Tuma and F. Reif (eds.), *Problem Solving and Education: Issues in Teaching and Research*. Englewood Cliffs, N.J.: Prentice-Hall, 1980.

16. R. Sherwood, C. Kinzer, T. Hasselbring, and J. D. Bransford, Macro-contexts for learning: Initial findings and issues. *Journal of Applied Cognition* 1 (1987):93–108.

17. N. R. Hanson, A picture theory of theory meaning. In R. G. Colodny (ed.), *The Nature and Function of Scientific Theories.* Pittsburgh: University of Pittsburgh Press, 1970.

18. D. J. Jefferson, Building a better mousetrap doesn't ensure success. *The Wall Street Journal* (Nov. 18, 1991).

19. D. Bohm, Further remarks on order. In C. H. Waddington (ed.), *Towards a Theoretical Biology,* Vol. 2. Chicago: Aldine Press, 1969.

20. From J. R. Hayes, *The Complete Problem Solver.* Philadelphia: Franklin Institute Press, 1981.

21. From G. Teague, Constraints on Effective Illustrations. Master's thesis, Tennessee Technological University, Cookeville, Tenn., 1985.

22. This is one version of a popular game called Nim. Nim originated thousands of years ago in Asia where it was played with 12 stones. This particular version of the game is described in M. F. Rubinstein and K. Pfeiffer, *Concepts in Problem Solving.* Englewood Cliffs, N.J.: Prentice-Hall, 1980.

23. H. Randall Todd, in *Parade Magazine.* July 1, 1990.

■ Suggested Readings

Practically Oriented Readings

Anderson, B. F. 1980. *The Complete Thinker.* Englewood Cliffs, N.J.: Prentice-Hall.

Halpern, D. 1989. *Thought and Knowledge: An Introduction to Critical Thinking* (2d ed.). Hillsdale, N.J.: Lawrence Erlbaum Associates.

Hayes, J. R. 1989. *The Complete Problem Solver* (2d ed.). Hillsdale, N.J.: Lawrence Erlbaum Associates.

Polya, G. 1957. *How to Solve It.* Garden City, N.Y.: Doubleday Anchor.

Rubinstein, M. F., and K. Pfeiffer. 1980. *Concepts in Problem Solving.* Englewood Cliffs, N.J.: Prentice-Hall.

Sternberg, R. J. 1986. *Intelligence Applied.* San Diego, Calif.: Harcourt Brace Jovanovich.

Wickelgren, W. A. 1974. *How to Solve Problems.* San Francisco: W. H. Freeman.

Theoretically Oriented Readings

Bransford, J. D., B. S. Stein, R. Arbitman-Smith, and N. J. Vye. 1985. Three approaches to teaching thinking and learning. In J. Segal, S. Chipman, and R. Glaser (eds.), *Thinking and Learning Skills: Relating Instruction to Basic Research*, Vol. 1. Hillsdale, N.J.: Lawrence Erlbaum Associates.

Humphrey, G. 1963. *Thinking: An Introduction to Its Experimental Psychology.* New York: Wiley.

Lochhead, J., and J. Clement (eds.). 1979. *Cognitive Process Instruction: Research on Teaching Thinking Skills.* Philadelphia: Franklin Institute Press.

Mandler, J. M., and G. Mandler. 1964. *Thinking: From Association to Gestalt.* New York: Wiley.

Mayer, R. E. 1991. *Thinking, Problem Solving, Cognition* (2d ed.). New York: W. H. Freeman.

Sternberg, R. J. 1985. *Beyond I.Q.: Toward a Triarchic Theory of Intelligence.* New York: Cambridge University Press.

Sternberg, R. J., and P. A. Frensch (eds.). 1991. *Complex Problem Solving: Principles and Mechanisms.* Hillsdale, N.J.: Lawrence Erlbaum Associates.

Tuma, D. T., and F. Reif (eds.). 1980. *Problem Solving and Education: Issues in Teaching and Learning.* Hillsdale, N.J.: Lawrence Erlbaum Associates.

Voss, J. F., D. Perkins, and J. Segal. 1990. *Information Reasoning and Education.* Hillsdale, N.J.: Lawrence Erlbaum Assoicates.

Wason, P. C., and P. N. Johnson-Laird. 1968. *Thinking and Reasoning.* Baltimore: Penguin.

Wertheimer, M. 1959. *Productive Thinking.* New York: Harper & Row.

CREATIVITY AND THE IDEAL FRAMEWORK

The uncreative mind can spot wrong answers, but it takes a creative mind to spot wrong questions.

Antony Jay[1]

One of the most common excuses we hear for why people are unable to solve problems is that they are just not creative. It is therefore important to ask, "Where is creativity in the IDEAL framework?" It may seem surprising, but processes for enhancing creativity *are everywhere* in the IDEAL model; they are involved in *identifying* problems and opportunities, *defining* goals, *exploring* possible strategies, and so forth. Our goal in this chapter is to explore ways to enhance creativity in the context of the IDEAL model.

Before we can explore ways to enhance creativity, it is important to define what we mean by creativity. Some people assume that only people in the performing or other arts are creative. In fact, creativity can be found in any problem-solving domain. For example, scientists can take creative approaches to constructing and testing theories, business leaders can be creative in identifying new ideas for products and services and in running their companies, and students can take creative approaches to their choice of topics for term papers and projects. Furthermore, not all artistic activities are creative. For example, drawing, sculpture, painting, dance, and music can be approached noncreatively as well as creatively. The important point is that any task can be approached from a creative or a less creative point of view.

David Perkins[2] reminds us that there are degrees of creativity; it is not something that you either have or don't have. It is also important to take a realistic view of creativity. Many people erroneously assume that someone is creative only if he or she is like Einstein or Bach or Picasso. But if you look for creativity only at that level of achievement you will miss the hundreds of opportunities to be creative each day. Children are naturally creative, and all adults continue to have this potential.

In this book we use the term *creative* to refer to the ability to solve problems in ways that are novel for the individual. An idea that you generate can be creative even if you were not the first person in history to think of it. What counts is your ability to approach and solve problems in ways that are not routine for you. A creative idea is also one that is appropriate to the situation, rather than simply novel but off the wall. As we discuss creativity within the IDEAL model, we will focus on ways to generate ideas that are *both novel and appropriate* to your goals.

Identify Problems and Opportunities

The ability to identify problems and opportunities is one of the most important steps in the creative process. As an illustration, consider creative journalists. One of their hallmarks is the ability to find important issues to work on—they don't simply choose any random problem or topic. Often they write about problems that others have missed or ignored. Similarly, creative scientists often begin by finding important problems with existing theories and methods that others have failed to notice. This can lead to new, productive research that otherwise might not have been pursued.

We saw in Chapter 2 that many successful inventions grow out of the process of identifying everyday problems and turning them into opportunities for useful products or services. However, not all inventions stem from problems that the inventor experienced personally or was the first to identify. For example, the surgeon Henry Heimlich identified an important problem when he read a report that choking was the sixth leading cause of accidental death. Although many other doctors had probably noticed this problem, Heimlich recognized it as an opportunity for a creative solution. He soon realized that two of the recommended treatments for choking victims—removing the object with a finger and slapping the victim on the back—would probably push the object deeper into the victim's throat. Heimlich's experience as a chest surgeon helped him realize that there would probably be enough air in the lungs to clear the victim's airway if someone pushed on the diaphragm. His invention, the Heimlich maneuver, is now recognized as the best lifesaving technique for choking victims.

Sometimes creative ideas stem from identifying problems in other people's solutions. For example, Cal Garland noticed that the styrofoam nuggets used to package delicate objects sent through the mail are bad for the environment. He realized that he could take advantage of material available at his lumberyard to provide a solution to the packaging problem that was better for the environment. Garland patented a machine that creates curls of paper-thin wood shavings that can provide packaging protection and then be used as garden mulch.[3]

The Importance of Encouraging Problem Identification

Unfortunately, our society often discourages people from identifying important problems that can lead to creative solutions. In some instances, people who have attempted to identify existing or potential problems have actually been fired from their jobs. A number of tragedies in our society might have been averted if employees had been encouraged to identify actual or potential problems. Examples include the *Challenger* space shuttle accident and the increased incidence of cancer from asbestos. In fact, the pressure to ignore problems in business and industry has been strong enough to motivate the U.S. Congress to pass the Whistleblowers Protection Act. The goal of this legislation is to protect people who believe that they have identified important problems. Ideally, people will come to realize more fully that the identification of problems can lead to opportunities for improvements.

One of us recently held a problem-solving workshop for a company that wanted to improve its operations. The workshop was designed to kick off a "quality month" during which everyone in the company would try to find opportunities for improvement. The first week was spent asking employees to identify problems in the company that, if solved, might improve working conditions and company operations. The most important problems would be selected by a committee and then worked on by cooperative teams for the remainder of the month. The problem identification phase of the project was especially productive, and the reactions of the employees were very interesting. Many mentioned that normally the act of identifying potentially solvable problems would be viewed as whining or complaining. Within the context of quality month, however, problem identification was linked with the discovery of opportunities and so was seen as valuable.

One way of using the IDEAL framework that we have found beneficial is to encourage people to identify problems in their own lives and then attempt to solve them creatively. We ask them to begin with problems that can be solved relatively quickly. The problems that people identify in these exercises tend to be quite interesting. Participants often remark that the exercise prompted them to pay much more attention to annoying or troublesome events rather than simply brush them aside as facts of life. For example, college students with whom we have worked have identified problems of dormitory life such as noise from a squeaky bathroom door that kept them awake (oiling it did not help), a tendency to turn off alarm clocks and go back to sleep, and a shortage of parking spaces. The students had noticed these problems before the IDEAL exercise, but they had not given much thought to the possibility of systematically attempting to solve them. By actively identifying problems and treating them as opportunities for creative solutions, the students often surprised themselves and discovered that they were able to solve problems in very interesting ways.

Problems with Tests of Creativity

An emphasis on the identification of problems and opportunities as an important step in the creative process helps clarify why it can be difficult to create paper-and-pencil instruments to measure creativity. For instance, one way people have tried to assess creativity is by measuring "divergent thinking." A test of divergent thinking might ask people to generate as many new uses for a brick as possible in a limited period of time. Such a test will indeed show that some people think of lots of uses (for example, bookends and doorstops) while others think of fewer uses. But it is not the mere quantity of new uses that is important; it is better to have a few really excellent answers than a host of mediocre ones.

From our perspective, there is something about the brick test that misses important aspects of the creative process. It explicitly asks people to generate new uses for a brick, rather than measuring their ability to identify new problems and opportunities. People who can generate ideas on a brick test are not necessarily going to notice opportunities for inventions such as those pictured in Chapter 2.[4]

Define Alternative Goals

The act of defining and redefining one's goals is a particularly important part of the creative process. Different goals suggest different lines of thought and so have a powerful effect on the solution strategies that we consider. We saw an example of this in Chapter 2 when we discussed James Adams's bruised tomato problem. One way to define the goal in this case was to design a mechanical tomato picker that was less likely to bruise tomatoes. An alternative goal was to design a tomato less likely to be bruised.

The Grocery Store Problem

The relationship between goals and creativity can be clarified by imagining a grocery store that is losing customers because they are annoyed at how long it takes to check out. If you were hired as a consultant to this company, what would you suggest?

We have given this problem to hundreds of people and find that many approach it in a very similar manner. They tend to generate solutions such as

- Train the cashiers to work faster.
- Purchase scanners and other technology to speed up the checkout process.
- Open up some cash-only lines for customers who are buying only a few items.
- Increase the number of checkout lines.

These are all potentially good solutions. Nevertheless, they address only one of a number of possible general goals. That goal is to speed up the process of getting customers through the checkout line. An alternative goal is to find ways to keep people from getting annoyed at slow checkout lines. This suggests a host of potential strategies, such as installing televisions that customers can watch while they wait in line, giving the customers free samples while they wait in line (the store can conduct market research at the same time that it helps with the checkout problem), and having live entertainment to amuse the customers.

Still another goal is to keep the store from having too many customers at any particular time of day. This suggests strategies that are different from the others. One is to get more of the store's regular customers to come at nonpeak hours. This might be accomplished by doubling the value of coupons during certain hours of the day, having special sales at certain hours, or holding special events such as services for the elderly at particular hours or a singles night.

In our experience with the grocery store problem, it is rare for people to step back and try to define alternative goals. Instead, most read the problem and almost immediately begin generating strategies. One way that we try to help them become more creative is by asking them to explicitly define a minimum of two or three different goals for each problem situation.

Additional Illustrations of the Importance of Defining Goals

We have used the strategy of defining at least two goals when working with students to identify their own problems. For example, we noted earlier that one problem identified by a college student was a squeaky bathroom door across the hall from her dormitory room that kept her awake. When she presented her problem to the class, she went beyond our request for two different goals and presented the following three:

- To eliminate the squeak (for example, by oiling the hinge or removing the bathroom door)
- To keep the sound from entering the dorm room (for example, by filling the space at the bottom of the dormitory door)
- To keep the sound from being bothersome (for example, by masking it with music or white noise)

As you can see, different goals suggested different types of possible strategies. Indeed, all the students in this class generated strategies that were much more interesting and creative than those we had seen in previous classes. What was new about this class was our request that the students generate at least two different goals to solve their problems. We had not used this instruction in previous years, and the students had not spontaneously generated multiple goals on their own.

The importance of carefully defining goals also apples to activities such as choosing a topic for a paper. This point is nicely illustrated by a student we shall call Judy who decided to write a paper on humor and came to one of us for consultation. In talking with her it became clear that her implicit goal was to describe what the "experts" on humor had to say. Her focus was on what they say rather than on what she wanted to know. Marlene Scardamalia and Carl Bereiter note that a common approach to writing is to engage in knowledge telling—people simply attempt to restate what they know or have read. They suggest that a much better approach to writing is a "knowledge transforming" approach. Here the goal is not simply to tell what you know or have read but to transform that knowledge in some useful way.[5]

To help Judy move beyond knowledge telling, we tried to get her to better define what she wanted to understand about humor. She was a nursing major with considerable experience and we asked how the study of humor might help people in the medical field. This eventually led Judy to think of such ideas as laughter's being the best medicine. Her goal eventually became much clearer: to determine whether humor is beneficial to sick people and to understand why. This approach to the problem of writing her paper enabled Judy to use her own knowledge about illness and the hospital setting. Furthermore, she now had a criterion for evaluating the adequacy of the theories proposed by the experts in terms of her goal. Needless to say, her paper turned out to be much more interesting (both to her and to us) than it would have been had she simply gone through the motions of comparing theories A, B, and C.

Lee Bolman and Terrence Deal[8] illustrate the value of considering multiple goals when trying to develop creative ways to improve organizations such as businesses, schools, or government agencies. They suggest that people thinking about ways to improve an organization should consider four goals: to improve the organizational structure, to improve the use and development of human resources, to improve political characteristics, and to improve the organization's image. They argue that these four subgoals can help people think of possibilities that they might otherwise fail to consider.

Balancing Routine and Nonroutine Thinking

It is important to recognize that most of what we do in life involves routine rather than nonroutine problem solving. Routine thinking is valuable because it allows us to solve problems quickly and without much effort. It would be very inefficient to approach every daily task by making your goals explicit and then redefining them in order to be more creative. Effective problem solving requires a delicate balance between going with the routine (because it is efficient) and taking the extra time to treat a situation as nonroutine and attempting to develop a more creative approach.

Studies in cognitive science suggest that in many situations, routine thinking and creative thinking may be complementary rather than antithetical. The reason is that people have limited attention spans, and real-world problems can easily overwhelm our processing capabilities. It is difficult to be creative when one is overwhelmed.

Remember the experience of first learning to drive a car? You had to consciously attend to particular aspects of driving such as putting on the turn signal, hitting the brake and clutch, looking in the rear-view mirror before changing lanes, and so forth. These tasks demanded so much of your attention that it was difficult to do something else simultaneously, such as carry on a conversation with a passenger. But as these components of driving became routine they demanded less and less attention, until finally you could drive and carry on a conversation at the same time. In general, routine tasks support creativity because they allow us to shift our attention to new aspects of a situation.

As an additional example of how routine and nonroutine thinking can be complementary, imagine that you are asked to coordinate a fund-raising banquet and the organizer wants you to make it an especially memorable occasion. This is a complex problem that can be broken down into a number of subgoals that are routine for people who do this type of thing often. These subgoals include finding a suitable location, arranging decorations, notifying and inviting guests, arranging entertainment, selecting a menu, preparing and serving food, and cleaning up. Attention to each of these subgoals does not guarantee that your banquet will be memorable, but if you overlook one of them the banquet will be a flop.

A task such as running a fund-raising banquet requires a combination of routine and nonroutine thinking. The more experience you have organizing banquets the more likely you will be to think of all the important subgoals. You can then decide where to focus your creative energies. Perhaps you will need special invitations, an extravagant dessert, entertainment, or an unusual theme and decorations. By first considering the routine subgoals, you will get a better idea of the creative options available. Furthermore, each of the subgoals has a number of routine components. All invitations have to meet certain prerequisites such as being sent out on time and being clear about the place and time; similarly, all meals require some sort of preparation and cleanup. You might proceed to question some of these routine components in an effort to think creatively, but you will certainly not change every one of them.

When to Search for Nonroutine Solutions

One signal to search for a nonroutine solution is that our familiar routines are not working as effectively or efficiently as we would like. A classic experiment by Norman Maier[7] illustrates the shortcomings of thinking about things in a routine rather than a novel manner. He presented a group of people with a problem in which two cords were suspended from a ceiling just far enough apart that you could not hold one and reach the other (see Figure 8). He asked the participants to find a way of tying the two cords together using anything they found in the room. On a table were several objects, including a pair of pliers. Can you solve the problem?

Even when given hints beforehand, many people failed to realize that the pliers could be used as a weight to create a pendulum. One cord set swinging with the pliers attached could be grasped while you held on to the other cord (see Figure 9). People failed to use the pliers as a weight because they saw only its most common function, a phenomenon known as *functional fixedness*. Incidentally, can you think of another way to solve this problem without removing the cords or tying an object to one of them? If you thought of standing on the table beneath the two cords to

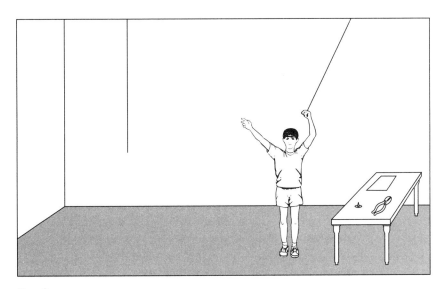

Figure 8

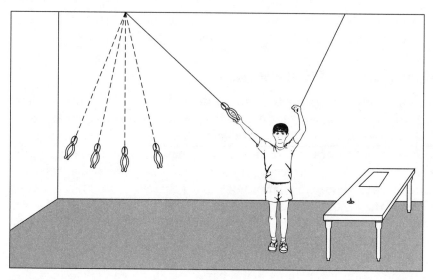

Figure 9

reach them more easily, you have mastered another strategy that is often overlooked because of functional fixedness.[8]

Routine thinking can also prevent us from developing effective solutions when we falsely assume that a new problem can be solved using a routine approach. This phenomenon is often referred to as *learning set*. Although learning sets can facilitate problem solving when dealing with problems that require similar solution strategies, they can limit our ability to explore other strategies. For example, many of our students have falsely assumed that the study techniques they used in many previous classes would work in a new course. It was only when they performed poorly on a test that they recognized the need to break out of this implicit set and treat the situation as nonroutine. We will address the importance of identifying assumptions that limit our creativity in more detail when we discuss the importance of looking back at the effects of using a strategy.

■ Explore Possible Strategies

Even after you have identified problems and opportunities and defined possible goals, there is still room to enhance your creativity. There are a number of strategies that can be used to find more creative ways to reach your goals. Many of these techniques are designed to help you access a greater range of personal knowledge and experience that might be relevant to the problem.

Fractionation

One strategy for enhancing the range of experiences we consider during problem solving involves what Edward deBono calls *fractionation*.[9] The goal of fractionation is to break a concept or idea into its component parts so that new thoughts are more likely to come to mind. For example, consider the problem of generating ideas for possible uses of bricks. Rather than focusing only on bricks per se, it is helpful to fractionate bricks into more basic properties and consider uses for each one. Thus, a brick has a certain color and weight, is rectangular and porous, holds heat but does not conduct electricity, and is rough and small enough to be picked up in one hand.

Most people find that fractionating the concept of a brick into component parts increases the number of potential uses they can generate. Furthermore, when people try to generate uses but do not employ the strategy of thinking about individual properties of bricks, their responses usually reflect assumptions about those properties. For example, a person who thinks of doorstops, paperweights, and bookends as uses for bricks is probably, without necessarily realizing it, thinking about the property of weight.

Here is another problem.

Consider ways to reduce the sound from highways.

Breaking this problem into its components can also help you generate novel ideas. For example, you might first think of the factors involved in the problem; that is, roads, cars and trucks, people (presumably the ones bothered by noise), and some medium (such as air) that carries sound. You could then think about the individual properties of each. For example, people have ears that might be covered to reduce the perception of noise, cars and trucks have tires that might affect the level of noise, and so forth. Such thinking can facilitate our access to ideas that may lead to creative solutions.

The Use of Analogies

Searching for analogies is another strategy for enhancing creative thinking. For example, John Hayes describes a meeting on the problem of campus housing.[10] Someone said, "We have BYOB (bring your own booze) parties; why not a BYOH (bring your own housing) university?" Hayes notes that, although this suggestion was partly meant as a joke, it was in fact quite beneficial, leading to a discussion of mobile housing units. In the past, discussion had focused only on conventional housing such as dorms, which are expensive to build and impossible to move around.

Analogies have played a key role in discoveries in science and technology. For example, Benjamin Franklin noticed that a pointed object would draw a much stronger spark than a blunt object in the vicinity of an electrified body.[11] At first he thought this was an unimportant observation. Until he recognized the analogy between clouds and electrified bodies, he did not realize that pointed rods of iron could be used to protect buildings and ships from damage by lightning. Similarly, Gutenberg's invention of the printing press was developed in part out of analogies he saw with the wine press and the punches used for making coins.

Another illustration of the key role analogies can play in great discoveries is provided in the reflections of August Wilhelm Kekule written 25 years after he published his model for the structure of the benzene molecule.[12]

> I turned my chair to the fire and dozed. . . . Again the atoms were gambolling before my eyes. This time the smaller groups kept modestly in the background. My mental eye, rendered more acute by repeated visions of this kind, could now distinguish larger structures, of manifold conformation; long rows, sometimes more closely fitted together; all twining and twisting in snakelike motion. But look! What was that? One of the snakes had seized hold of its own tail, and the form whirled mockingly before my eyes.

Using the analogy of a snake biting its own tail, Kekule developed a model for the ringlike structure of the benzene molecule that profoundly affected the science of organic chemistry.

In addition to facilitating the discovery of new ideas and the creation of new inventions, analogies provide alternative frameworks for interpreting familiar facts. For example, in a recent period of stock-market decline, one analyst criticized the gloomy predictions of most of his colleagues and argued instead that the market would experience a substantial gain. His reasoning was based on an analogy with a diving board—the more downward pressure placed on a diving board, the greater the tendency for it to push back upward. We question the appropriateness of this analogy, but the market did experience a bullish period shortly thereafter. Even imperfect analogies may sometimes be useful if they lead to creative solutions. The effect of analogic thinking on creativity was perhaps best expressed by William Gordon when he said that analogies make the strange familiar and the familiar strange.[13] Both increase the probability that we will think about things in new rather than routine ways.

Brainstorming

In 1957, Alexander Osborn described the concept of brainstorming.[14] His goal was to use a group setting to increase the production of creative ideas. One of the most important characteristics of a brainstorming session is that participants adopt an attitude of complete friendliness and an openness to suggestions. At first, wild ideas are encouraged—the wilder the better. Further, members of the brainstorming group must agree to withhold their evaluation of ideas until later in the session; criticism is therefore ruled out. This rule is extremely important. Since novel ideas often differ from conventional wisdom, premature evaluations can prevent one from appreciating their value. Premature evaluations in brainstorming sessions are often referred to as "idea killers" because they hinder creative thought.

A variation on brainstorming is to ask group members to write down their ideas on sheets of paper and then exchange them so that others can make modifications and suggestions. This procedure, called brainwriting, has sometimes been found to be even more effective than brainstorming.[15]

Writing as a Discovery Technique

Another strategy for discovering new ideas is to explore a topic in writing. Since written language persists over time, written ideas can be subjected to more intense scrutiny. Writing is often thought to be a way of expressing ideas rather than creating new insights. That people should think this is probably a reflection of the way society and educational institutions typically view writing and communication skills. Usually they are taught independently of subjects such as physics, psychology, and mathematics. However, many experienced writers, speakers, and researchers say that the development of ideas occurs to a great degree during the process of putting ideas into a communicable form.

Here is a simple example of discovery that took place during the writing of this book. We knew that we wanted to have a section on the use of analogies, and because we assumed that all uses of analogy were similar, we thought that one section on analogies would be adequate. As we began writing, however, it became clear that analogies can be used in very different ways. For example, they are often used as a basis for arguments (see Chapter 4). Earlier in this chapter, we also argued that analogies can be used to facilitate the generation of new ideas, and in a later chapter we discuss how they can help in the communication of ideas. In retrospect, these different uses of analogies seem obvious to us, but they were not obvious before. Writing and other forms of communication (such as teaching) help us discover ideas and distinctions of which we were not at first aware.

Incubation

In the preceding discussion we assumed that one continues to work on a problem until it is solved. However, if you have ever worked on a difficult problem for some length of time (on ideas for a speech or paper, for example) you have probably found that, at some point, you had to stop thinking about it for a while. This is not merely because of mental fatigue; often one is able to think about other things. Instead, the reason for stopping is that the same old answers keep coming up. People get locked into a particular way of thinking and need to break out.

The term *incubation* refers to something that happens during the period when one has stopped working on a problem. For example, some people purposely think about a problem before going to bed so they can sleep on it. They hope that ideas will incubate (hatch) during the night and fresh insights will be available when they wake up. And indeed, this sometimes seems to occur. Many scientists have written about having flashes of insight after they stopped thinking about a problem and did something else (took a trip, read a novel, or slept).[16] The following quotation is from the French mathematician Henri Poincaré.[17]

> *One evening contrary to my custom, I drank black coffee and could not sleep. Ideas rose in crowds; I felt them collide until pairs interlocked, so to speak, making a stable combination. By the next morning, I had established the existence of a class of Fuchsian functions, those which come from the hypergeometric series; I had only to write out the results, which took but a few hours.*

In Poincaré's case, a great deal of preparation preceded the insight; he had spent a large amount of time working on his problem. The same is true for other scientists who have reported the role of insight in their work. The entire process has been broken down into four phases: (1) preparation, when you work hard on a problem and understand it; (2) incubation, when you stop working on the problem; (3) illumination, when a new insight occurs; and (4) elaboration, when the implications of the insight are worked out.

An interesting question is "What happens during incubation?" One answer is that the unconscious mind works on the problem. A weakness of this view is that we don't know what the unconscious mind is or does. Nevertheless, if you believe that the unconscious does its best work when it is not interfered with by the conscious mind, then the best procedure is probably to avoid thinking about the problem you want to solve, perhaps by going to sleep.

Another view of the benefits of incubation is that, with time, we cease making implicit assumptions that are preventing an adequate solution. Land, the inventor of the Polaroid Land Camera, once described insight as "the sudden cessation of stupidity."[18] This is consistent with the view that incubation helps us stop making inappropriate assumptions. Like the unconscious process theory, this view of insight suggests that we not think about the problem during the incubation phase. However, this view also suggests that during the preparation phase of problem solving we should try to make our assumptions as explicit as possible to increase the likelihood that alternatives will emerge.

Still another view of incubation is that it enables us to process new information that may provide a clue for a solution. When problem solvers focus only on the problem to be solved, they may miss information that could serve as clues. However, if they keep the problem in the back of their minds while doing other things, they may increase the probability of encountering useful clues.

Consider the following list of words and phrases:

Cowbell

Chopsticks

Trumpet

Roof

Tree

These probably don't suggest anything special; they probably don't produce an insight or the feeling of "aha!"

Now assume that you have been trying to comprehend the following statement: "The food was uneaten because the wood was warped." Assume also that after working on it for a while you stop and do other things, one of which is to read the list of words above. This time, items on the list (such as *chopsticks*) may provide a clue for problem solution.[19] If you had kept working on the problem you probably would not have read the list. Furthermore, if the problem had not been in the back of your mind, the insight afforded by the word *chopsticks* would not have occurred to you.

Charles Darwin notes that while trying to develop a theory that would account for the data he had collected on similarities and dissimilarities among different species, he happened to read an essay by Thomas Malthus on population.[20] According to Darwin, the essay helped him formulate the theory of evolution despite the fact that it was about a different topic. Had Darwin simply sat in his room pondering the data, he might not have read Malthus's article. And if Darwin had not kept the general problem of accounting for his data in the back of his mind, Malthus's work would not have had the clue value it did.

This perspective on incubation suggests that we can take an active role, rather than merely sleeping or not thinking about a problem. We can talk with others, read books, look at magazines, view scenery, and so forth. If we keep the problem in the back of our mind, we may find a host of clues that can help us generate creative ideas.

Creativity Checklists

Another way to increase our ability to access knowledge and experiences that might be relevant to a problem is by using special lists designed to help people get around the constraints of routine thinking. Like fractionation, creativity checklists are meant to expand the range of experiences and strategies that we consider during problem solving. Alexander Osborn[21] created one of the more famous creativity lists.

Creativity checklists can be useful in helping us get beyond routine thinking. Although checklists such as Osborn's are limited to certain types of problems, you can construct your own checklists to increase the number of strategies to consider during problem solving. You can experience the effects of using a creativity checklist by thinking about ways to modify a thumbtack and then performing the tasks in the checklist below, which was designed by Gary Davis and William Roweton.[22]

1. Add or subtract something
2. Change color
3. Change the materials
4. Change by rearranging the parts
5. Change shape
6. Change size
7. Change design or style

Creativity checklists are somewhat controversial because they often depend on the use of prompts formulated by others. Also, repeated use of the same checklist may promote a routine approach to problem solving that eventually limits creativity. We recommend that creativity checklists be used only after other strategies for enhancing creativity have been tried.

■ Anticipate and Act

The anticipate and act phase of the IDEAL model can help us uncover inappropriate assumptions that may be limiting the creativity of our thinking. For instance, we noted earlier that functional fixedness and learning set can prevent people from solving a problem because they assume that it requires routine thinking. In many situations we are unaware or unwilling to admit that we are making certain assumptions. These assumptions may guide our behavior and thoughts without our knowing it. For instance, a male business executive who is unaware of his belief that women cannot be effective managers may be biased in favor of hiring only male managers. One strategy that psychologists have used to uncover such biases or assumptions is to get people to make predictions or anticipate outcomes. Thus, we could ask the business executive to predict the success of two job applicants by looking at resumes that were identical in every way except gender. Predictions like these could be used to uncover other assumptions that might bias jurors, patients, voters, and others.

Anticipating outcomes can also help us to uncover fundamental assumptions in other areas. For example, to probe people's understanding of certain fundamental laws of physics, the researcher Michael

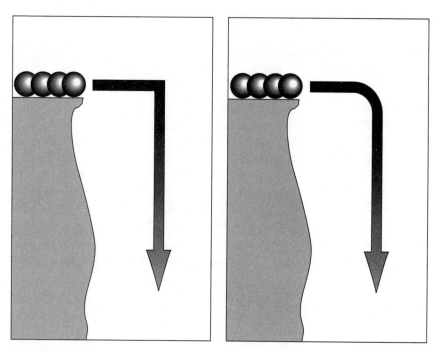

Figure 10 Inaccurate predictions.

McCloskey asked students to predict the path a ball will travel when it rolls off the edge of a cliff.[23] The answers students gave illustrate some common misconceptions or faulty assumptions about the laws of physics. Two of these are shown in Figure 10. In reality, the ball will move forward as it descends, following a path that closely approximates a parabola.

Scientists often explore the adequacy of their theoretical assumptions by performing thought experiments that involve anticipating outcomes. A good example of how such thought experiments can be used to explore and evaluate assumptions was provided by Albert Einstein.[24] Einstein imagined a person riding on a streetcar that was headed away from a large clock. He then tried to predict how the clock would appear to the traveler if the car were to travel at the speed of light. He reasoned that since the light reflecting off the clock would be traveling at the same speed as the observer, the observer would always see the same image of the clock and therefore time or the clock would appear L have stopped. The results of this thought experiment helped Einstein to understand the inadequacy of the assumption that time is an absolute and to formulate a new, relativistic concept of time. To explore the use of predictions and thought experiments further, try to imagine what the observer would see if the streetcar were traveling faster than the speed of light (the answer appears in Appendix A).

The Importance of Anticipating Positive as Well as Negative Outcomes

The opposite of failing to anticipate problems that may arise from new ideas is thinking too narrowly and failing to anticipate the good that can come from them. In the late 1930s and early 1940s, Chester Carlson approached numerous companies with a new idea for copying documents that was based on the principles of photoconductivity and electrostatics. All but one of the companies rejected his idea. One of the reasons given was that office workers already had an effective method—carbon paper—for making multiple copies of documents. Many thought there would be little demand for an expensive machine that performed virtually the same function. Others found fault with the quality of the image that Carlson's machine produced.[25]

Those early criticisms of the invention assumed that the new machine's primary consequence would be to replace carbon paper and that the quality of the image it produced could not be improved. In fact, Carlson's invention had applications that went far beyond the purpose of carbon paper. For example, his machine could be used to duplicate documents and graphic images that were prepared in other offices, making it unnecessary to retype or redraw them. Unlike carbon paper, the copy machine could also produce a large number of copies with the same image quality.

The problems that Carlson experienced gaining acceptance for his machine demonstrate how easy it is to find fault with any new idea or invention. It is therefore important to look back at initial criticisms and determine whether they are based on inappropriate assumptions. For example, in Carlson's case the copy machine had many more applications than the critics thought. Similarly, it is important to determine whether a new idea or invention can be modified to overcome a fault. In the case of the copy machine, the quality of the image was greatly improved in subsequent development work. Carlson's invention (xerography) quickly became a big success for the Haloid Corporation (now the Xerox Corporation), and modern versions of the machine are a part of almost every office environment.

Using Focus Groups to Anticipate Outcomes

As discussed in Chapter 2, one approach to anticipating the effects of new ideas is to convene focus groups that are asked to provide feedback on possible new ideas or products. Members of these groups often point out problems that are obvious in retrospect but were not recognized beforehand. For example, we have worked with several groups that were planning large research projects on the uses of computer technology in the classroom. The projects were budgeted for computers and modems so that teachers and students could communicate by computer through modems plugged into telephone lines. These plans seemed fine until we talked to some teachers who revealed to us an obvious flaw in our thinking: Most classrooms do not have a telephone. To install phone lines in each of the classrooms involved in the project would have been quite expensive.

The question of who to talk with to help anticipate the effects of various ideas is very important. In the previous example, our tendency was to talk only with computer experts, since that was the technology we were implementing. If we had not talked to the classroom teachers, we would have failed to realize that the lack of phone lines in the classroom was a problem. People often convene focus groups without thinking much about whom to include. If you choose people with very different kinds of experiences, there will be a much higher probability of getting feedback that will save you from costly mistakes later on.

It can also be important to have focus groups work with actual prototypes rather than simply to imagine a new idea. The more concrete the prototype and the more realistic the setting for its use, the higher the probability that potential problems will be found and fixed.

A Checklist That Can Facilitate the Anticipation of Consequences

Sidney Parnes and Harold Harding discuss checklists such as the one below that can be helpful in anticipating the effects of new ideas and products.[26] You might want to modify this list to suit your own problems.

1. Effects on your objective?
2. Individuals and/or groups affected?
3. Costs involved?
4. Tangibles involved (material, equipment, etc.)?
5. Moral or legal implications?

6. Intangibles involved (opinions, attitudes, feelings, aesthetic values, etc.)?
7. New problems caused?
8. Difficulties of implementation and follow-up?
9. Repercussions of failure
10. Timelines, etc.?

For any problem, these questions can be answered in terms of both potential negative and positive outcomes. In fact, an effective approach to anticipating outcomes is to imagine both worst-case scenarios and best-case scenarios. As these are imagined (and sometimes acted out) in detail, we find that a number of ideas are considered that otherwise would not come to mind. Our suggestions are consistent with Edward deBono's PMI (plus, minus, interesting) strategy. He suggests that creativity can be enhanced if we consider the "plus" aspects of an idea, the "minus" aspects, and the points that seem "interesting."[27] Creative problem solvers often get new insights during the anticipate phase of problem solving. These insights can reveal new opportunities and problems that were previously overlooked.

■ Look and Learn

Long-term efforts to enhance your creativity will not be successful unless you actively look at the effects of your actions and attempt to learn from them. Furthermore, you need to look at them from the perspective of learning something general about enhancing creativity. For example, imagine that you have failed to anticipate some effect of a new idea and discover it only after trying out the idea. You may have developed a novel way to make a presentation to a group of people, for example, and found that it fell flat because the audience expected something much more conventional. What do you do?

A natural reaction is to feel awful and to put the situation out of your mind and get on with other work. But failure can be an excellent teacher. We have therefore learned to ask such questions as "What assumptions were being made about the situation that were erroneous?" and "How could we have gotten the right kind of feedback in advance by using the right people for the situation?" As we explore these questions, we develop ideas about improving our ability to be both novel and appropriate.

Uncovering Implicit Assumptions

We noted earlier that people can uncover inappropriate assumptions by anticipating outcomes. Another important part of looking back at our problem-solving strategies is to examine implicit assumptions that might interfere with creative problem solving. For an illustration of how certain assumptions can interfere with creativity, try to solve the following puzzles as quickly as possible:

1. A superpsychic can predict the score of any game before it begins. How is this possible?
2. Two men played five games of checkers. Each won three games. Please explain.
3. Add one line to IX to make six.

Most people have a difficult time solving these verbal puzzles, especially the first and third. The reason is that they are making assumptions that block the solutions.

Consider the first problem. You probably assumed that the superpsychic could predict the final score of any game. But the question really asks about the score of any game before it begins. Once you make this assumption about the score to be predicted the answer is easy: zero to zero.

In the second problem, you probably assumed that the two men played each other. Once you realize that this assumption is unnecessary, the problem is easy to solve.

The third problem is difficult for people who assume that they must restrict themselves to working with roman numerals and that a line is necessarily straight line. The problem becomes much simpler when you break out of these assumptions. You can add a curved line (an S) to IX to make SIX.

The idea of examining routine assumptions that are taken for granted is important in all areas of inquiry. As an illustration, consider the Copernican revolution. Copernicus was a careful and creative scientist who eventually solved a problem that others before him had failed to solve: how to account for the irregular movements of the planets in the heavens. Astronomers had collected data indicating where various planets were at particular points in time (for example, during different months), but no one had been able to come up with a satisfying theory that explained why planetary movement appeared to deviate from the regular paths that were predicted.[28] After years of study, Copernicus finally created a theory that nicely explained the apparently irregular movements of the planets. To do so, however, he had to make a radical assumption. Before Copernicus, everyone had taken for granted that the sun and the other planets revolve around the Earth, and indeed, it looks that way to the naked eye. Copernicus argued that this assumption made it impossible to explain the movement of the planets. His theory began with the alternative assumption that the Earth and the other planets revolve around the sun. This assumption was considered absurd and so radical that Copernicus was condemned by the Catholic Church.

Several lessons can be learned from the example of Copernicus. One is that unnecessary assumptions (that the sun and the other planets revolve around the Earth) can make it impossible to solve a problem. We have discussed this point before, but it is so important that it bears repeating. Another is that it is easy to overlook basic assumptions that reduce the creativity of our responses to problems.

People who work with business executives have noted an assumption that keeps many of them from exploring new avenues for training and employment. The assumption is that one is too old to try something new. David Schwartz describes a 40-year-old man, Cecil, who wanted to receive training for a better job but felt that he was too old.[29] A common response to this type of problem is to suggest that "you are only as old as you feel" or to say something like, "Ruth and Jim changed jobs at your age and look at how well they are doing." The problem with such suggestions is that people often *feel* old because they believe they *are* old. It is also easy to see Ruth and Jim as special cases whose situations differ in important ways from one's own.

Schwartz approached the problem in a way that directly challenged Cecil's basic assumptions. He asked Cecil to say when a productive career began ("About 20" was the answer) and then when such a career usually ends ("Between 65 and 70"). Schwartz thus helped Cecil to realize that, at 40, he hadn't even approached the halfway point of his career.

Searching for Inconsistencies

Our discussion of Copernicus illustrates a general strategy that can prompt an examination of basic assumptions—the strategy of searching for inconsistencies. Copernicus wanted to create a theory that explained irregularities in the movements of the planets, but his initial attempts resulted in theories that were inconsistent with the actual data. His continued failure to formulate a successful theory eventually served as a signal that some of his assumptions must be erroneous. Had Copernicus not cared about formulating a precise theory consistent with all the data, the need to question basic assumptions would probably never have occurred to him.

The strategy of searching for inconsistencies is also used by efficient technicians, doctors, and others when they are trying to evaluate their diagnoses of a problem. For example, a particular problem (a dead battery) usually has an associated set of symptoms (the engine won't start or turns over slowly, or the lights are dim). If the observed facts are not consistent with these symptoms (the lights are very bright even though the motor won't start), there is reason to doubt or reject the diagnosis of a dead battery. People often fail to evaluate the adequacy of their assumptions because they do not notice their inconsistency with observed facts. For example, in the next paragraph the implicit assumption is inconsistent with certain facts. See if you can identify those facts.

> I left work at 4:30 P.M. on Friday and got caught in the usual rush-hour traffic. When I arrived home I decided to take a shower before preparing for my trip that weekend. After packing my clothes and putting food out for the cat I decided to make a sandwich. To my horror the refrigerator was not working. Since I would be gone all weekend it was important to get it fixed before leaving early next morning. I immediately looked in the phone book and called the only refrigerator repair service. Unfortunately, no one answered the phone. This was very aggravating since the advertisement said it was open until 5 P.M. Monday through Friday and the clock on my kitchen wall showed it to be 20 minutes before 5. In desperation, I went out and bought a new refrigerator at the all-night department store.

Did you notice any facts that appeared inconsistent with the problem's being specific to the refrigerator? That the clock in the kitchen read 4:40, which is only 10 minutes from the time the person left work (and took a shower, packed, and fed the cat), could indicate that the electrical power in the kitchen was not operating properly. To evaluate further the assumption that the problem was localized in the refrigerator, it would have been helpful to check other appliances in the kitchen and the circuit-breaker panel. By searching for inconsistencies between what we observe and what we assume to be true, we can discover assumptions that limit our ability to respond creatively to novel problems and reenter the IDEAL cycle.

The IDEAL Cycle And Creativity

We noted in Chapter 2 that problem solvers usually do not simply start with the I in IDEAL and proceed in a linear order until they get to the L. Instead, they move very flexibly and frequently through the IDEAL cycle a number of times. Different ways of reentering the IDEAL cycle are more or less creative. A less creative approach may be to see that something doesn't work (the look and learn part of the cycle) and then to try again with only a small change in procedure. A more creative approach may be to rethink one's assumptions and redefine the problem from a very different point of view.

Edward deBono[30] distinguishes between vertical thinking (proceeding systematically from a single concept or definition) and lateral thinking (seeking alternative ways of defining or interpreting a problem). He states:

> Logic is the tool that is used to dig holes deeper and bigger, to make them altogether better holes. But if the hole is in the wrong place, then no amount of improvement is going to put it in the right place. No matter how obvious this may seem to every digger, it is still easier to go on digging in the same place than to start all over again in a new place. Vertical thinking is digging the same hole deeper; lateral thinking is trying again elsewhere.

These comments suggest that an important aspect of creative problem solving is to ask yourself whether you are making assumptions about the nature of a problem that are limiting your ability to find solutions.

During an afternoon seminar on problem solving that one of us was teaching, a bird flew through the open window and fluttered frantically around the room. It was possible that the bird might be injured or people could get hurt. The teacher announced that this was a real-world problem to be solved. (What else could he do, given that the seminar was on problem solving?) Fortunately for the teacher, he was eventually able to solve the problem.

In considering his thought processes, the teacher realized that he was not successful until he had moved through the IDEAL cycle several times and had reformulated some of his initial definitions of the problem.

For example, he defined his goal first as "How can I catch the bird?" and next as "How can I catch the bird without hurting either it or myself?" Neither of these definitions led to a solution. Approximately two minutes after the bird entered the room, the teacher redefined the goal as "How can I get the bird to leave the room?" This led to a strategy that worked on the first try (see Appendix A).

■ Summary

Creativity is the ability to generate ideas and that are both novel and appropriate. Everyone is creative to some degree, and we can all improve our ability in this area. From the perspective of the IDEAL framework, efforts to enhance creativity involve each component of IDEAL.

A hallmark of creative individuals is their ability to identify important problems and opportunities that others have missed or taken for granted. Tests of divergent thinking do not tap this ability and hence miss a very important aspect of creative behavior. By actively attempting to identify important problems and opportunities, people can enhance their creativity.

Creativity can also be enhanced by learning to define a minimum of two different goals for any problem, rather than jumping right to the generation of possible solution strategies, as most people do. Attention to goals helps us uncover a host of unexamined assumptions that can block our ability to think in nonroutine ways.

Once goals are defined, there are a variety of strategies for thinking more creatively about them. Examples include the use of the PMI (plus, minus, interesting) strategy, the fractionation strategy, analogies, creativity checklists, brainstorming, and incubation (sleeping on the problem). It is important not to evaluate ideas prematurely, because evaluations can act as idea killers that hamper nonroutine thought.

Since the goal of being creative is to generate ideas and behave in ways that are both novel and appropriate, it is very important to anticipate the effects of implementing novel strategies. There are many strategies that enhance the probability of anticipating both negative and positive outcomes that might otherwise be unforeseen.

The ability to be creative depends in part on our ability to make aspects of complex problems routine so that our attention is not overwhelmed. If you look at a situation and decide that your responses were not as creative as you desired, it can be helpful to ask whether part of the problem is that you were overwhelmed by the complexity of the task.

Our ability to learn from our experiences can be enhanced by thinking in terms of distributed intelligence and creativity. Theorists such as Roy Pea note that a powerful strategy is to create relationships with other aspects of our environment, including technology, and, most important, with other people.[31] Attempts to learn from experience are enhanced when we consider not only how to improve our own attitudes and skills but also how to put together creative, collaborative teams.

Creative individuals usually reenter the IDEAL cycle from new perspectives rather than from the same perspective. Part of being creative is having the patience to continue to explore a problem rather than giving up too soon and accepting solutions that are easy but routine.

Appendix C contains an IDEAL problem navigation guide that people have found valuable in enhancing their ability to identify important problems and to generate novel solutions to them. We recommend that you try it on problems that are important and relevant to you.

■ Exercises

Use the IDEAL Problem Navigation Guide (in Appendix C) to help you work through a real-world problem and explore creative alternatives. Follow the suggestions given in this chapter and remember to define at least three different goals for solving your problem.

1. Generate some inventions (ones that you make up as well as ones you already know about) that can help people appreciate tropical fish while remaining in their homes (one invention would be an aquarium). Generate as many as you can in three minutes.
2. Six normal drinking glasses are standing in a row. The first three are full of water; the next three are empty. By handling and moving only one glass, change the arrangement so that no full glass is next to another full glass, and no empty glass is next to another empty one.
3. When my cousin comes to visit me in my apartment, why does he always get off the elevator five floors below my floor and walk the rest of the way? Generate as many reasons as you can.
4. How could you make a tennis ball go a short distance, come to a dead stop, then reverse itself and go in the opposite direc-

tion? *Note:* Bouncing the ball is not permitted, nor may you put a spin on the ball and roll it (this is really a form of bouncing it) or tie anything to the ball.

5. Look at the nine dots below. Connect all of them using only four straight lines, never retracing a line or removing your pen or pencil from the paper as you draw.

●   ●   ●

●   ●   ●

●   ●   ●

6. Try solving this mystery. A county sheriff arrived at the scene of an apparent homicide and found the victim lying on the side of the road, dead. The only clue to the crime was a pair of tire tracks left on the little-traveled dirt road. The sheriff followed the tracks to a country farmhouse less than a mile away. Although there were three men sitting on the front porch, the sheriff was certain that the man he wanted for questioning was sitting in the middle, even though he knew that none of the men had a car and none had mud on his boots. How did the sheriff know he should question the man sitting in the middle?

7. Do you see any inconsistencies in the following passage? If so, are there ways they might be resolved? The man was worried. His car came to a halt, and he was all alone. It was extremely dark and cold. The man took off his overcoat, rolled down the window, and got out of the car as quickly as possible. Then he used all his strength to move as fast as he could. He was relieved when he finally saw the lights of the city, even though they were far away.

8. A farmer ate two eggs every morning for breakfast. He had no chickens; nobody ever gave him any eggs; and he never bought, borrowed, begged, or stole any eggs. Where did he get the eggs?[32]

9. A goat is tied to a rope. The rope is only 5 feet long, yet the

goat can reach a pile of hay that is 10 feet away. How is this possible?

10. In 1969 it was reported that a young woman gymnast in New York City fell from a window sill on the 25th floor and was not badly hurt. There was nothing special to cushion the fall or reduce the impact. How was this possible?

11. Jim and Tom find a long piece of pipe in a vacant lot. It's big enough that each boy can just manage to squeeze into it and crawl from one end to the other. If Jim and Tom go into the pipe from opposite ends, is it possible for each to crawl the entire length of the pipe and come out the other end?[33]

12. How can a boy stand behind his mother and at the same time have his mother stand behind him? No stepmothers or grandmothers are involved.

13. A man walked through a pouring rain for 20 minutes without getting a single hair on his head wet. He didn't wear a hat, carry an umbrella, or hold anything over his head. His clothes got soaked. How could this happen?[b]

14. Several years ago a new baby was born to Bill's family. This new baby wasn't Bill's son or daughter, his brother or sister, his nephew or niece. In fact, it was not his relative. How is this possible?[34]

▮ Notes

1. A. Jay, *Management and Machiavelli; An Inquiry into the Politics of Corporate Life*. New York: Holt, Rinehart & Winston, 1967.

2. D. N. Perkins, *The Mind's Best Work*. Cambridge, Mass.: Harvard University Press, 1981.

3. Styrofoam blitz. *Time* (July 6, 1992):20.

4. W. T. Brown, Creativity: What are we to measure? In J. A. Glover, R. R. Ronning, and C. R. Reynolds (eds.), *Handbook of Creativity*. New York: Plenum Press, 1989.

5. M. Scardamalia and C. Bereiter, Higher levels of agency for children in knowledge building: A challenge for the design of new knowledge media. *Journal of the Learning Sciences* 1 (1991):37–68.

6. L. G. Bolman and T. E. Deal, *Reframing Organizations: Artistry, Choice, and Leadership*. San Francisco: Jossey-Bass, 1991.

7. N. R. F. Maier, Reasoning in humans II: The solution of a problem

and its appearance in consciousness. *Journal of Comparative Psychology* 12 (1931):181–194.

8. Experiments demonstrating functional fixedness were conducted by K. Dunker, On problem solving, *Psychological Monographs* 58, no. 5 (1945).

9. E. de Bono, *Lateral Thinking: Creativity Step by Step.* New York: Harper & Row, 1970.

10. J. R. Hayes, *Cognitive Psychology: Thinking and Creating.* Homewood, Ill.: Dorsey, 1978.

11. See A. Koestler, *The Act of Creation.* New York: Macmillan, 1964.

12. See note 11.

13. W. J. Gordon, *Synectics: The Development of Creative Capacity.* New York: Harper & Row, 1961.

14. A. F. Osborn, *Applied Imagination.* New York: Scribners, 1957.

15. See A. B. Van Gundy, *Managing Group Creativity.* New York: American Management Association, 1984.

16. See note 2.

17. H. Poincaré, Mathematical creation. In G. H. Halstead (trans.), *The Foundations of Science.* New York: Science Press, 1913.

18. See G. I. Nierenberg, *The Art of Creative Thinking.* New York: Simon & Schuster, 1982.

19. This analysis of insight is from J. D. Bransford and K. E. Nitsch, Coming to understand things we could not previously understand. In J. F. Kavanagh and W. Strange (eds.), *Speech and Language in the Laboratory, School and Clinic.* Cambridge, Mass.: MIT Press, 1978.

20. See note 2.

21. A. F. Osborn, *Applied Imagination* (3d rev. ed.). New York: Scribners, 1963.

22. G. A. Davis and W. E. Roweton, Using idea checklists with college students: Overcoming resistance. *Journal of Psychology* 70 (1968):221–226.

23. M. McCloskey, Intuitive physics. *Scientific American* 248 (1983):122–130.

24. Einstein's thought experiments. L. K. Barnett, *The Universe and Dr. Einstein.* New York: New American Library, 1962. See also T. Kuhn, A function for thought experiments. In P. N. Johnson-Laird and P. C. Wason (eds.), *Thinking: Readings in Cognitive Science.* Cambridge, England: Cambridge University Press, 1977.

25. For more on Chester Carlson and his invention see J. E. Brittain, "Chester Floyd Carlson," *Dictionary of American Biography* 28, no. 8

(1988):70–72; An idea looking for a company. *Appliance Manufacturer* (November 1988:33–38).

26. S. J. Parnes and H. F. Harding (eds.), *A Source Book for Creative Thinking*. New York: Scribners, 1962.

27. E. de Bono, The CoRT thinking program. In J. Segal, S. Chipman, and R. Glaser (eds.), *Thinking and Learning Skills: Relating Instruction to Basic Research,* Vol. 1. Hillsdale, N.J.: Lawrence Erlbaum Associates, 1985.

28. S. Toulmin and J. Goodfield, *The Fabric of the Heavens: The Development of Astronomy and Dynamics.* New York: Harper, 1961.

29. D. Schwartz, *The Magic of Thinking Big.* New York: Cornerstone Library, 1981.

30. E. debono, *New Think*. New York: Basic Books, 1967.

31. R. Pea, Practices of distributed intelligence and designs for education. To appear in G. Salomon (ed.), *Distributed Cognitions*. New York: Cambridge University Press, in press.

32. From D. A. Hindman, *1800 Riddles, Enigmas and Conundrums*. New York: Dover Publications, 1963.

33. From M. Gardner, *Perplexing Puzzles and Tantalizing Teasers*. New York: Simon & Shuster, 1969.

34. Personal communication, Grant Gong. June 1990.

∎ Suggested Readings

Practically Oriented Readings

Adams, J. L. 1986. *Conceptual Blockbusting: A Guide to Better Ideas* (3d ed.). Reading, Mass.: Addison-Wesley.

Anderson, B. F. 1980. Chap. 4, "Creative Thinking," in *The Complete Thinker*. Englewood Cliffs, N.J.: Prentice-Hall.

Anderson, H. H. (ed.). 1959. *Creativity and Its Cultivation*. New York: Harper & Row.

de Bono, E. 1970. *Lateral Thinking*. New York: Harper & Row.

Gordon, W. J. 1961. *Synectics: The Development of Creative Capacity*. New York: Harper & Row.

McKim, R. H. 1980. *Experiences in Visual Thinking* (2d. ed). Monterey, Calif.: Brooks/Cole.

Osborn, A. F. 1963. *Applied Imagination: Principles and Procedures of Creative Problem Solving* (3d rev. ed.). New York: Scribners.

Theoretically Oriented Readings

Amabile, T. M. 1983. *The Social Psychology of Creativity*. New York: Springer-Verlag.

Bradshaw, G. F., P. W. Langley, and H. Simon. 1983. Studying scientific discovery by computer simulation. *Science* 222:971–975.

Barron, F. 1969. *Creative Person and Ceative Process*. New York: Holt, Rinehart & Winston.

Brown, S. I., and M. I. Walter. 1985. *The Art of Problem Posing*. Hillsdale, N.J.: Lawrence Erlbaum Associates.

Glover, J. A., R. R. Ronning, and C. R. Reynolds (eds.). 1989. *Handbook of Creativity*. New York: Plenum Press.

Koestler, A. 1964. *The Act of Creation*. New York: Macmillan.

Kuhn, T. S. 1962. *The Structure of Scientific Revolutions*. Chicago: University of Chicago Press.

Perkins, D. N. 1988. Creativity and the quest for mechanism. In R. J. Sternberg and E. E. Smith (eds.), *The Psychology of Human Thought*. Cambridge and London: Cambridge University Press.

Stein, M. I. 1974. *Stimulating Creativity*. New York: Academic Press.

Sternberg, R. J. (ed.). 1988. *The Nature of Creativity: Contemporary Psychological Perspectives*. Cambridge and London: Cambridge University Press.

Taylor, I. A., and J. W. Getzels (eds.). 1975. *Perspectives in Creativity*. Chicago: Aldine.

Watzlawick, P., J. H. Weakland, and R. Fisch. 1974. *Change: Principles of Problem Formation and Problem Resolution*. New York: W. W. Norton.

Weisberg, R. W. *Creativity: Genius and Other Myths*. 1986. New York: W. H. Freeman.

CHAPTER

4

INTELLIGENT CRITICISM

The most important factor in the training of good mental habits consists in acquiring the attitude of suspended conclusion, and in mastering the various methods of searching for new materials to corroborate or to refute the first suggestions that occur.

John Dewey[1]

Our discussion in Chapter 3 examined various ways that the IDEAL framework can help people develop more creative approaches to problem solving. We noted that some strategies for enhancing creativity, such as brainstorming, require postponing the critical evaluation of ideas to stimulate idea generation. At some point, however, effective problem solvers must critically evaluate their ideas by *anticipating* outcomes and by *looking* at the effects of a strategy once it has been acted upon.

■ The Importance of Evaluating Arguments

In addition to evaluating our own ideas, it is equally if not more important to develop the skills necessary to evaluate other people's ideas and arguments. Whether we are scientists, business executives, doctors, lawyers, or consumers, we must learn to evaluate the claims, arguments, and beliefs that confront us daily.

The Effects of Failing to Evaluate Ideologies

Throughout history people have harmed each other and committed atrocities because of their belief in political, social, religious, or economic ideas that seemed to justify such actions. It is often difficult for us to imagine people accepting ideas that would justify killing millions of people in the Holocaust or blowing up an airplane full of innocent civilians. William Dember notes that it is fashionable to think that the perpetrators of such atrocities were people whose "emotions overshadowed their thinking." But Dember suggests that we consider the opposite conclusion: that ideology came to rule their emotions.[2] In fact, numerous examples of atrocities committed in almost all societies are difficult to attribute to emotion. For example, the U.S. government forced Native Americans to give up much of the land their ancestors had occupied for centuries. Many of the Native Americans who refused were killed by soldiers. More recently, the U.S. government interned thousands of American citizens of Japanese ancestry during World War II. These actions were justified on the basis of a political and economic ideology that stressed the importance of protecting the country and allowing it to grow.

The powerful effects that ideology can have on people's actions and their sense of right and wrong has been noted by many observers. For example, Arthur Koestler states:[3]

> We are thus driven to the unfashionable conclusion that the trouble with our species is not an excess of aggression, but an excess capacity for fanatical devotion. Even a cursory glance at history should convince one that individual crimes committed for selfish motives play a quite insignificant part in the human tragedy, compared to the numbers massacred in unselfish loyalty to one's tribe, nation, dynasty, church or political ideology.

IDEAL and the Evaluation of Arguments

Throughout this chapter we will examine how to use the IDEAL framework to think about and evaluate arguments critically. When you first hear an idea or argument you may begin to *identify* a problem with it ("something seems to be wrong here"). You may then *define* the goal of your criticism more precisely. For example, your first goal may be to determine the factual accuracy of the argument; this calls for an *exploration* of various strategies for verifying the evidence presented. You may then *anticipate* the outcome of certain strategies (such as reading a textbook or searching through a computerized database) and *act* on those that seem most promising. Finally, you can *look* at the effects. If they are

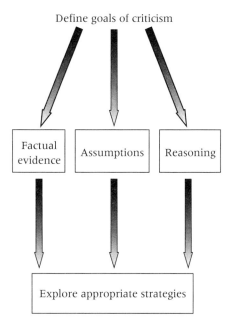

Figure 11

negative—that is, if you are unable to show that the argument is factually inaccurate—you may reenter the IDEAL cycle and redefine your goals (for example, to determine whether the argument's conclusions follow logically or whether the argument is based on inappropriate assumptions).

■ Three Ways of Critically Evaluating Arguments

We will examine three general goals in evaluating arguments. These goals involve the evaluation of facts, reasoning, and assumptions. By "facts" we mean the data that people use as the basis for their arguments. "Reasoning" refers to the steps people take in connecting facts or data to their conclusions. "Assumptions" form the basis of an argument and may or may not be reasonable (see Figure 11).

The three goals for critically evaluating arguments can be illustrated by Vincent Bugliosi's description of a famous murder trial that he prosecuted in California.[4] Since there were no eyewitnesses, the prosecution was based solely on circumstantial evidence. Near the end of the trial, the defense lawyer tried to convince the jury that the defendant was innocent. He reminded the jury that the argument of the prosecuting attorney was based on circumstantial evidence and argued that a trial of this type is like a chain. A chain is only as strong as its weakest link, and the defense lawyer said that the jury needed a strong chain to convict the defendant. He then proceeded to show not only one weak link in the chain, but several.

Imagine that you are the prosecuting attorney in this trial. You speak to the jury after the defense finishes its presentation. To convince the jury that the defendant is guilty, you need to do more than comprehend what the defense lawyer has said to the jury. You also need to criticize his argument and communicate your ideas clearly and persuasively.

There are several ways to evaluate arguments. One is to focus on factual accuracy. For example, the defense attorney may have stated (erroneously) that a jury may not reach a guilty verdict on the basis of circumstantial evidence alone. Given this argument, you could challenge the accuracy of the defense attorney's facts.

A second way is to determine whether the reasoning is logical and consistent. A person may begin with accurate facts, but the conclusion drawn may be invalid. For example if the defendant drinks beer and a wine bottle was found near the victim, this does not prove that the defendant is innocent.

A third way to evaluate an argument is to question its underlying assumptions. The facts may be correct and the arguments sound only *given* the truth of various assumptions. However, a creative person may be able to come up with a set of assumptions that differ from those made previously. In the California trial, for example, Bugliosi questioned a basic assumption made by the defense attorney: He argued that trials based on circumstantial evidence are analogous to a *rope* rather than a chain. A rope is composed of a number of independent strands; several of these can break without having much effect on the overall strength of the rope. Bugliosi acknowledged that there were indeed a few questionable strands, but he emphasized that the rest of the evidence was more than strong enough to convict the defendant. (For what it's worth, Bugliosi won the case.)

The Analysis of Factual Claims

Suppose you win $10,000 in a contest and want to invest the money. An investment counselor offers you a once-in-a-lifetime opportunity: He knows someone who is willing to part with an ancient coin for a fraction of its worth. You examine the coin and observe that it indeed looks authentic. The counselor emphasizes that since the coin is very old (the date stamped on it is 42 B.C.), it should be worth at least what you are being asked to pay (which is $9100). He also explains that the seller is willing to part with the coin at this low price only because he needs the money immediately and it usually takes about a month to sell an antique coin at its fair value. Would you buy the coin? Why or why not?

If you decided to buy the coin you also bought a faulty argument. One of the facts used to support the claim that the coin is ancient cannot be true. To stamp a coin 42 B.C., the coin maker would have had to know in advance not only the exact year of the birth of Christ, but also that his birth would be the basis for dating in the future. Since this is extremely doubtful, the coin clearly is a fake.

A claim that a coin was minted in 42 B.C. is not necessarily false. It is possible to find a coin this old. The problem with the argument is not the claim itself but *the evidence for the claim* (that the date was printed on the coin). Geologists and archaeologists make claims about the age of various entities (fossils and skeletons), but they do so by providing evidence that seems reasonable given current scientific knowledge (they often use radioactive isotopes to date items). Effective critics pay careful attention to the nature of the evidence on which claims are based.[5]

Invited Inferences That Do Not Follow from the Data

You can learn a lot about the importance of paying attention to data by studying advertisements. By law, advertisers cannot lie; for example, it would be illegal to advertise that a coin stamped 42 B.C. is authentic. Nevertheless, advertisements often prompt us to make "invited inferences" about messages that, from a logical or scientific perspective, do not follow. Consider the following claim.

> Scientific studies show that our brand (brand A) is unsurpassed by any other brand on the market.

How do you interpret this statement? Many people assume that brand A has been shown to be superior to other brands. This is only an invited inference, however. *Legally,* "unsurpassed" means that the researchers have found no differences in the effectiveness of brand A versus other brands.

Here is another example of a possible claim.

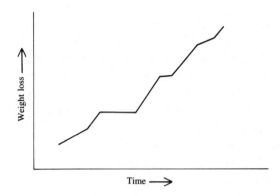

Figure 12 A graph illustrating weight loss as a function of time.

> Dogs prefer our brand of food by a ratio of 2 to 1.

What is missing here is any explicit mention of what was used for comparison. The advertised brand could have been compared to uncooked cabbage, for example. Such information is often omitted in the hope that consumers will make the invited inference that a reasonable comparison group was used.

Look at the graph in Figure 12, which appeared in an advertisement for a new weight-reducing product. Many people who see this graph conclude that, by using the product advertised, they could lose a lot of weight in a short period of time. However, if you examine the graph more carefully you will notice that the units of weight loss and time are not specified. The conclusion that the product is highly effective is only an invited inference. It is possible, for example, that in actual tests the new product produced a reduction of only an ounce in six months. When analyzing graphs and charts it is always important to check the units of measurement to evaluate the claims being made.

Scientific "Facts"

It would be unfair to imply that the purpose of all advertisements is to mislead. Many ads are designed to inform us about products that are quite good. Furthermore, misleading arguments are by no means confined to advertising. Arguments found in newspapers, textbooks, conversations, and even scientific articles may be based on questionable facts.

The following data show the number of deaths per million boat passengers in 1973:[6]

Canoe (motor)	0.14
Canoe (no motor)	1.66
Sailboat (auxiliary motor)	0.44
Sailboat (no motor)	0.52

When asked to draw conclusions on the basis of these data, many people state that there are fewer deaths in boats with motors, and they go on to explain why these are safer. For example, a motor provides an alternative means of transportation in case of an accident like a broken arm or a torn sail; also, a motor allows one to travel faster and hence avoid such problems as storms and high winds. In general, people think the data show that *boats with motors are safer than boats without motors.* This statement, therefore, appears to be a fact.

If you think about it, however, you will recognize a problem with this "factual" statement, which is that there are many differences between boats besides the presence or absence of motors. For example, white-water canoes would never have a motor, whereas canoes used on calm lakes (which are generally safer than fast-moving streams) would be much more likely to have one. And only the larger sailboats (those less likely to capsize) are likely to have motors. Finally, inexperienced sailors are more likely to have smaller, less stable boats. Given these considerations, it is questionable that motors alone account for differences in safety. Indeed, in many situations (such as canoeing on a fast river or sailing a small boat on a windy lake) it seems that the presence of a motor could make a boat less safe.

Many types of claims are based on similar types of data. For example:

> At a meeting of educators, a committee chairman reported on a study that had just been completed. Questionnaires had been sent to teachers; two of the questions asked were: "How much do you like computers?" and "How much experience have you had with computers?" The data showed that the people who claimed to have had the most experience with computers also liked them better. Based on these data, the chairman drew the following conclusion: "We can see that the more people are exposed to computers the more they will like them."

Do the data support this factual claim? It is quite possible that exposure to computers increases people's liking for them. Nevertheless, the data presented by the committee chairman do not really support this claim. The chairman is suggesting that experience with computers *causes* people to like them. But the opposite is also possible; namely, that people who like computers are apt to seek to learn more about them, and such people therefore have more experience with them. It is the degree of liking that causes the contact with computers.

The data do not allow us to conclude that liking causes contact with computers, that contact causes liking, or that each affects the other. The reason is that the data involve only correlations between two variables. Evidence for a correlation between variables (liking and contact with computers or motors on boats and safety) does not necessarily include evidence that either variable causes the other. Indeed, both might be caused by a third variable. For example, it is not difficult to find a positive correlation between increases in teacher salaries and increases in alcohol consumption. This doesn't necessarily mean that teachers use the additional money to buy liquor. Instead, the correlation is probably due to some third variable that affects raises as well as consumption. A likely candidate would be growth in the general economy which would allow schools to pay teachers more and increase the disposable income of other people as well.

Correlation Versus Cause and Effect

The preceding discussion illustrates a common mistake in reasoning: *Correlational data are often interpreted as indicating cause and effect.* There are times, however, when it is valid to conclude that one thing is caused or affected by another. It is important to understand the nature of the evidence necessary to make such a claim. For example, what kinds of data would provide convincing evidence that as people's contacts with computers increase, they like computers more?[7] The following paragraphs illustrate one approach to this problem.

Imagine that 100 people are randomly assigned to two groups. This means that everyone has an equally likely chance to be in either group; names could be put in a hat and the first name drawn assigned to group 1, the second to group 2, the third to group 1, and so on. If the assignment to groups is truly random, we would expect that each group would have had, on average, approximately equal experience with computers (many in each group would probably have had none) and liking for computers.

Assume that all receive a questionnaire asking about their experience with computers and their liking for computers. We can then arrange it so that members of the two groups have different experiences. For example, the people in group 1 work with computers for an hour a day for two weeks, and the people in group 2 (the control group) do no work with computers. At the end of the experiment we give everyone another questionnaire that asks them to rate their liking for computers. If experience with computers increases the degree to which people like them, we should find that those who received computer training will like computers more than before and that these in the control group will not. This would allow us to conclude that an increase in experience with computers increases the degree to which people report liking them.

However, even this claim may be an overgeneralization. First, it implies that experience with computers affects all people positively. Second, it suggests that any type of experience with computers (learning to program in BASIC as well as playing video games) is equally likely to increase liking. A more finely tuned experiment could be conducted as follows.

The participants are assigned to groups on the basis of how much they think they will like computers (a great deal, pretty much, or not at all). Half the members of each group are then given computer experience, and the other half acts as the control (receiving no computer experience). After two weeks, people are again asked to rate the degree to which they like computers.

Given such an experiment, it is possible to assess whether experience with computers affects different groups in different ways. For example, people who think they will like computers a great deal or pretty much may like them more after computer training, whereas people who think they will not like computers may actually like them less after training. However, these results may hold for some types of experiences with computers (such as learning to program in BASIC) but not for others. In assessing a factual claim such as that more experience with computers increases people's liking for them, we therefore have to consider the nature of the evidence carefully. For example, we need to know something about the people being discussed, and we need information about the nature of the computer training they received.

Additional Illustrations of Factual Claims

Here are some more examples of factual claims and of the evidence used to support them. See if you can spot problems with these claims (answers appear in Appendix A).

College professors are asked to indicate the degree to which they agree with various statements. One is "Students who turn in papers that are typed tend to get higher grades than students who do not type their papers." Most of the professors surveyed indicate that they agree with this statement. On the basis of these data, a typewriter company recommends that students learn to type so that they can get better grades. Do the data support this conclusion? Why or why not?

Sid Slye wants to sell you a special gas-saving device for your car for only $100. "How do I know it works?" you ask. "That's easy," says Sid. "I have one on my car and it gets 45 miles per gallon. My other car doesn't have one, and it gets only 25 miles per gallon." Is this enough information to convince you that the device works?

The number of people who send in a $1 rebate form is found to be related to their average annual income in the following manner.

Income	Number of people
Less than $20,000	10,000
$20,000–$40,000	7,000
Over $40,000	4,000

Can you conclude from these data that people who make more money are less likely to worry about collecting rebates? Why or why not?

Evaluating the Reasoning of Arguments

In the preceding discussion we emphasized situations in which the facts used to support arguments were questionable. For example, the claim that people should be encouraged to put motors on their canoes might be based on the "fact" that canoes with motors have been shown to be safer than canoes without motors. However, this claim is not supported by the data presented. It is therefore important to analyze the nature of the evidence used to support factual claims.

Another way to analyze arguments is to assume that we begin with an accurate fact (a premise) and ask how we can use it to make a logical point. That is, what must we do to ensure that our conclusions follow logically from a set of premises or facts?[8]

Here is a claim that seems to be supported by the study of history: "Many scientific theories that later proved valid were first ridiculed." In medicine, for example, Pasteur's idea that diseases are transmitted by germs too small to see with the naked eye was considered by many to be totally unrealistic.

How might the fact that many valid scientific theories were at first ridiculed be used in an argument? Imagine that you have a theory that is criticized by several other scientists. A reporter suggests that you give up in the face of such criticism. A possible response would be "Look, history shows that many valid theories were at first ridiculed. Therefore, the fact that some people ridicule my theory does not prove it is wrong."[9] Another possible response would be "Look, history shows that many valid theories were at first ridiculed. Therefore, the fact that my theory is being ridiculed shows it is correct."

You probably feel much more comfortable with the first argument than the second. Only in the first argument does the conclusion seem to follow from the premise on which it is based. The two arguments illustrate a type of reasoning known as *categorical syllogistic* reasoning.

Argument 1

Some theories that have been criticized have turned out to be valid (major premise).
My theory is being criticized (minor premise).
Therefore, it could turn out to be valid (conclusion).

Argument 2

Some theories that have been criticized have turned out to be valid (major premise).
My theory is being criticized (minor premise).
Therefore, it is valid (conclusion).

Using Venn diagrams, Figure 13 represents the relationship among theories that are initially criticized, theories that are accepted, and theories like yours. These diagrams are a powerful tool for analyzing arguments in detail. The use of Venn diagrams makes it clear that the second argument is not logically sound.

Imagine that the facts of history were somewhat different. For example, suppose that all (rather than some) theories that later turned out to be valid were criticized initially. Now could one conclude that criticism of a theory proves that it is true? The answer is no; many invalid theories

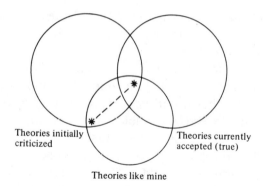

Figure 13   Note that "my theory" could fall into either of the two places in the diagram marked by asterisks. If it falls into the space designated by the asterisk on the left, the theory would not be currently accepted as true.

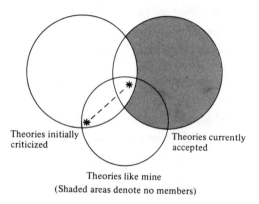

Figure 14   Note that "my theory" could fall into either of the two places in the diagram marked by asterisks. If it falls into the space designated by the asterisk on the left, the theory would not be currently accepted as true.

could also have been criticized initially. This is illustrated by the Venn diagrams shown in Figure 14.

Consider one more hypothetical historical fact, that all new theories initially criticized turned out to be valid. Given this premise, you would be in a much stronger position to make the argument that the existence of criticism proves your theory is valid (see Figure 15). However, the historical fact on which this argument is based is not true.

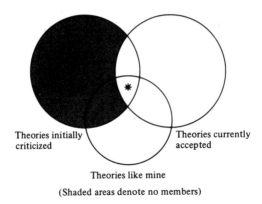

Theories initially criticized

Theories currently accepted

Theories like mine

(Shaded areas denote no members)

Figure 15   Note that "my theory" must be accepted because, in this instance, all theories that were initially criticized are currently accepted as true.

If–Then Arguments

Many arguments we make follow an "if–then" structure. You are undoubtedly familiar with a very simple if–then statement known as a guarantee: "If you are not satisfied with our product, [then] we will refund your money." Another example is insurance policies: "If you have a car accident, we will pay for damages." The if–then statement is used to describe a relationship between two events; it tells us what should happen (we will be able to get our money back) if certain events (we are not satisfied with the product) occur. Each if–then argument includes what is called an *antecedent* (if you are not satisfied with our product) and a *consequent* (we will refund your money). When we are given a clear if–then statement and find the antecedent condition to be true (we are not satisfied with the product), we can rightfully expect the consequent condition also to be true (we will to get our money back). This type of argument illustrates a type of reasoning known as *conditional syllogistic* reasoning.

If–then statements occur in a variety of settings. For example, suppose again that you are a lawyer in a trial. This time you are a defense lawyer. You have established that the defendant has an ironclad alibi for 9 to 12 A.M. on the day of the murder. You might therefore want to argue, "If the murder occurred between 9 and 12 A.M., my client is innocent." The form of this argument is "If A, then B."

Assume that the time of the murder is established at 10 A.M. Your argument would then be "If the murder occurred between 9 and 12 A.M., my client is innocent (because of the airtight alibi). The murder did occur during this time; therefore, my client is innocent." The general form of this argument is "If A, then B; A, therefore B." This is a valid argument.

Suppose we try to reverse the argument. That is, if the client is truly innocent, can we conclude that the murder therefore took place at the time of his alibi; that is, between 9 and 12 A.M.? The answer is no; the murder could have taken place at any number of times. The form of this argument is "If A, then B; B, therefore A." Philosophers refer to this form of argument as the fallacy of affirming the consequent (where A is the antecedent and B is the consequent). This is an invalid form of argument.

It is instructive to note that many tests of scientific theories take the form, "If A (this theory is correct), then B (the following results should be obtained)." For example, a theory of the effects of imagery on memory might predict that people who form images of information will remember more than people who do not form images (see Chapter 6 for a discussion of imagery). Assume that an experiment is conducted, and the prediction holds. Can we conclude that the imagery theory is correct? Note that the form of this argument would be "If A (the imagery theory is correct), then B (the group told to form images should remember more); B (the imagery group did remember more), therefore A (the imagery theory is correct)." As noted above, this is an invalid form of argument because it rests on the fallacy of affirming the consequent. For this reason logicians caution that one cannot prove a theory correct. Instead, one can only say, "These results are consistent with the theory" or "These results provide support for the theory."

There are two more if–then argument forms; one is "If A, then B; not A, therefore not B." Returning to the trial example, this translates as "If the murder occurred between 9 and 12 A.M., my client is innocent. The murder did not occur during this time; therefore, my client is not innocent." This is not an argument you would want to make as a defense lawyer. Fortunately, it also involves what philosophers call the fallacy of denying the antecedent and is an invalid form of argument. In this case, it is possible that the client was fishing alone at a remote cabin, but no one else may have known it; hence, he could not prove that he was not at the scene of the murder when the victim was killed. Nevertheless, the absence of an alibi does not prove the presence of guilt.

The fourth form of if–then argument is "If the murder occurred between 9 and 12 A.M., my client is innocent. My client is not innocent, therefore the murder did not occur between 9 and 12 A. M. " Although as a defense lawyer you might be reluctant to admit that your client is not innocent, the form of this argument is valid. The form is "If A, then B; not

Table 1

ILLUSTRATIONS OF VALID AND INVALID ARGUMENT FORMS

Argument	Valid or Not Valid
1. If A is true, then B is true. A is true. Therefore, B is true.	Valid
2. If A is true, then B is true B is true. Therefore, A is true.	Not valid; fallacy of affirming the consequent
3. If A is true, then B is true A is not true. Therefore, B is not true.	Not valid; fallacy of denying the antecedent
4. If A is true, then B is true B is not true. Therefore, A is not true.	Valid

B, therefore not A." It is this form of argument that can be used to disprove a hypothesis; that is, one can argue, "If this hypothesis is true, then the following experimental result should be obtained. The result was not obtained; therefore (assuming that the study was carried out appropriately) the hypothesis cannot be true." We will discuss the limitations of this form of reasoning later.

Many people seem to be unfamiliar with the valid and invalid forms of conditional reasoning when testing their own hypotheses. For example, our discussion suggests that finding evidence that confirms a hypothesis (If A, then B; B is true, therefore A could be true) is much less decisive than finding evidence that is inconsistent with a hypothesis (If A, then B; not B, therefore not A). Researchers such as Peter Wason[10] have found that people have a tendency to evaluate a hypothesis by only searching for information that would be consistent with it. Wason and others refer to this predisposition as a "confirmation bias" and note that it often leads people to have more confidence in their initial hypothesis than they really should. A confirmation bias may cause people to ignore simple tests that would disconfirm a faulty hypothesis.

The four basic forms of if–then arguments are presented in Table 1. Since many people have a difficult time remembering these abstract rules, a simple example may help you generate the correct rules on your own. Start with an antecedent such as "If it snows six feet tonight" and add the consequent "then public schools will be closed tomorrow." Assume that this relationship will always be true. To determine if any particular form of argument is valid (B is true; therefore A is true) simply examine how those arguments would be represented in terms of the familiar case. For example, to remember if situation 2 (in Table 1) is valid, consider the following: Schools are closed today (B is true); can we therefore conclude that it snowed six feet the night before (A is true)? Obviously this is not a valid conclusion, since school may be closed for other reasons (such as a holiday, a fire, or summer vacation). If school is not closed (B is not true), can we conclude that it did not snow six feet the night before (A is not true)? This is a valid conclusion. Try generating the other situations in Table 1 using this model and then try to solve a different set of arguments without referring to the table. For example, consider the premise "If it is a triangle, then it is red." Now try to answer the following questions: If the shape is not a triangle, is it not red? If it is not red, is it not a triangle? (See Appendix A for answers.)

The Consistency of Arguments

Another important feature of valid arguments is that they are logically consistent. The search for inconsistencies plays an important role in a many areas. Consider again a court of law. A witness may provide information inconsistent with his or her previous testimony or may describe an event in a manner inconsistent with other people's testimony. The effective trial lawyer searches for such inconsistencies and makes sure the jury realizes they exist.

An advertisement that appeared in a Tennessee newspaper announced in bold type the following "A 45-piece tool set for only $10.00." It went on to describe the pieces included: a hammer, a set of screwdrivers, a set of Allen wrenches, a retractable metal tape measure. The offer seemed too good to be true. Further, the advertisement described a free case that could be used to organize the tools and store them neatly. The advertisement stated that the case allowed you to fold the entire set of 45 tools into just 1 inch of space.

The information about storing the tools in 1 inch of space was totally inconsistent with our previous assumptions about the set of tools; namely, that it included a full-sized hammer, a set of normal-sized screwdrivers, and so forth. We reasoned that either the tools must be minuscule (like a jeweler's screwdrivers and hammer) or the information about the 1 inch of storage space must have been a printing error. Our bet is that the advertisement did not contain a printing error and that the tools are indeed minuscule and worth considerably less than $10.00. Note that people who failed to see the inconsistency between their assumption about the tools and the information about storage space were probably angry when they received the product. But the writers of the advertisement would undoubtedly claim that it told people what to expect and therefore doesn't qualify as outright fraud.

When scientists attempt to construct formal theories that explain phenomena, one of the criteria of a successful theory is that it be internally consistent. In contrast, many of our everyday beliefs have not been subjected to the rigors of scientific analysis and do not form a system that is internally consistent.

Consider everyday beliefs that can be expressed in proverbs such as "He who hesitates is lost." This is undoubtedly good advice, but so is "Haste makes waste." Yet the two contradict each other. Additional examples of proverbs that seem contradictory are

Nothing ventured, nothing gained.
Better safe than sorry.

Absence makes the heart grow fonder.
Out of sight, out of mind.

Many hands make light work.
Too many cooks spoil the broth.

If you attempted to create a formal theory of advice based on proverbs, you would have to deal with this appearance of inconsistency. One way might be to assume that each of the proverbs provides advice that is appropriate in some contexts. You would then need to define the contexts in which they did and did not apply. For example, the proverb "Many hands make light work" seems to be appropriate when there is a task to be done (such as beautifying a yard) that can be divided into relatively independent components (raking dead leaves, mowing the grass, trimming around the bushes and fence). In contrast, "Too many cooks spoil the broth" is appropriate when several people are given responsibility for the same task (such as baking a cake) and each approaches it in a different way.

It is instructive to define the contexts in which each of the other two proverbs are and are not appropriate. As you do so, you will begin to appreciate how looking for inconsistencies and then attempting to resolve them can lead to new insights that previously were taken for granted, such as the need to define the conditions of applicability of an idea. Harold Kushner[11] provides a fascinating look at one person's attempt to create a logically consistent set of beliefs to explain people's relationship to God.

The search for inconsistencies is very important in science. For example, in discussing the search for black holes in space, Nigel Calder describes the work of scientists who studied a galaxy of stars orbiting the galaxy's center.[12] The scientists knew that the speed of rotation of stars around a center or core depends on the mass of the core. The speed of the stars being studied was calculated and found to be extremely fast, approximately 250 miles per second. Based on this information it was possible to calculate the mass of the core necessary to sustain such movement. The calculations revealed that the mass must be enormous, roughly 5000 million times greater than the sun's.

Calder notes that the scientists also had access to an electronic light detector that allowed them to measure the amount of light (brightness) generated by the core being studied. He states, "If there was an enormous number of stars at the core, corresponding to the mass, the heart of the galaxy would be very bright indeed." (Note the if–then reasoning used.) When the scientists measured the light they found only a relatively faint glow, not a dazzling display; the appearance of the core was therefore not what one would expect if it were composed of stars. Calder goes on to observe that *the information about the appearance of the core was inconsistent with calculations of the mass of the core, unless the core contained a black hole.* The detection of a possible inconsistency was therefore very important; it showed the need to postulate something—a black hole—that would allow the apparent inconsistency between the appearance and the mass of the core to be resolved.

■ The Analysis of Key Assumptions

Our previous discussion emphasized two general classes of strategies for detecting flaws in arguments: (1) evaluate the accuracy of factual claims and (2) look for logical flaws and inconsistencies. The third strategy is to evaluate the assumptions on which an argument is based.

The evaluation of assumptions is especially important. For example, the fact that most arguments are based on sets of assumptions can make it difficult to apply some of the idealized rules of logic discussed earlier. Consider the premise "If John invents a better mousetrap, he will become rich." From our previous discussion we can conclude that it is not valid to argue that John must have invented a better mousetrap because he is now rich (that is, it is invalid to reason "If A, then B; B is true, therefore A is true"). Similarly, we know that it is not valid to say that John will never become rich because he did not invent a better mousetrap (it is invalid to reason "If A, then B; not A, therefore not B"). However, imagine that at some time in the future we meet John and find that he has never become very wealthy. Can we conclude that John never invented a better mousetrap? Logically, the form of the argument is "If A, then B; not B, therefore not A." As discussed earlier, this is a valid form of argument.

However, the logical forms discussed earlier represent ideal situations. In reality, John may have invented a better mousetrap but never have marketed it successfully, or people may have stopped buying mousetraps. What appears to be a valid argument logically (If A, then B; not B, therefore not A) has become an ambiguous situation in the real world. One reason for this ambiguity is that the truth of the relationship expressed in our premise ("If John invents a better mousetrap, then he will become rich") *depends on the existence of other conditions or assumptions* (that mousetraps continue to be purchased, that John employs a good marketing strategy, or that John finds a financial backer). Generally, whenever we include events and observations from the real world in our relationships, we import additional assumptions or conditions that may not be obvious immediately. However, these assumptions may have an important effect on the reasonableness of the arguments we make.[13]

Assumptions and Inconsistencies

Basic assumptions must also be analyzed to detect inconsistencies. For example, anyone familiar with political debates has probably witnessed at least one in which the politicians present facts or statistics that seem to contradict one another. How is it possible for such inconsistencies to occur? Although politicians may occasionally make factual errors, more often than not the collection of facts involves subjective judgments or assumptions. For example, two politicians may argue about changes in workers' income during one of their administrations. The incumbent may argue that workers' wages increased 30 percent during his administration. The challenger may argue that workers' salaries actually declined by 5 percent during the same period. Neither of the statistics cited by the politicians is necessarily wrong; they may simply be based on different assumptions. Thus, the challenger may have taken into account the rate of inflation during the survey period and adjusted wages accordingly, while the incumbent did not.

Earlier, we discussed several cases in which an apparent inconsistency was resolved by making a different assumption. For example, the inconsistency between a set of 45 full-sized tools and a 1-inch storage case was resolved by assuming that the tools were miniature rather than full-sized. Similarly, the scientists described by Calder found that the appearance of the galaxy's core was inconsistent with calculations of its mass *unless* they assumed the existence of a black hole. Much scientific theorizing involves the creation of new concepts and theories that resolve seeming inconsistencies.

Everyday comprehension also involves assumptions that resolve inconsistencies. Here are some simple statements that appear to contain inconsistencies unless you make the appropriate assumptions.[14]

> The floor was dirty because Sally used the mop.

> John is able to come to the party tonight because his car broke down.

> The dress wrinkled because Jill ironed it.

Examples of assumptions that make sense of these statements appear in Appendix A.

Now consider the following problem.

> A woman called the police and stated that she had just murdered her husband by shooting him. The police went to the house and found that, sure enough, the man had just been shot. Despite the woman's fingerprints on the gun and her testimony (she also passed a lie detector test), the courts were unable to punish her by putting her in jail or sentencing her to death. Why?

At first glance, this problem seems to involve an inconsistency between what we know about murder and what we know about the law.

Most people try to resolve this apparent inconsistency by making assumptions, such as "She really didn't do it," "It was an accident," or "She is insane so she cannot be prosecuted." However, in this problem the woman did commit the crime, she is perfectly sane, and the reason she was not sent to jail or put to death has nothing to do with legal technicalities (for example, the police failing to read her her rights). See if you can come up with an assumption that makes the apparent inconsistency disappear (the answer appears in Appendix A).

The Reasonableness of Assumptions

The fact that assumptions play such an important role in evaluating facts, logical arguments, and apparent inconsistencies has an obvious but important implication: We must carefully evaluate the reasonableness of the assumptions that form the basis of arguments. At the beginning of this chapter, for example, we discussed a murder trial in which the defense attorney made an analogy between a trial based on circumstantial evidence and a chain. The remainder of his argument to the jury was consistent with this analogy. The prosecuting attorney made an alternative analogy, that a trial based on circumstantial evidence is more like a rope than a chain. This allowed him to counter a number of points the defense attorney had made; for example, he argued that a few weak points in the overall testimony were not enough to prove the defendant's innocence.

Many arguments are based on analogies that, if analyzed, are found to be based on questionable assumptions. Otherwise, such arguments might seem to make sense, and we would make assumptions and draw conclusions that should probably not be drawn.

Consider again the scientist who is asked why he doesn't give up his theory in the face of criticism. The scientist may respond, "Your question reminds me of a story about Louis Pasteur. He was ridiculed unmercifully when he first suggested his germ theory of disease. As we all know, however, he got the last laugh."

What kind of argument is the scientist making by his reference to Pasteur? The argument might simply be "Because a new theory is ridiculed it is not necessarily invalid." On the other hand, the scientist may purposely be using an ambiguous argument to encourage an invited inference, such as "This situation is just like Pasteur's; therefore, the theory must be true." The scientist's reference to Pasteur illustrates a form of reasoning by analogy that is quite common in everyday situations. To evaluate such arguments, it is important to ask whether a particular analogy is appropriate, and if so, what its exact implications are supposed to be.

Consider a controversial topic, such as whether couples should have sex before marriage. One response to this question is to say, "You wouldn't buy a car without taking it out for a test drive, would you?" Although some might agree with this argument, others may be offended by the inappropriateness of the analogy. For example, unlike a car, a spouse does not become one's property, and unlike problems with a car, those between couples are usually a two-way street. Furthermore, although people usually don't feel guilty after taking a test drive, many feel guilty after premarital sex.

You can undoubtedly find additional problems with the test-drive analogy, but the basic point is clear: The analogy carries with it a host of assumptions that are inappropriate and misleading. Assumptions have powerful effects on our reasoning and it is therefore important to analyze those we make as well as those we are invited to make by others.

At the beginning of this chapter, we noted that many ideologies are closed systems that are difficult to crack because they are based on assumptions considered to be immutable. For example, imagine a person whose beliefs are based on the assumption that you are the enemy and that one's enemy can never be trusted. Unless you can show that those assumptions are faulty, it is doubtful that any logical argument you make will be convincing. Thus, in addition to critically evaluating ideas, we also need to be able to communicate our arguments effectively. In Chapter 5 we will examine how the IDEAL framework can be applied to problems of communication.

■ Summary

Ideologies can play a powerful role in motivating human action. Throughout history, a great deal of suffering has resulted from the uncritical acceptance of ideologies that have motivated people to harm one another. It is therefore important for people not to necessarily accept everything they hear or read. They need to be intelligent critics who can *identify* possible flaws in their own arguments as well as in arguments made by others. Subsequently, they can *define* the goal of their critical analysis (for example, to evaluate the accuracy of factual claims), *explore* strategies for analyzing and correcting an argument, *anticipate* outcomes and *act* on the most promising strategies, and *look at* the effects. If the argument still seems faulty, they can reenter the IDEAL cycle and try again.

There are three general goals to adopt when evaluating an argument. One is the possibility that the argument is based on inaccurate factual claims. Note that people who make such claims are not necessarily trying to be misleading or dishonest. Instead, they may simply fail to realize that their interpretations are in error.

A second cause of faulty arguments is the use of inappropriate logic or reasoning strategies. Someone may begin with an acceptable factual claim ("Many theories that later turned out to be true were at first ridiculed") but end up with a conclusion that does not follow from the facts ("Therefore, since my theory is being criticized, it must be true"). Similarly, arguments can contain inconsistencies. For example, an author may at first state that the views of a historical figure never changed on a particular issue yet provide an example later on indicating that they did.

A third reason for criticism involves the assumptions that form the basis of an argument. An argument will often seem valid if we grant the underlying assumption ("Since war is inevitable, we should make the first strike"). However, once the basic assumption (that war is inevitable) is identified and questioned, an argument will frequently lose its force. The use of analogies and metaphors also involves assumptions that may or may not be appropriate. Unless these are analyzed, they can lead us astray.

■ Exercises

Use the IDEAL Problem Navigation Guide (in Appendix C) to help you work through a problem involving critical thinking in the real world. Remember to consider the goals identified in Figure 11.

1. What do you conclude from the statement "Nine out of ten doctors surveyed recommended this product"?
2. A car maker compared its luxury car to four other well-known European luxury cars. Its car outperformed each of the four other cars, which were more expensive. It outperformed one of the other cars on a braking test, another on acceleration, another on cornering, and another on interior noise. What can you conclude about the performance of the car that outperformed each of the other cars tested?

3. A recent advertisement boasted that more than 70 percent of the owners of Toyota Corollas, Honda Civics, Ford Escorts, and Chevrolet Cavaliers actually preferred the new Dodge Shadow. The survey was based on 100 respondents (about 25 owners of each type of vehicle). Assuming that the facts described are accurate, what can you conclude?

4. What additional information would you need to evaluate the claim, "American schoolchildren scored lower on mathematics achievement tests than did children in all other industrialized countries"? (Assume that all children were of comparable ages and took comparable achievement tests.)

5. Can you trust the factual claims made in the advertisement on the facing page?

6. What are some possible problems with the following factual claim?

   Our teachers are better than those at University X. Students who have graduated from our university average $10,000 more per year than students who graduated from University X.

7. A school survey reveals that students who have computers at home earn significantly better grades than students who do not have computers at home. Should the school recommend that parents buy their children computers?

8. In 1927, Elton Mayo began a study to investigate the effects of illumination intensity on worker productivity. One of his findings revealed that when the illumination level was increased, productivity went up. If you were the plant manager, would you increase the lighting provided for workers at the plant? Why or why not?

9. If all men in Scottberg live on Gorky Street and no people who live on Gorky Street love strawberry pie, can we logically conclude that some men who live in Scottberg love strawberry pie?

10. If all xenos are oxons and some oxons are red, can we conclude that all xenos are red?

11. If all xenos are oxons and all zeeps are xenos, can we conclude that all zeeps are oxons?

12. If all pennies are nickels and all silver coins are nickels, can we conclude that all pennies are silver?

13. Assume that the following is true: "If I go to the party I can-

not do my homework." If I did not do my homework, can you conclude that I went to the party?

14. Assume that the following is true: "If the annual inflation rate rises above 7 percent, then the Federal Reserve Bank will raise interest rates." If the inflation rate is not above 7 per-

cent, we can one conclude that the Federal Reserve Bank did not raise interest rates?

15. Assume that the following is true: "Putting more money into public education will not necessarily improve education." Can we conclude that we can improve public education if we do not put more money into public education?

16. To test a theory that RNA is used to store information in the brain, scientists injected 20 people with RNA. They found that the 20 people performed no better on a memory test after they were injected with RNA than before. Have they disproved the theory that RNA is used to store information in the brain?

17. A publication reports that people in hospitals who are depressed recuperate much more slowly and less completely than people who are not depressed. The article goes on to advocate increased psychological counseling for depressed patients to improve their chances of recovery. What type of factual evidence probably supports this conclusion? Are there alternative explanations for this evidence?

18. Read the following game rules and then answer the questions below.

This is a two-player game. The players start at opposite corners of a checkerboard. The players move around the outside edge only. The object of the game is to reach the other player's corner first. Each player rolls the dice, and the player with the highest roll goes first. This player also picks a direction, either clockwise or counterclockwise. The other player must move in the opposite direction. On each turn the dice are rolled and the player with the highest roll advances one square on the board. The other player does not move on that turn. Players cannot occupy the same square at the same time.

   a. Does the player who moves first have an advantage?
   b. How long will the average game last?
   c. If you played 100 games, how many could you expect to win?

Many riddles involving logical reasoning center around the problem of differentiating a liar from one who tells the truth. Here are two.

19. You are at a road junction with two alternative paths and need directions about which path to take to the nearest town, but you don't know if the only person there to help you is a liar or

truthful. If he is truthful he will always answer truthfully; if he is a liar, he will always answer untruthfully. Using only one question, how can you find out which path is correct?

20. There are two brothers; one always tells the truth and the other always lies. The truthful brother is very knowledgeable and always answers correctly; the liar is very poorly informed and always thinks things are just the opposite of how they really are. Since the liar is both poorly informed and lies, he will usually answer questions identically to his brother. For example, the liar would answer yes to the question, "Is two plus two equal to four?" because he thinks that two plus two is not equal to four, but he lies about it. Can you ask one question requiring a yes or no answer that will tell you which brother you are talking to?

◼ Notes

1. J. Dewey, *How We Think.* Boston: D. C. Heath, 1910.
2. W. N. Dember, Cognition, motivation, and emotion: Ideology revisited. In R. R. Hoffman and D. S. Palermo (eds.), *Cognition and the Symbolic Processes: Applied and Ecological Perspectives.* Hillsdale, N.J.: Lawrence Erlbaum Associates, 1991.
3. A. Koestler, *Janus.* New York: Random House, 1978, p. 14.
4. V. Bugliosi, *'Till Death Us Do Part.* New York: Bantam, 1979.
5. See D. Huff, *How to Lie with Statistics.* New York: W. W. Norton, 1954.
6. These data are from the National Safety Council, 1973.
7. More extensive discussion of experimental designs can be found in D. G. Elmes, B. H. Kantowitz, and H. L. Roediger III, *Research Methods in Psychology* (4th ed.). St. Paul, Minn.: West, 1992; D. Radner and M. Radner, *Science and Unreason.* Belmont, Calif.: Wadsworth, 1982; D. H. McBurney, *Experimental Psychology* (2nd. ed.). Belmont, Calif.: Wadsworth, 1990; M. Mitchell and J. Jolley, *Research Design Explained* (2nd. ed.). Fort Worth: Harcourt Brace Jovanovich, 1992.
8. More extensive discussions of reasoning can be found in M. Scriven, *Reasoning.* New York: McGraw-Hill, 1976; S. Toulmin, *The Uses of Argument.* Cambridge, England: Cambridge University Press, 1958; S. Toulmin, R. Rieke, and A. Janik, *An Introduction to Reasoning.* New York: Macmillan, 1979.

9. See M. Gardner, *Fads and Fallacies in the Name of Science*. New York: Dover, 1957.

10. P. C. Wason, Reasoning about a rule. *Quarterly Journal of Experimental Psychology* 20 (1968):273–281.

11. H. S. Kushner, *When Bad Things Happen to Good People*. New York: Avon, 1981.

12. N. Calder, *Einstein's Universe*. New York: Penguin, 1980.

13. T. Kuhn, *The Structure of Scientific Revolutions*. Chicago: University of Chicago Press, 1962.

14. These examples are from J. D. Bransford and N. S. McCarrell, A sketch of a cognitive approach to comprehension. In W. Weimer and D. Palermo (eds.), *Cognition and the Symbolic Processes*. Hillsdale, N.J.: Lawrence Erlbaum Associates, 1974.

▌Suggested Readings

Practically Oriented Readings

Anderson, B. F. 1980. Chap. 3, "Reasoning," in *The Complete Thinker*. Englewood Cliffs, N.J.: Prentice-Hall.

Beardsley, M. C. 1950. *Thinking Straight: Principles of Reasoning for Readers and Writers*. Englewood Cliffs, N.J.: Prentice-Hall.

Campbell, S. K. 1974. *Flaws and Fallacies in Statistical Thinking*. Englewood Cliffs, N.J.: Prentice-Hall.

Fogelin, R. J. 1978. *Understanding Arguments: An Introduction to Informal Logic*. New York: Harcourt Brace Jovanovich.

Halpern, D. F. 1989. *Thought and Knowledge: An Introduction to Critical Thinking* (2d. ed.). Hillsdale, N.J.: Lawrence Erlbaum Associates.

Huff, D. 1954. *How to Lie with Statistics*. New York: W. W. Norton.

Radner, D., and M. Radner. 1982. *Science and Unreason*. Belmont, Calif.: Wadsworth.

Scriven, M. 1976. *Reasoning*. New York: McGraw-Hill.

Toulmin, S., R. Rieke, and A. Janik. 1979. *An Introduction to Reasoning*. New York: Macmillan.

Whimbey, A., and R. Lochhead. 1982. Chap. 4, "Verbal Reasoning Problems," Chap. 6, "Analogies," Chap. 7, "Writing Relationship Sentences," and Chap. 8, "How to Form Analogies," in *Problem Solving and Comprehension*. Philadelphia: Franklin Institute Press.

Zechmeister, E. B. and J. E. Johnson. 1992. *Critical thinking: A Functional Approach*. Belmont, Calif.: Wadsworth.

Theoretically Oriented Readings

Egan, D. E., and D. D. Grimes-Farrow. 1982. Differences in mental representations spontaneously adopted for reasoning. *Memory and Cognition* 10:297–307.

Hempel, C. G. 1966. *Philosophy of Natural Science*. Englewood Cliffs, N.J.: Prentice-Hall.

Kahneman, D., P. Slovic, and A. Tversky (eds.). 1982. *Judgment Under Uncertainty: Heuristics and Biases*. Cambridge, England: Cambridge University Press.

Kuhn, T. S. 1962. *The Structure of Scientific Revolutions*. Chicago: University of Chicago Press.

Mayer, R. E. 1991. *Thinking, Problem Solving, Cognition* (2d ed.). New York: W. H. Freeman.

Paul, R. W. 1986. Dialogical thinking: Critical thought essential to the acquisiton of rational knowledge and passions. In J. B. Baron and R. J. Sternberg (eds.), *Teaching Thinking Skills: Theory and Practice*. New York: W. H. Freeman.

Wason, P. C., and P. N. Johnson-Laird. 1972. *Psychology of Reasoning: Structure and Content*. Cambridge, Mass.: Harvard University Press.

EFFECTIVE
COMMUNICATION

What is there greater than the word which persuades the judges in the courts, or the senators in the council, or the citizens in the assembly, or at any other political meeting?

Plato[1]

In the preceding chapters we discussed ways to improve creativity and develop effective criticism. For your ideas to have an important impact, they must at some point be communicated to others. Without effective communication skills, good ideas can easily be ignored. In this chapter we will examine how the IDEAL framework can be applied to communication problems and opportunities.

■ The Importance of Identifying Communication Problems

The first step in developing an effective approach to communication is to *identify* the existence of potential problems. Although we communicate with many people every day, most of our communication involves relatively routine thinking. We may greet people, conduct transactions at a bank, or discuss recent news events with people at work—activities that are relatively routine. Sometimes these routine attempts to communicate break down, and we must identify the problem before serious consequences result. For example, most of us have at one time or another made a comment that was meant to be funny but was misinterpreted by a friend as an insult. If we do not identify the existence of such a communication problem, we could lose a valued friendship.

In addition to identifying problems that arise in relatively routine communications, we must also identify those that arise in nonroutine situations, such as making a presentation to a large group of people we don't know. We have seen many attempts to communicate fail when the goal of communicating with a large group of strangers was approached in the same way as more routine types of communication such as talking to a small group of friends. To develop effective communication skills, we must first recognize situations that require nonroutine approaches and treat them as opportunities to develop creative solutions. To help you do this, we will focus on three ways to think about your communication goals.

Three Ways of Defining Communication Goals

Once a communication problem has been identified, it is important to define your communication goals. For example, when you are applying for a job your goal may be to convince the employer that you have something important to contribute to the organization. It is important to recognize that your goal always involves a message (for example, that you have something important to contribute), an audience (the prospective employer), and a presentation medium (a personal interview, letter, or group presentation). These subgoals are represented by the acronym MAP—message, audience, presentation medium—and are illustrated in Figure 16.

Failure to consider each of these components of your communication goals can frustrate your overall attempt to communicate. For example, if you tried to convince a prospective employer that you are easy to get along with by means of the same communication strategy that you might use to invite a friend to a party, the prospective employer might misunderstand the message and think that you are not a diligent worker. The way you define each of these subgoals can influence the strategies you use for communication. We will consider in the following discussion how these subgoals affect the strategies that should be explored for effective communication. Later in the chapter we will consider the importance of *anticipating* outcomes before *acting* on your communication strategies. We will also consider the importance of *looking* back and *learning* from your attempts to communicate.

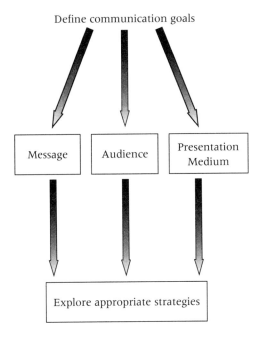

Define communication goals

Message | Audience | Presentation Medium

Explore appropriate strategies

Figure 16

■ Message

Sometimes people adopt a message that is actually ambiguous but that they want to seem clear. For example, imagine that your goal is to win an election. If the electorate (your audience) includes people with conflicting sets of beliefs, you may purposely try to be ambiguous. Thus you might say, "You know what is needed and I am going to do it," in the hope that everyone will make the invited inference that you agree with his or her ideas. The goal of ambiguity may not be lofty, but it seems to be one that people sometimes adopt.

We will assume, however, that your goal is to be clear rather than ambiguous. You therefore need to have a clear idea of your message. This may seem obvious, but it is amazing how often people are unclear about what they really want to communicate. They have a general idea of their message but when asked to put it into words, they often discover that it's not so easy to do.

Consider the following introduction to a presentation on economics.[2]

> *The persistent economic woes that now plague the United States will not be vanquished, or even substantially curbed, until new currents of thought emerge within the federal government that will force it to commence with the difficult policies required to assuage our present problems.*

Daniel Fader describes his interactions with the economics student who wrote this introduction. Fader's first request was that he state what he meant by the sentence. The student's response to Fader's question was as follows:

> *Well, yeah, America's worst economic problems won't be solved until the government, until the government, comes up with some tough new policies.*

Fader asked the student why he had not written this, instead of the "woes" and "plague" and "vanquished" and "assuage." The student's answer is revealing.

> *That's just the kind of stuff you use to write about economics and things like that.*

It is possible that some audiences are more impressed by sophisticated-sounding words than by the clarity of the message, but this has not been our experience. Most people value presentations that provide a clear and concise statement of the key ideas.

Fader's strategy for helping the economics student better understand his message was simple but powerful. He had the student restate the message in his own words and keep the statement as simple as possible. Fader notes that as the student tried to paraphrase his introduction, he developed a much better understanding of the issues. In the end, he began his presentation by advising the government to develop tough new economic policies based on economic *facts* rather than economic *politics*.[3] This was a much clearer introduction to the message the student wanted to present.

Some people use the strategy of reformulating their message into two or three "talking points" that summarize the essence of what they wish to communicate. This can be very beneficial in helping you clarify what you want to say.

◼ Audience

As you clarify your message it is also important to define your audience. Different communication strategies are necessary depending on the knowledge, interests, attitudes, and customs of the people you plan to address. Obviously, it would not be wise to speak English to a group of people who understood only French. Even when people can speak your language, however, you must communicate differently depending on what they know. For example, if you wanted to help third and fourth graders learn something about problem solving, you could probably find a way to do so, but it is doubtful that you would suggest that they read this book. Most children in the third and fourth grades can read, but they do not have enough knowledge to understand many of the concepts and examples used in this book.[4]

Differences in Background Knowledge

Here is a message that can be meaningful to the right audience. Try to figure out how it can be made to make sense.[5]

> If the balloons popped, the sound would not be able to carry since everything would be too far away from the correct floor. A closed window would also prevent the sound from carrying, since most buildings tend to be well insulated. Since the whole operation depends on a steady flow of electricity, a break in the middle of the wire would also cause problems. Of course the fellow could shout, but the human voice is not loud enough to carry that far. An additional problem is that a string could break on the instrument. Then there could be no accompaniment to the message. It is clear that the best situation would involve less distance. Then there would be fewer potential problems. With face-to-face contact, the least number of things could go wrong.

Most people have a difficult time understanding this passage. Given the information in Figure 17, however, it makes sense (look at the picture and then read the passage again). The passage would be quite comprehensible if you delivered it to an audience that already possessed the relevant background information. However, the same message would make no sense to people who did not possess that information.

We often need to discuss a topic even though many members of our audience do not possess extensive background knowledge about it. If you are a lawyer, for example, you may need to communicate information about biology, psychiatry, or physics to the members of a jury. The use of metaphors, analogies, and concrete examples can be very helpful in such situations. Consider Nigel Calder's use of metaphor and analogy to explain about a black hole in space, which he describes as "a great starswal-

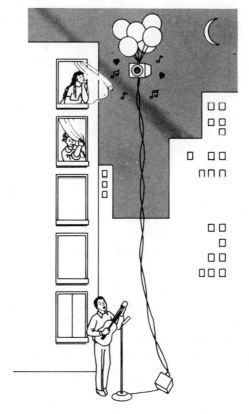

Figure 17   A picture that allows people to understand the passage about the balloons.

lower. . . . When stars or gas [come] close to it they [swirl] in faster and faster like water approaching a plug hole."[6] This is a very helpful analogy *provided* that people already know what it is like for water to swirl down a drain or plug hole. To evaluate the appropriateness of analogies and examples, you must know something about your audience's knowledge base.

Factual information may also need to be presented in different ways depending on your audience. For example, imagine that you want to make the following claim: "By the time they graduate from high school, American children have watched an average of 18,000 hours of television." Whether or not your audience will understand the significance of this depends on how familiar they are with thinking in terms of thousands of hours. Usually you will need to make such a fact more meaningful. For example, you might tell your audience that this figure amounts to several hours of TV viewing each day, or you could point out that 18,000 hours is more than most of these students have spent in school. The units and comparisons that are most meaningful will depend on what your audience already knows.

One of the major limitations of school-based instruction in communication is that the presenter's audience is usually very limited, consisting of the teacher and fellow students. But in everyday life, one has to communicate with people who have different levels of knowledge, experience, and expectations. In these circumstances, it is important to explore what the audience already knows about your topic and what it expects from you.

Technical Jargon Versus Doublespeak

Knowledge of your audience will also help you decide whether to use technical language or everyday English. The use of technical jargon can greatly improve the efficiency of communication. For example, a phrase such as "an A-B, A-C retroactive interference paradigm" is an extremely efficient way for a scientist to communicate, *provided* that the intended audience is familiar with this technical term.

Technical jargon can also be used for other purposes. One is to make a message less direct and hence less objectionable. For example, Edwin Newman, an authority on the uses and abuses of the English language, notes that in today's world people are often "outplaced" rather than "fired."[7] Similarly, someone who does not own a car is "transportation disadvantaged." Still another example of jargon designed to make unwelcome information more palatable is "strategic retrograde action," which was used to describe retreat during the Vietnam War.

William Lutz uses the term *doublespeak* to refer to technical jargon that is used to deliberately mislead or deceive people.[8] For example, when President Reagan proposed a $3 billion tax increase, his advisors described it as a "revenue enhancement" so that Reagan would seem to be honoring his pledge not to raise taxes. When the Reagan administration proposed a plan to increase the federal gasoline tax by 5 cents a gallon, it was disguised as a "user's fee" imposed on those who use cars and gasoline. Some forms of doublespeak are even more sinister. For example, Lutz notes that the investigative reporters Donald Bartlett and

James Steele uncovered the following passage in the U.S. Tax Reform Act of 1986.

> *In the case of a partnership with a taxable year beginning May 1, 1986, if such partnership realized net capital gain during the period beginning on the first day of such taxable year and ending on May 29, 1986, pursuant to an indemnity agreement dated May 6, 1986, then such partnership may elect to treat each asset to which such net capital gain relates as having been distributed to the partners of such partnership in proportion to their distributive share of the capital gain or loss realized by the partnership with respect to each asset.*

Lutz notes that this passage specifically created a tax loophole for the partners of Bear Stearns and Companies, Inc., that saved them approximately $8 million in taxes. Some other examples of doublespeak are listed below.

Unlawful or arbitrary deprivation of life	Killing
Nonperforming assets	Bad debt
Sexual reassignment surgery	Sex-change operation
Wood interdental stimulator	Toothpick
Portable hand-held communications inscriber	Pencil
Indefinite idling	Laying off workers
Downsizing personnel	Laying off workers
Headcount reductions	Laying off workers
Negative employee retention	Laying off workers

Communication Across Cultures

The task of creating messages appropriate to a particular audience can be especially difficult when dealing with members of different cultures or subcultures. Since most of us tend to take our cultural knowledge for granted, we often fail to realize that others may not share our view of the world. For example, researchers have presented Americans and natives of India with written descriptions of an American wedding and an Indian wedding.[9] Although members of both groups knew something about weddings, they frequently misinterpreted aspects of the other culture's ceremony. The description of the American wedding included the fact that the bride wore "something old, something new, something borrowed, something blue." The Americans knew that this was part of a tradition, but many of the Indians interpreted it differently. They felt sorry for the bride because she had to borrow and wear old clothes.

The Indians' and Americans' misinterpretations of each other's weddings were unlikely to have serious international ramifications. Nevertheless, it is easy to imagine situations in which differences in interpretation can have unfortunate consequences. For example, the cliché "When the going gets tough, the tough get going" is usually interpreted as a statement of the importance of self-determination. Members of another culture, however, could see it as an attempt to bully by reference to a threat of war.

Cross-cultural communication is often a problem for companies doing business in other countries. For example, an article in the *Wall Street Journal* described an incident in which a U.S. firm asked its Japanese distributor to advertise a new product.[10] The Japanese distributor agreed. A year later the owner of the U.S. firm found that not a single advertisement had been placed. He later discovered that in Japan "yes" does not necessarily mean "Yes, I will do it." Instead it often means "Yes, I understand."

Communication often involves nonverbal as well as verbal messages. Like verbal messages, nonverbal messages can be misinterpreted across cultures. One example of this is eye contact. In the United States, it is generally considered important to "look people in the eye"; if you glance into an American's eyes and then quickly look away, you are likely to be perceived as unsure of yourself or even rude. In other cultures, however, direct eye contact can have other meanings. In some Native American tribes young children are taught that it is disrespectful to look an elder in the eye, and eye contact by others can seem disrespectful. Likewise, Native American children are often perceived as uninterested by their white teachers because they tend to look away.[11]

Expectations of the Audience

An important question to ask about your audience is what its implicit rules of conduct are likely to be. For example, we have attended meetings at which the name of the game was for the speaker to present a lot of hype about his or her ideas and the advantages for the audience in adopting them. There was no serious discussion about the weaknesses as well as the strengths of the ideas and about how the ideas might be improved. Imagine that you want to talk about weaknesses as well as strengths but you are at a meeting where all the other speakers are trumpeting only the strengths of their ideas. If you come on with a serious discussion of both strengths and weaknesses, you may well seem boring and weak compared with the other speakers. It is very important to make sure that your goals fit in with the audience's expectations. If you want to keep your standards high, you will probably find yourself turning down invitations to speak in some settings where the expectations do not match your own.

Several years ago one of us went to an academic symposium that was attended by more than 500 people and featured four nationally known speakers. Each speaker spoke for about 20 minutes, followed by questions and comments. The room became tense as the fourth speaker presented data that called into question a theory that the first speaker had published several years earlier. After the fourth speaker finished, the moderator asked the first speaker if he wanted to reply. You could have heard a pin drop as the first speaker approached the podium. He began, "About my paper where I argued that. . . ." Then he paused and, with a grin, said, "Can I take that back?" The room broke into applause.

This first speaker's courage taught us a powerful lesson. Science is based on respect for data rather than for slick performances. The speaker demonstrated his respect for the data, and the audience greatly appreciated his acknowledgment. But not all audiences are like this.

Presentation Medium

The third component of MAP is the presentation medium you use when presenting your message. Possible formats include oral presentations, written presentations, interactive software, and interactive multimedia. Each of these is discussed below.

Some Advantages of Speaking

Given a choice between a friendly face-to-face conversation and writing a letter or paper, most people prefer the conversation. One reason is that most people speak much faster than they write. The slowness of writing is one of the major reasons that people do not like it. They think that its slowness interferes with their thinking, which can seem quite fast.

Another advantage of speaking over writing is that speakers can convey more in different ways. They can use facial expressions, gestures, and different intonations to make their messages clear. In addition, speakers usually have a number of chances to clarify their meaning, since the audience can ask questions or indicate it does not understand. In contrast, writers are usually isolated from their audience, and they are unable to rely on outside sources of information such as gestures. Writers must therefore work hard to state their ideas clearly and avoid ambiguity. Many people do not like this extra work.

Some Advantages of Writing

Although writing *does* need to be less ambiguous than spoken language and *is* slower, it has its advantages. An extremely important one is that writing persists over time and space and so can be analyzed with considerably more care than can spoken language. Indeed, some theorists argue that the invention of written language was one of the hallmarks of human development because it enabled people to become more precise in their analysis of arguments.

One way to appreciate the greater precision of written language is to compare written and spoken sentences. If you tape-record everyday conversations and then type them word for word, you will be amazed at the number of false starts, pauses, "um's," and other imperfections. The linguist Wallace Chafe provides the following illustrations.[12]

> *I'm feeling OK now (laugh), but uh I had last week I thought I was (laugh) dying. You heard that I fainted in the shower.*

When we are listening to others we tend not to notice all the false starts and pauses. When we write, however, we are expected to produce sentences that are well organized. We therefore need to plan and evaluate our statements more carefully.

That written language persists over time and space also has advantages that go beyond the level of individual sentences. Since written information can be stored, it is easier to compare earlier statements with those made later on. This can lead to the detection of inconsistencies and enable the writer to rethink his or her ideas.

An additional advantage of writing over speaking is that it does not require that we begin at the beginning and proceed until we reach the end. *Papers can be written in any order we choose.* Interestingly, many students do not realize this at first and may spend hours trying to find "the perfect" introductory sentence or paragraph. Experienced writers often skip the introduction or spend very little time on it at first because they know that they will get a better idea of their thesis as they write and will end up redoing the introduction anyway. Experienced writers can also work on different parts of a paper at different times. For example, if at some point you will have to supply background on your main character, you can write this at any time—such as when you need to incubate other ideas. Writing permits a great deal of flexibility in the strategies you use.[13]

Effective Use of Visual Aids

Visual aids can greatly facilitate communication regardless of whether you intend to communicate orally or in writing. For example, one of us recently participated in a committee that was set up to explore salary inequities across disciplines at the university. One of the administrators interviewed by the committee was certain that there were inequities across disciplines and said that although he had tried for years to convince the faculty of the problem, he had never been successful. The committee realized that it needed a simple way to illustrate the salary inequities so that even people who did not feel comfortable with numbers could understand. A visual representation similar to the one the committee used is shown in Figure 18. The committee's report generated such a strong reaction from the faculty that action was soon taken to correct the problem.

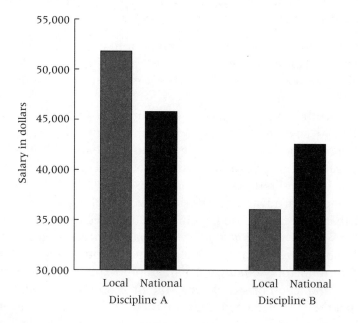

Figure 18

It is important to realize, however, that not all visual strategies facilitate communication. The effectiveness of an illustration ultimately depends on whether it helps clarify the underlying message and whether it can be seen and understood by the audience. We have seen numerous presentations in which tables or charts were used that presented too much information too quickly. In other cases, presenters fail to enlarge the information sufficiently for the audience to see important details. Edward Tufte[14] has described many of the problems that can detract from the effectiveness of visual illustrations.

Interactive Computer Programs

Modern computer technology makes it possible to create new forms of communication that combine some of the advantages of spoken and written messages. Programs that interact with users (that is, with your audience) are one example. Imagine that you want to write a letter to your mother, but you want to program it on a computer and store it on disk rather than write it down on paper. You might write the program so that when your mother uses the disk with her computer, the message on her screen reads: "Hi, Mom. I have several things to tell you. Please choose the topic you want to start with."

Your computer program might then provide a menu of topics, such as (1) "How I spent my summer vacation," (2) "When I could come to visit," and (3) "Why I want to get married next month." By selecting 1, 2, or 3, your mother could read about each topic in the order she chooses. In addition, you could program tests that increased the probability that your intended message was conveyed. For example, after your mother had read part of your message, you could provide choices allowing her to indicate her reaction. Thus you might ask, "What do you think about what I've just told you?" Choices might be (1) "I'm elated," (2) "It's okay, but certainly not great," or (3) "You are disinherited." Your program could then respond in different ways depending on your mother's answer (that is, on how she interacted with your program). If she chose option 3 ("You are disinherited"), for example, your program could respond with "Wait a minute, you must have misunderstood something," and so forth. Interactive computer programs have the potential to provide interactive communication in which answers depend on questions. In addition, the message can persist in space and time.

Multimedia Presentations

Another way to apply modern technology to communication problems involves multimedia presentations that combine voice, text, still pictures, and moving video. These can all be controlled at the touch of a computer button and so can be used in extremely powerful ways. In a presentation, video, sound, and other resources can be used to illustrate one's points. Each medium has different strengths. For example, we find that some points simply cannot be made forcefully by talking about them, but their significance immediately becomes apparent in a short videoclip. In other cases, people prefer written documents over videos because they want to analyze the information in detail.

Multimedia technology is already changing the standards people have for effective presentations. In many circles it is no longer sufficient simply to talk to the audience and use overheads that list the main points. Instead, audiences want to see and hear what the speakers are talking about. The good side of these changes is that people are learning to use the new resources to communicate in powerful new ways. The bad side is that multimedia can make it easier for glitz to win out over substance. Ultimately, however, audiences will demand substance from multimedia presentations.

■ Evaluating the Effectiveness of Your Attempts to Communicate

Anticipate Outcomes and Act

Often it is difficult for the person who delivers the message to anticipate the consequence of using a particular communication strategy. One reason is that the creator of the message is usually much more familiar than the audience with the communication goals. As a result, he or she can infer missing information and hence fail to detect communication gaps. It is also difficult to anticipate how the audience's attitudes and expectations may affect its understanding of the message.

One of the most common strategies used by effective communicators to help them anticipate the effects of a particular communication strategy is to test it on other people. Ideally, those from whom you get feedback should be similar to the intended audience, especially if you want to assess your communication strategy. Many of the issues we considered in our discussion of focus groups (see Chapter 3) are relevant to anticipating the effects of communication strategies.

In some cases it is relatively easy to anticipate the outcome of using a particular communication strategy. For example, if you know the size of the room where a presentation will be given, it is easy to determine whether the audience will be able to see your visual aids clearly. However, anticipating how the audience's expectations and attitudes will interact with your communication strategies is more difficult to assess and may require that you obtain outside input. Similarly, editors and publishers often solicit comments from individuals whose opinions may be representative of the intended audience for a new article or publication.

Look and Learn

Once you have acted on your communication strategy it is important to look at the effects to learn from your experience. This is especially important if your goal is to become an effective communicator, since people are rarely outstanding at this the first time they try.

Audience feedback can be an important source of information about the effectiveness of your strategies and the appropriateness of your goals. For example, the questions people ask can help you evaluate whether you defined the nature of your audience correctly and used communication strategies that allowed people to relate your message to their own experiences.

Videotaping your presentation can also provide an effective way of looking back at your presentation (at mannerisms, intonation, gestures, answers to questions) and can help you improve your effectiveness. We have observed many instances of a speaker's communication goals being disrupted by an annoying presentation style or an inability to answer questions without becoming defensive. Critically reviewing a videotape of your own presentation can help you identify potential problems and better define your goals for improvement.

The IDEAL framework and the MAP configuration shown in Figure 16 provide a useful framework for looking at the effects of your attempts to communicate and learning from them. For each component of MAP, ask yourself if you failed to identify potential problems, clearly define your goals, explore a wide enough range of strategies, or anticipate the effects of various strategies. If your experiences are like ours, you will find that there is something useful to learn from every attempt to communicate.

Summary

After you have gone through the problem-solving process, have generated some exciting, creative ideas, and are ready to communicate them to an important audience, three subgoals must be clearly defined to plan an effective communication strategy. These subgoals are message, audience, and presentation, or MAP: define the *message* you plan to present, define the *audience* to which you will present it, and define the *presentation* format (oral, written, interactive, multimedia) that you plan to use. Each of these subgoals affects the selection of an effective communication strategy.

In considering your message, explore strategies for clarifying what you really want to say. Although this may seem obvious, it is an important step that is often overlooked.

It is also important to carefully define the audience. A message that is perfectly comprehensible to one audience may be a complete mystery to another. When we attempt to communicate across cultures we run into additional problems, since what is understood may be very different from what we intended.

Also, consider the audience's expectations of a presentation. Does it expect glitz, hype, and cheerleading or a serious analysis of issues? Failure to address this question can lead to serious mismatches between audience and presentation.

When choosing a presentation format, explore the advantages and disadvantages of different media, including oral communication, writing, visual illustrations, interactive software, and multimedia.

Finally, it is important to evaluate attempts to communicate and learn from them. The IDEAL approach, together with the MAP subgoals, provides a useful framework for evaluating effects.

Exercises

Use the IDEAL Problem Navigation Guide in Appendix C to help you work though a real-world communication problem. Remember to consider each of the MAP subgoals illustrated in Figure 16 when you define your goals.

■ Notes

1. B. Jowett, *The Dialogues of Plato*, Vol. 1. New York: Random House, 1937.
2. From D. Fader, Narrowing the space between language and text. In P. L. Stock (ed.), *F Forum: Essays on Theory and Practice in the Teaching of Writing*. Upper Montclair, N.J.: Boynton Cook, 1983.
3. See note 2.
4. See especially T. C. Anderson, Role of the reader's schema in comprehension, learning and memory. In R. Anderson, J. Osborn, and R. Tierney (eds.), *Learning to Read in American Schools: Basal Readers and Content Texts*. Hillsdale, N.J.: Lawrence Erlbaum Associates, 1984.
5. From J. D. Bransford and M. K. Johnson, Contextual prerequisites for understanding: Some investigations of comprehension and recall. *Journal of Verbal Learning and Verbal Behavior* 11 (1972):717–726.
6. N. Calder, *Einstein's Universe*. New York: Penguin, 1980.
7. Cited in *Simply Stated: The Monthly Newsletter of the Document Design Center, American Institute for Research* 32 (Dec. 1982–Jan. 1983).
8. W. Lutz, *Doublespeak: From "Revenue Enhancement" to "Terminal Living," How Government, Business, Advertisers, and Others Use Language to Deceive You*. New York: Harper & Row, 1989.
9. M. S. Steffensen, D. Joag-Deci, and R. C. Anderson, A cross-cultural perspective on reading comprehension, *Reading Research Quarterly* 15 (1979):10–29.
10. H. Klein, Firms seek aid in deciphering Japan's culture. *The Wall Street Journal* (Sep. 1, 1983):27.
11. See R. Freedle, Interaction of language use with ethnography and cognition. In J. H. Harvey (ed.), *Cognition, Social Behavior and the Environment*. Hillsdale, N.J.: Lawrence Erlbaum Associates, 1981.
12. From W. L. Chafe, Speakers and writers do different things. In P. L. Stock (ed.), *F Forum: Essays on Theory and Practice in the Teaching of Writing*. Upper Montclair, N.J.: Boynton Cook, 1983.
13. Excellent discussions of writing can be found in L. Flower, *Problem-Solving Strategies for Writing*. New York: Harcourt Brace Jovanovich, 1981; S. Pearl, Understanding composing. *Composition and Communication* 31 (1980):363–369; C. Bereiter and M. Scardamalia, *The Psychology of Written Communication*. Hillsdale, N.J.: Lawrence

Erlbaum Associates, 1987; P. L. Stock (ed.), *F Forum: Essays on Theory and Practice in the Teaching of Writing*. Upper Montclair, N.J.: Boynton Cook, 1983.

14. E. R. Tufte, *The Visual Display of Quantitative Information*. Cheshire, Conn.: Graphics Press, 1983.

■ Suggested Readings

Practically Oriented Readings

Flower, L. 1981. *Problem-Solving Strategies for Writing*. New York: Harcourt Brace Jovanovich.

Theoretically Oriented Readings

Flower, L., V. Stein, J. Ackerman, M. J. Kantz, K. McCormick, and W. C. Peck. 1990. *Reading to Write: Exploring a Cognitive and Social Process*. New York: Oxford University Press.

Freedle, R. 1981. Interaction of language use with ethnography and cognition. In J. H. Harvey (ed.), *Cognition, Social Behavior and the Environment*. Hillsdale, N.J.: Lawrence Erlbaum Associates.

Hull, G. H. 1989. Research on writing: Building a cognitive and social understanding of composing. In L. B. Resnick and L. E. Klopfer (eds.), *Toward the Thinking Curriculum: Current Cognitive Research*. Alexandria, Va.: American Society for Curriculum Development.

Pearl, S. 1980. Understanding composing. *Composition and Communication* 31: 363–369. Scardemalia, M., and C. Bereiter. 1987. Knowledge telling and knowledge transforming in written composition. In S. Rosenberg (ed.), *Advances in Applied Psycholinguistics*, Vol. 2, *Reading, Writing, and Language Learning*. Cambridge, England: Cambridge University Press.

Sommers, N. 1980. Revision strategies of student writers and experienced adult writers. *Composition and Communication*, 31:378–388.

Steffensen, M. S., D. Joag-Deck, and R. C. Anderson. 1979. A cross-cultural perspective on reading comprehension. *Reading Research Quarterly* 15:10–29.

Stock, P. L. (ed.). 1983. *F Forum: Essays on Theory and Practice in the Teaching of Writing*. Upper Montclair, N.J.: Boynton Cook.

PART 2

A MODEL FOR ACQUIRING NEW KNOWLEDGE

6 IMPROVING MEMORY SKILLS

The unassisted hand and the understanding left to itself possess but little power. Effects are produced by means of instruments and helps, which the understanding requires no less than the hand.

Sir Francis Bacon, 1620[1]

In Part 1 we explored ways of using existing knowledge more effectively to solve problems. We also noted that many problems require specialized knowledge—knowledge that we must first learn and remember. In Part 2 we consider ways of improving our ability to acquire new knowledge.

The goal of this chapter is to explore strategies that can increase our ability to remember information. These strategies operate like other useful tools that human beings have developed. Like a good hammer, for example, a memory tool can help us perform tasks that otherwise would be difficult or even impossible. However, just as a hammer may be appropriate for some tasks but not for others (pounding nails versus tightening a bolt, for example), a particular memory strategy may or may not be appropriate, depending on the nature of the problem. The exploration and eventual selection of strategies must therefore be preceded by *identification* of the particular memory problem to be solved and by a careful *definition* of one's goals. The appropriateness of particular strategies can then be evaluated by *anticipating* the outcome of using them, *acting* on those that seem most promising, and *looking* back at their effects to see if they have helped to accomplish the defined goals. These are all components of the IDEAL model discussed in Chapter 2. This model will provide the basis for our discussion of improving memory performance. We begin with an analysis of a simple memory task.

■ Remembering as Problem Solving

A father we know purchased a new combination lock for his son to use in the gym at school. His son read the directions and then asked to borrow a pen. The reason, the son explained, was to write the combination of the lock inside his tennis shoes and gym bag.

This is an excellent illustration of everyday problem solving that involves the need to remember information. First and foremost, the son *identified* the existence of a potential problem. If he locked his locker but did not know the combination to the lock, he would be unable to get to his clothes. Locks often have to be cut off of lockers because people fail to recognize the existence of this potential problem.

The son also *defined* his goals for solving the problem, at least implicitly. He asked himself, "How can I make sure I know this combination without having to memorize and risk forgetting it? After *exploring* possible strategies he decided to write the combination inside his tennis shoes and gym bag. The son explained that he had first thought about writing the combination inside his street shoes but then changed his mind. Implicitly, at least, he *anticipated* the effect of this potential strategy and realized that it would not work. Although he would be wearing street shoes to the gym, his street shoes would be locked in his locker during gym class.

The boy's father pointed out a different strategy for remembering the combination—an elaboration strategy. He noted that the first number, 13, was his son's age; the second number, 8, was the month of his son's mother's birthday; and the third number, 14, was the age his son would be on his next birthday. At first the son was skeptical of this strategy but later found that it worked well.

The combination lock problem is one of thousands that revolve around the task of remembering information. The father and son each used strategies that, while different, were both effective in helping them accomplish their goals.

Examples of Different Strategies

To understand how different memory goals require different types of strategies, consider the following problem. The list below contains 25 words; spend approximately 1½ minutes studying the list (approximately 4 seconds per word). Then, without looking at the list, write down as many of the words as you can. Please begin now.

couch potato hat trumpet boat desk carrot shirt piano cat chair
watermelon pants harp airplane table bread coat violin bicycle bed
tomato glove drum truck

People take a variety of approaches to such memory problems. We will
discuss these differences from the perspective of the IDEAL framework.

We assume that all people *identify* the existence of a problem since
they have been told that there is a problem to be solved. Most people
define the goal as recalling as many words as possible in any order. They
therefore *explore* strategies such as organizing related words and recalling
them in categories. For example, couch, desk, chair, and bed; trumpet,
piano harp, and drum; and so forth.

Categorization strategies can be very useful for remembering. However, as with all memory strategies, their usefulness is strongly dependent
on the memory goal. Imagine that the preceding task had been to recall
the words in their exact order of appearance. Now a categorization
strategy would no longer be optimal. A better strategy would be to construct a story that uses each word in the order in which it appears (for
example a couch potato wearing a hat played a trumpet while sailing in
his boat. Then he went home to his desk and . . .).

As an additional example, assume that the goal is to recall all the
words in reverse order, and to do this quickly. The categorization strategy
is not appropriate, and the story strategy also leads to problems because
it is difficult to tell a story from end to beginning. However, the peg-word
strategy that will be discussed later in this chapter is excellent for achieving this goal.

Here are some additional memory goals that could be adopted for
the list of 25 words.

1. Remember the words that contain at least one e.
2. Remember the two-syllable words.
3. Remember the words that occur third, fifth, tenth, and
   twentieth on the list.
4. Remember the words that are homonyms (those that have
   at least two distinct meanings, such as traffic jam and
   strawberry jam).
5. Remember the words in alphabetical order.

Each of these goals requires the use of different strategies for learning.
Effective problem solvers must be flexible; they must define their goals

carefully and use different strategies depending on the nature of the memory problem they are asked to solve.

If you have ever taken an exam, you know the importance of clarifying your goals ahead of time. For example, it is especially important to know whether it will be an essay exam or a multiple-choice exam. For an essay exam, you need to explore strategies that will help you organize and remember information without strong retrieval cues; you might therefore generate acronyms (discussed later) and use other procedures for helping you retrieve relevant information. For multiple-choice exams, retrieval is less important because each choice is in effect a potential retrieval cue. For multiple-choice exams, it is usually better to pay attention to definitions and make sure that you have learned the distinctions among terms that you need to know.

We discuss various strategies in more detail later. For the moment, it is important to note that people's approaches to the preceding memory problem also differ with respect to the anticipate/act and look/learn components of the IDEAL process. For example, some people begin by *anticipating* the effects of different strategies, *acting* on one they think will work, and *looking* at the effects. If one strategy does not work, they may change strategies as they proceed through the list. In contrast, other people use the same strategy throughout the entire task. Differences in the anticipate/act and look/learn components become even more apparent if the task is changed. For example, imagine that the problem is to study until you are confident of your ability to recall all the words on the list. Effective learners will undoubtedly change their strategy if the initial one seems ineffective and concentrate their attention on words they *cannot* recall rather than on those that they *can* recall.

The Effectiveness of Different Strategies

If you experiment with memory problems like the one just presented, you will undoubtedly find that some of the strategies are more effective than others. For example, the simple strategy of repeating each word several times will usually result in poorer recall than such strategies as organizing words into categories or making up a story (and perhaps supplementing it with images) that links all of the words.[2] Later we discuss why some strategies are better than others.

As we said earlier, the appropriateness of a strategy depends on the nature of the memory problem you are trying to solve. Suppose you look up a new phone number and want to remember it only long enough to walk across the room to dial. You are therefore attempting to solve a problem of short-term rather than long-term memory. An effective strategy in this case is simply to repeat the number to yourself as you walk across the room. Interestingly, even this simple strategy involves a relatively sophisticated level of problem solving. Studies with kindergarten children show that, although they may want to remember information, many children do not realize that they need to repeat it.[3] Not surprisingly, those who did not repeat the information also did not remember it well.

Returning to the earlier problem, 25 is far too many words to hold in short-term memory by simple repetition (generally, we can hold only five to nine units of information in short-term memory).[4] The problem requires that we store the words in long-term memory for which such strategies as simple repetition are not as effective as those involving categorization or the construction of stories and images. Similarly, the latter strategies are effective only for certain types of memory problems.

The remainder of our discussion of memory is organized into three sections. The first concerns the processes of human memory, an understanding of which can help you remember more effectively. We will show, for example, the although attention is a prerequisite for remembering, it does not guarantee it. The second section explores some strategies for remembering that have been devised over the centuries. By using these strategies, people often find that they can solve memory problems they had assumed were too difficult for them. In the final section we discuss the importance of adapting memory strategies to your own situation and inventing new ones when necessary.

Understanding Basic Memory Processes

Researchers in cognitive psychology have discovered some basic principles of human memory that are very useful in helping people learn to solve memory problems. We explore three of them: attention, elaboration, and retrieval.

Attention

Imagine that you are a student and need to learn a great deal of information in a short time. You missed several classes, so a friend has tape-recorded lectures from a history class and an economics class. Since you are so pressed for time, you design a system that allows you to play the history lecture into your left ear and the economics lecture into your right ear at the same time. Will this method allow you to learn twice as much in the same amount of time?

If you have ever attempted to study when people are interrupting you, you probably answered no to this question. It is very difficult to attend carefully to more than one source of information at a time, especially if both messages contain information that is unfamiliar.[5]

Attending to the Right Information

Even when we hear or read only a single message, we can easily miss some of the information. Read the following passage once:

> Many foods cost too much. Food costs would diminish if farm land was not so costly. In addition, tractors and additional tools cost way too much. Politicians should also diminish any tax on farm products. A high tax on such products hurts us all.

Now try to remember as much about this passage as you can without looking back. If you studied the passage, the chances are quite good that you can easily recall its main points. However, without looking back at the passage, suppose you have 10 seconds to answer a different question: "How many words in the passage contain the letter *e*?" You might be able to estimate the number of e's by recalling the words and checking each one, but this will take a considerable amount of time and you will probably make mistakes. Although most passages of this length include a considerable number of *e*'s, this one does not. (You may have noted that the wording was a little strange; that's because it only used words that do not contain an *e*).

You would have been able to answer the question about the number of *e*'s in the passage much more easily if you had known about it beforehand. You would then have know to focus your attention on this problem as you read. Had you done so, however, chances are you would have missed something about the meaning of the passage. Even in a passage this simple, there is more to attend to than we can process in a single trial. It is important to define your memory goals ahead of time so you can attend to the relevant information.[6]

Elaboration Processes

The preceding discussion illustrates the importance of attending to information that is relevant to your memory goal. Researchers have also found that memory is affected by our ability to relate new information to previous experience and knowledge. This is known as "elaboration." An example of how elaboration can facilitate remembering was presented at the beginning of this chapter; it involved of a father's and son's strategies for remembering the combination to a lock. The father elaborated on the information by making it meaningful. To remember the number 13, he elaborated by relating it to the current age of his son.

In many situations people elaborate information without thinking about it. For example, consider the following sentence.

John was late for work because of the snow.

Most people will automatically elaborate this sentence by relating it to experiences they have had traveling to or from work or school during a snowstorm. Routine elaborations such as these make it easier to understand and remember information, but they also depend on our ability to relate new information to our own past experiences.

Frequently, however, elaboration requires more conscious effort, especially when the relationship between the new information and previous experience is not obvious. College students often tell us about classmates who can sit through a lecture without taking notes and remember almost everything. In contrast, they can remember very little, and they worry that their memory is poor. We try to help these students understand that remembering information is comparatively effortless or difficult depending on what one already knows about a topic. If you know a lot about a topic, it is much easier to elaborate the information and remember what you hear or read.

Please try the following experiment. Spend no more than 4 seconds reading each of the sentences listed below, and *read each one only once. Most important, try not to use any elaboration strategies such as generating images or thinking of people you know.*

John walked on the roof.

Bill picked up the egg.

Pete hid the axe.

Jim flew the kite.

Frank flipped the switch.

Alfred built a boat.

Sam hit his head on the ceiling.

Adam quit his job.

Jay fixed the sail.

Ted wrote the play.

Now try to answer the following questions without looking back at the preceding sentences.

Who built the boat?

Who picked up the egg?

Who walked on the roof?

Who quit his job?

Who flew the kite?

Who fixed the sail?

Who hit his head on the ceiling?

Who wrote the play?

Who flipped the switch?

Who hid the axe?

Most people have a very difficult time remembering who did what, despite the fact that each statement is comprehensible. If you really read these sentences without trying to elaborate them, you could probably remember only two or three at the most. To remember more of the sentences you would have to use more sophisticated elaboration strategies, such as thinking of someone you know with a particular name (for example, a friend named John) and imagining him walking on the roof.

Such sentences become easier to remember if your knowledge base does much of the work for you. As an illustration, spend approximately 4 seconds reading each of the sentences below. As in the earlier task, *do not attempt to use any sophisticated strategies. Instead, process each sentence as effortlessly as you can.*

Santa Claus walked on the roof.

The Easter bunny picked up the egg.

George Washington hid the axe.

Benjamin Franklin flew the kite.

Thomas Edison flipped the switch.

Noah built a boat.

Wilt Chamberlain hit his head on the ceiling.

Richard Nixon quit his job.

Christopher Columbus fixed the sail.

William Shakespeare wrote the play.

Now answer the following questions without looking back at the list.

Who built the boat?

Who picked up the egg?

Who walked on the roof?

Who quit his job?

Who flew the kite?

Who fixed the sail?

Who hit his head on the ceiling?

Who wrote the play?

Who flipped the switch?

Who hid the axe?

Most people can remember this second list of sentences almost effortlessly. When information is easily related to our knowledge or previous experience, it is relatively easy to remember. When information is difficult to relate to previous experience, we need to make use of nonroutine elaboration strategies.

Many people do not automatically use effective elaboration strategies when they are confronted with information that requires nonroutine thinking. For example, James Turnure, Nissan Buium, and Martha Thurlow[7] found that retarded children (those with intelligence scores of around 70) do not elaborate relationships that are difficult to remember, and consequently their memory performance is much lower than that of students with higher intelligence test scores. Turnure and his colleagues noticed dramatic improvements in the memory scores of retarded children when they were prompted to elaborate confusing relationships in an effective way. We have found important differences in the effectiveness of elaboration strategies used by successful and less successful fifth graders confronted with nonroutine learning tasks.[8]

Retrieval Processes

Researchers who study human memory emphasize the difference between *encoding* or *storing* information and *accessing* or *retrieving* it later on.[9] You have probably had the experience of trying to remember a person's name or a certain word and feeling that it was right on the tip of your tongue. You know from these experiences that retrieval processes are an important part of remembering.

The following demonstration experiment is designed to illustrate the importance of retrieval processes. Spend 3 to 5 seconds reading each of the sentences in the list below, and read through the list only once. As soon as you finish, remove the list from sight and write down as many of the sentences as you can. Please begin now.

A brick can be used as a doorstop.

A ladder can be used as a bookshelf.

A wine bottle can be used as a candleholder.

A pan can be used as a drum.

A record can be used to serve potato chips.

A guitar can be used as a canoe paddle.

A leaf can be used as a bookmark.

An orange can be used to play catch.

A newspaper can be used to swat flies.

A TV antenna can be used as a clothes rack.

A sheet can be used as a sail.

A boat can be used as a shelter.

A bathtub can be used as a punch bowl.

A flashlight can be used to hold water.

A rock can be used as a paperweight.

A knife can be used to stir paint.

A pen can be used as an arrow.

A barrel can be used as a chair.

A rug can be used as a bedspread.

A telephone can be used as an alarm clock.

A scissors can be used to cut grass.

A board can be used as a ruler.

A balloon can be used as a pillow.

A shoe can be used to pound nails.

A dime can be used as a screwdriver.

A lampshade can be used as a hat.

Most people are able to recall between 10 and 16 sentences. However, we are interested in those that were not recalled. What happened to them? Did you fail to encode them because of a lapse of attention? Did you attend to them, yet forget them quickly? Are they actually in memory but can't be found?

Most people who participate in this experiment are convinced that they learned more than they can recall. They believe they are simply unable to find all the information that has been stored. This suggests that there may be important differences between storing information and retrieving it later on.

Appropriate retrieval cues can help us find stored information that we were not at first able to retrieve. Without looking back at the preceding list of sentences, read the potential retrieval cues in the list below. These words are the subjects (the first noun) of the sentences you just tried to recall. Read each cue and see if it reminds you of a sentence from the list. Keep track of how many sentences you remember so that you can compare this number to your first attempt without the help of cues. Please begin now.

flashlight	lampshade
sheet	shoe
rock	guitar
telephone	scissors
boat	leaf
dime	brick
wine bottle	knife
board	newspaper
pen	pan
balloon	barrel
ladder	rug
record	orange
TV antenna	bathtub

You should find a substantial increase in the number of remembered sentences. Many people find that cues frequently produce an "aha!" experience; they are reminded of information that was stored but not retrieved during the first recall trial. Such experiences suggest that memory requires not only storage, but also retrieval. Many of the memory strategies that we discuss later in this chapter are designed to help you retrieve information that you have learned.

■ Strategies for Remembering

The ancient Greeks invented some powerful strategies for solving many types of memory problems.[10] One strategy is called the method of loci, or the use of familiar locations. It requires a familiar sequence of visual images that can be recalled easily and used as retrieval cues. One such sequence would be scenes you know from a familiar route, such as one through your house (for example, through the front door, to various places in the living room, and into the kitchen).

Here's how to use the scene you have imagined. Basically, you need to (1) form an image of each object to be remembered, and (2) place it in your imagined scene. Thus, if the first object is "horse," you might imagine it jumping through the front door of your house. If the second object is "rocket," you might imagine a huge rocket in the second location you come to in the living room (such as the couch). Ideally, the visual scene you use should have as many locations as there are objects to remember, and you should proceed through your scene in a natural order that is easy to remember. In addition, it can be helpful to form images that have vivid and unique interactions.

Below is a list of 10 words for you to attempt to remember by using the method of loci. Spend enough time on each word to form an image of it and of its place in a scene that is vivid and unique.

carrot	trumpet
moose	pillow
helicopter	scissors
Indian	goat
chicken	cherry

Without looking back at the list, try to recall the words in the order in which they occurred by using the retrieval cues in your familiar path. Now try to recall them in reverse order. This can be done easily by reversing the direction in which you move through your imaginary scene.

For another memory problem, recall as quickly as possible the fifth word from the preceding list, then the third, then the seventh, and so forth. Although it is possible to use the method of loci to achieve this goal, it would be very cumbersome and time-consuming to walk through all the scenes while counting them. A much better strategy for solving this type of memory problem is to use images indexed to a numerical code. The peg-word system is one such strategy. In the peg-word system we form associated images using objects that rhyme with numbers. For example, try forming interactive images of the objects in the peg-word scheme below combined with those in the previous word list (imagine the first word, carrot, in a bun, for example, and the second word, moose, with a shoe on its antlers).

One is a bun

Two is a shoe

Three is a tree

Four is a door

Five is a hive

Six is a stick

Seven is heaven

Eight is a gate

Nine is a dime

Ten is a hen

With the peg-word system, you should be able to recall any numbered item in a list by using the number as a cue to retrieve the word and images that were paired with it. Of course, this strategy requires that you become familiar with the peg-word scheme so that the images can be retrieved easily.

Interactive Imagery

The key feature of both the method of loci and the peg-word system is the creation of images that link something you want to learn with something you already know. Interactive imagery strategies have been studied by a number of researchers and have been found to work extremely well for most people.

We have devised a demonstration experiment to illustrate the role of interactive imagery in memory. Please follow the instructions accurately, otherwise the demonstration will not work. Sixteen pairs of words are listed below. *Simply read each word pair as you go through the list; try to do nothing more (spend approximately 4 seconds per pair)*. Please begin now.

clock sheep

telephone dog

cloud ring

rabbit shovel

bear ice cube

fox lamp

tree radio

pencil cloud

book fence

stove owl

mountain egg

robin flute

tent movie

key snake

snow elephant

rock baby

In the list below is the first half of each of the 16 pairs of words you just read. When you read each word, try to think of the word that went with it, but do not look back at the previous list. Keep track of the number of times you are successful.

rabbit	stove
book	bear
mountain	pencil
rock	tent
telephone	key
robin	clock
cloud	tree
snow	fox

Most people find it very difficult to remember which words go together. Note that the instructions were simply to read each word pair and nothing more. If you found that most of the words above called to mind the other half of the pair, chances are you used strategies similar to those discussed below.[11]

The following experiment is designed to illustrate the power of interactive imagery in remembering. As in the last experiment, you will see 16 pairs of words. This time, however, do not simply read each word as you proceed through the list. Instead, try to generate a vivid image that relates the two words in each pair. (For example, if the word pair were chicken–flag, you could imagine a chicken holding a flag in its mouth.)

newspaper arrow	fork ball
bathtub whale	rain tuba
deer roller skates	apple magazine
rope football	cup yardstick
cake lawn mower	cigar piano
worm house	taxicab flower
fan gun	hat lion
shark peach	bus spear

The list below contains the first word from each of the pairs above. Keep track of the number of times these words enable you to remember the second member of each pair. Most people find that their performance with this list is much better than their performance with the first list (unless, of course, they cheated earlier and used a strategy that integrated the pairs of words).[12]

rain	worm
gar	fan
cake	fork

shark	apple
deer	hat
newspaper	rope
bathtub	bus
cup	taxicab

Remembering Faces and Names

A problem faced by many people is an inability to remember the names of new acquaintances. One solution to this problem is to use a strategy known as the image-name technique, which is similar to the imagery strategy discussed above.[13]

The image-name technique establishes a link between a unique feature of an individual's face and a feature of his or her name. First you need to examine a person's features and try to identify those that most distinguish his or her face from other faces. For example, identify the unique features of the face in Figure 19 and make up a word or phrase that helps you remember the unique features. Use the letters in the word or use the first letter of each word in the phrase to remind you of a facial feature. When you are finished, turn the page and see if you can select that face from the others in Figure 20.

Figure 19 Try to remember this face.

Figure 20   Try to identify the face that you saw earlier.

This strategy should help you distinguish similar faces from one another (which can be important if you witness a crime, for example), but it will not necessarily help you remember the name that goes with each face. To remember names, identify a facial feature that you can associate with the person's name or with the syllables of the name. The picture in Figure 21 provides an illustration of how this correspondence can be developed.

If you practice the image-name strategy (faces and names are provided at the end of this chapter) you should become able to learn names quite effectively. This strategy can also be used for other purposes. For example, waiters and waitresses can use it to remember what customers order, and salespersons can use it to remember the family background and interests of the clients they serve.

Figure 21 Remembering names and faces. Distinctive facial features might include the beard and the glasses. Distinctive relationships between the facial features and the name (Bart Stein) might include letting "beard" remind you of a bar (for Bart) and "glasses" remind you of beer glasses, called steins (for Stein).

Harry Lorayne describes a variation of the image-name technique that may be more effective in certain situations. He recommends forming a collection of picture equivalents for common names that can be called upon when needed. Some picture equivalents for common names are listed below. For this strategy to be effective, you would need to expand the collection to include many more common names. You might even want to include picture equivalents for surnames and titles if that is information you often need to remember. Each picture equivalent should be associated in some way with the name.[14]

Ann	ant
Bonnie	bony
Rosita	rose eater
Sherry	cherry
Adam	atom bomb
Bill	dollar bill
Tom	tom cat

When you meet someone with a name for which you have a picture equivalent, you can form an interactive image that relates a distinctive visual feature of the person to your picture equivalent. For example, if you meet a woman with a prominent forehead named Bonnie, you could form an image of bone protruding from her forehead. As you become more familiar with your picture equivalents, it will require less and less effort to form these interactive images.

Acronyms and Acrostics

A powerful strategy for facilitating memory is the creation of acronyms. These are especially useful for retrieving information that you have encoded and stored. Assume, for example, that you want to remember the component processes involved in problem solving that were discussed in Chapter 2. An excellent way to do this is to think of the acronym IDEAL, which can serve as a retrieval cue for information about the individual components (identify, define, explore, anticipate/act, and look/learn). Effective learners often create their own acronyms to remember information they need to know. For example, to remember the three major sections of this chapter, you might create the acronym USA, for *understanding* basic memory processes, *strategies* for remembering, and *adaptations* and inventions of memory strategies.

Some acronyms have become so widely accepted that they are used in place of the words they represent (an example is radar, which stands for radio detecting and ranging). The use of acronyms is similar to the practice of forming abbreviations for complex or specialized terms or names. DNA, RNA, and IQ are examples. It is very common for experts to invent a shared language or mental shorthand by means of acronyms and abbreviations. This can facilitate communication between experts but make it difficult for those outside the field to understand. In contrast, business leaders often use acronyms and abbreviations to help consumers remember their names or obtain their services. Some examples are

IBM
3-M
Dial 526-FILM for theater information

A related strategy for remembering important terms is to think of a short phrase comprising words whose initial letters represent the information to be remembered. For example, to remember the notes of the G clef, it is helpful to use the phrase "Every good boy does fine." Such phrases are called acrostics. Both acrostics and acronyms can be effective tools because they substitute easily remembered words or phrases for more complex and unrelated concepts; in short, they substitute an easier memory task for a more difficult one. These strategies work as long as the letters function effectively as retrieval cues. However, they may not be very effective for remembering unfamiliar words or concepts. For example, most people would not find the word "bunt" to be a good acronym for the names Baum, Ulpa, Nidia, and Treim, because the names themselves are so unfamiliar. Similarly, an acrostic would be ineffective if it were too complex to be remembered.

Adapting and Inventing Memory Strategies

So far in this chapter we have focused on analyzing basic memory processes and giving examples of powerful memory strategies. This will provide the foundation for improving your ability to invent your own ways to solve memory problems. Invention is important because a particular strategy may or may not be optimal depending on how much you already know about what is to be remembered and your specific goals. The more inventive you can be, the better your memory will become.

Because the effectiveness of memory strategies varies as a function of goals and personal knowledge and experience, it is important to learn to invent strategies that suit your purposes. Thus, depending on the situation, you might invent acronyms and acrostics or special rhymes and rules. Assume, for example, that you want to remember whether the head of a school is a principle or a principal. You could create a memory aid, such as "The head of the school should be a pal."

Examples of Memory Problems

Listed below are some common memory problems. Try to invent techniques for solving them. Possible answers (your own might be better) are provided in Appendix A.

> In accounting, people must learn that the left column is used for entering debits and the right column is used for entering credits. Devise a scheme for remembering which is which.

People who spend a lot of time in the woods (hikers, campers, and hunters) need to know which kinds of snakes are poisonous and which are not. In general, snakes that have adjacent red and black stripes have no poison whereas those that have adjacent red and yellow stripes do. Devise a memory scheme that will help people remember which type of snake is which.

In boating, the term "port" is used for left and "starboard" for right. Devise a way to remember these facts.

The combination of a new lock is 11–8–14. Devise a memory strategy that will help you remember it.

In each of the problems presented above, the amount of information that needs to be remembered is rather small. What is difficult about each one is that it is easy to confuse one thing with another (for example, to confuse "port" with right rather than left). The ability to reduce this kind of confusion is an important criterion for any memory technique's effectiveness.

Strategies for External Storage

A powerful strategy for enhancing memory is to store information externally (on paper) rather than to attempt to remember it directly. This may seem obvious, but even here there is considerable room for invention. Different ways of organizing information affect the ease of performing a task.

Imagine that you write a grocery list containing 15 items, such as milk, cereal, apples, and dog food. Once you get to the grocery store there are several ways you might use this list. One is to get the first item on your list, then the second, and so forth. However, if the items are not organized according to the sections in your grocery store, you will be forced to make a number of trips back and forth throughout the store.

Another way to use the grocery list is to walk to one section of the store (the dairy section, for example) and scan your list for all items that may be found there. Next, walk to another section of the store (pet foods) and scan your list again. This is more efficient than walking back and forth across the store, but unless your list is organized in a way that fits the organization of your grocery store, it is still not optimal.

Storing information in a way that enables us to obtain easy access to relevant information is especially important when the amount of information stored is large. Consider a phone book for a large city. The information it contains is organized in a way that makes it relatively easy to find a phone number or street address if you know the person's name. It also makes it easy to determine the number of people in that city who have the same last name. However, imagine that you want to know the phone numbers of all the people who live on 21st Avenue or in the eastern part of the city. You would have to search through every entry in the phone book to find this information. Needless to say, this would be a tedious procedure.

In many situations externally stored information (a data base) needs to be searched from a variety of perspectives. If you run a business, for example, you may want to call or send announcements to everyone who lives in the area where it is located. Or you may want to send mailings only to those whose income is over a certain amount, or only to those who have visited your store during the past year. Similarly, if you are taking notes on articles and books, you may sometimes want to refer only to those by certain authors or about particular topics. As the example of the phone book indicates, it can be very difficult to store information in ways that permit easy access to such categories.

Fortunately, modern computer technology is making it possible to gain access to data bases using a variety of search categories. For example, computerized data bases in libraries can allow you to search for articles on the basis of information about the author, title, date of publication, subjects covered, and key words used in the article. A computerized data base of cookbook recipes might allow you to search for recipes on the basis of title, important ingredients, country of origin, or nutritional value. Computers therefore provide a powerful means of enhancing memory. Even with computers, however, you must choose the format for representing and retrieving information that is most appropriate to your needs. Since the computer's ability to search for information depends on how data bases are organized and how you query them, your ingenuity will have important effects on what the computer can do.

■ Summary

In this chapter, our discussion emphasized the relationship between remembering and problem solving. People who are good at remembering information develop effective problem-solving skills. First, they are able to identify situations that may cause memory difficulties ("This is too much information to hold in short-term memory" or "If I am not careful

I will get confused and forget whether *port* means right or left"). Second, they define their goals appropriately ("I want to remember whether *starboard* refers to the right or left"). Third, they explore a variety of strategies and select those that are appropriate to their goals. Fourth, they anticipate the effects of different strategies and act on those that are most promising. Fifth, they look at the effects of particular strategies on performance (that is, on their ability to remember) and consider how to approach future memory problems. If their performance has been poor, they reenter the IDEAL cycle and may redefine their goals or select or invent different strategies. They then act on these new strategies and look at the effects, continuing to improve their memory skills.

It is important to understand the relationship between strategy selection and how we define our memory goals. First, particular strategies (simple repetition or categorization, for example) are appropriate for some goals but not for others. Second, it can be useful to examine some of the basic research on memory. For instance, researchers find that it is difficult to attend to multiple sources of information, and even with only one source we must still decide what aspects of that information are important. Elaboration also plays an important role in remembering information. While elaboration may be relatively effortless in some situations, it can require a great deal of effort in others. Another research finding is that storage of information does not guarantee its retrieval, and the selection and evaluation of strategies must take into account the nature of the retrieval environment. If no retrieval cues are going to be provided, for example, you need to generate a retrieval scheme of your own. In addition, the probability that particular retrieval cues will be effective can be increased (by forming interactive images, for example). Finally, the improvement of memory skills is an ongoing process. A major challenge is to become skilled at inventing new memory techniques for solving problems that you may confront in everyday life.

■ Exercises

1. Carefully read the passage below once, then turn to Appendix B and answer the questions about it.

   You are the driver of a bus that can hold a total of 72 passengers (there are 36 seats that can each hold 2 passengers). At the first stop, 7 people get on the bus. At the next stop, 3 people get off and 5 get on. At the next stop, 4 people get off and 2 get on. During each of the next two stops, 3 passengers get off and 2 get on. At the next stop, 5 passengers get off and 7 get on. When the bus arrives at the next-to-the-last stop, 2 people get on and 5 get off.

Develop acronyms or other techniques for remembering the following.

2. The order of the cranial nerves is olfactory, optic, oculomotor, trochlear, trigeminal, abducens, facial, auditory, glossopharyngeal, vagus, spinal-accessory, and hypoglossal.
3. You should set the clock one hour ahead in the spring and one hour back in the fall (for daylight savings time).

Devise strategies for remembering the following.

4. The combination to your new lock is 22–4–9.
5. Balsam fir trees have smooth twigs; eastern hemlocks have rough twigs.

Devise a strategy to help you remember the correct spelling of each word below.

Correct spelling	Common misspelling
6. across	accross
7. facilitate	facillitate
8. development	developement

Devise a technique for remembering the facts associated with each of the following names.

9. Edmund Hillary	First to climb Mount Everest
10. Hubert Booth	Invented the vacuum cleaner
11. John Sculley	Chairman of Apple Computer Corp.

Devise a strategy to remember the name associated with each face below.

12. Harriet Eisely

13. Lynn Foreman

14. Rose Lipman

15. Devise a strategy to help you remember that dromedary camels have one hump and Bactrian camels have two humps.
16. Devise a strategy to help you remember that polygyny refers to the practice of having more than one wife at a time and that polyandry refers to the practice of having more than one husband at a time.
17. Many types of computer programs (word processors, spreadsheets) allow you to build simple keystroke commands (CTRL-A) that execute complex functions. These simple keystroke commands are called macros. If you use a program

that allows you to build macros, try to construct a set of easily remembered keystrokes to execute the functions that you frequently use in the program.

■ Notes

1. F. Bacon, *Novum organum*. First book, Aphorism 2, 1620.
2. Studies of the effectiveness of various types of memory strategies include G. H. Bower and M. C. Clark, Narrative stories as mediators for serial learning. *Psychonomic Science* 14 (1969):181–182; F. L. M. Craik and R. S. Lockhart, Levels of processing: A framework for memory research. *Journal of Verbal Learning and Verbal Behavior* 11 (1972):671–684; F. L. M. Craik and M. J. Watkins, The role of rehearsal in short-term memory, *Journal of Verbal Learning and Verbal Behavior* 12 (1973):599–607; T. S. Hyde and J. J. Jenkins, Differential effects of incidental tasks on the organization of recall of a list of highly associated words, *Journal of Experimental Psychology* 82 (1969): 472–481; D. Rundus and R. C. Atkinson, Rehearsal processes in free recall: A procedure for direct observation. *Journal of Verbal Learning and Verbal Behavior* 9 (1970):99–105; M. A. McDaniel and G. O. Einstein, Bizarre imagery as an effective memory aid: The importance of distinctiveness. *Journal of Experimental Psychology: Learning, Memory, and Cognition* 12 (1986):54–65.
3. T. J. Keeney, S. R. Cannizzo, and J. H. Flavell, Spontaneous and induced verbal rehearsal in a recall task. *Child Development* 38 (1967):953–966.
4. G. A. Miller, The magical number seven plus or minus two: Some limits on our capacity for processing information. *Psychological Review* 63 (1956):81–97.
5. Research and theories dealing with attention are discussed by D. Kahneman, *Attention and Effort*. Englewood Cliffs, N.J.: Prentice Hall, 1973; D. L. LaBerge, Attention. *Psychological Science* 1 (1990):156–162.
6. Studies illustrating how particular strategies may or may not be effective depending on the testing context include C. D. Morris, J. D. Bransford, and J. J. Franks, Levels of processing versus transfer appropriate processing. *Journal of Verbal Learning and Verbal Behavior* 16 (1977):519–533. H. L. Roediger, Implicit memory: Retention without remembering. *American Psychologist* 45 (1990):1043–1056;

B. S. Stein, Depth of processing re-examined: The effects of precision of encoding and test appropriateness. *Journal of Verbal Learning and Verbal Behavior* 17 (1978):165–174.

7. J. E. Turnure, N. Buium, and M. L. Thurlow, The effectiveness of interrogatives for prompting verbal elaboration productivity in young children. *Child Development* 47 (1976):851–855.

8. B. S. Stein, J. D. Bransford, J. J. Franks, R. A. Owings, N. J. Vye, and W. McGraw. Differences in the precision of self-generated elaborations, *Journal of Experimental Psychology: General* 11, no. 1 (1982):390–398.

9. E. Tulving, Cue-dependent forgetting. *American Scientist* 62 (1974):74–82.

10. F. Yates, *The Art of Memory*. London: Routledge & Kegan Paul, 1966.

11. M. A. McDaniel and G. O. Einstein, Bizarre imagery as an effective memory aid: The importance of distinctiveness. *Journal of Experimental Psychology: Learning, Memory, and Cognition* 12 (1986):54-65.

12. R. R. Hunt and M. Marschark, Yet another picture of imagery: The roles of shared and distinctive information in memory. In M. A. McDaniel and M. Pressley (eds.), *Imagery and Related Mnemonic Processes*. New York: Springer-Verlag, 1987; B. S. Stein, The effects of cue-target uniqueness on cued recall performance. *Memory and Cognition* 5 (1977):319–322.

13. Strategies for linking faces and names are discussed in K. L. Higbee, *Your Memory: How It Works and How to Improve It*. Englewood Cliffs, N.J.: Prentice-Hall, 1977; H. Lorayne and J. Lucas, *The Memory Book*. New York: Ballantine, 1974.

14. H. Lorayne, *Remembering People: The Key to Success*. New York: Stein & Day Publishers, 1975.

■ Suggested Readings

Practically Oriented Readings

Bellezza, F. S. 1982. *Improve Your Memory Skills*. Englewood Cliffs, N.J.: Prentice-Hall.

Bower, G. H. 1970. Analysis of a mnemonic device. *American Scientist*, 58:496–510.

Cermak, L. S. 1976. *Improving Your Memory*. New York: McGraw-Hill.

Higbee, K. L. 1977. *Your Memory: How It Works and How to Improve It.* Englewood Cliffs, N.J.: Prentice-Hall.

Lorayne, H., and J. Lucas. 1974. *The Memory Book.* New York: Ballantine.

Luria, A. R. 1968. *The Mind of a Mnemonist.* New York: Basic Books.

Theoretically Oriented Readings

Ellis, H. C., and R. R. Hunt. 1989. *Fundamentals of Human Memory and Cognition* (4th ed.). Dubuque, Iowa: W. C. Brown.

Klatzky, R. L. *Human Memory: Structure and Process* (2d ed.). 1980. San Francisco: W. H. Freeman.

McDaniel, M. A., and M. Pressley (eds.). 1987. *Imagery and Related Mnemonic Processes.* New York: Springer-Verlag.

Matlin, M. W. 1989. *Cognition* (2d ed.). New York: Holt, Rinehart and Winston.

Neisser, U. 1982. *Memory Observed: Remembering in Natural Contexts.* San Francisco: W. H. Freeman.

Neisser, U., and E. Winograd (eds.). 1988. *Remembering Reconsidered: Ecological and Traditional Approaches to the Study of Memory.* New York: Cambridge University Press.

Reed, S. K. 1992. *Cognition* (3d ed.). Pacific Grove, Calif.: Brooks Cole.

Roediger, H. L., and F. I. M. Craik (eds.). 1989. *Varieties of Memory and Consciousness: Essays in Honour of Endel Tulving.* Hillsdale, N.J.: Lawrence Erlbaum Associates.

Zechmeister, E. G., and S. E. Nyberg. 1982. *Human Memory: An Introduction to Research and Theory.* Monterey, Calif: Brooks Cole.

LEARNING WITH UNDERSTANDING

Education is the acquisition of the art of the utilisation of knowledge.

Alfred North Whitehead[1]

In Chapter 6 we discussed strategies for remembering information. The effective use of memory strategies will enable you to remember important information, such as a person's name, when you are confronted with a particular retrieval cue, such as that person's face. However, suppose your goal in learning is not simply to remember information but to understand it so that you can apply it in creative ways to the solution of problems that arise in the future. There are important differences between remembering information and understanding how to use it to solve novel problems.

As an illustration of the difference between remembering and understanding, consider a friend of ours who discovered that he had an allergy to milk products and was given a pill by his doctor to help him digest milk. The doctor told him to take the pill 30 minutes before eating a meal. The statement "Take the pill 30 minutes before eating" was easy for our friend to remember. However, one day he encountered an unanticipated problem: He had just finished a meal that included milk products and suddenly realized that he had forgotten to take his pill. His goal was to decide what to do. Would it do him any good to take the pill now, or should he cancel his next appointment in anticipation of a reaction to the milk? Might it actually be harmful to take the pill after eating? Our friend could not answer these questions for himself, because he had no understanding of the relationship among milk products, his digestive system, and the pill provided by the doctor. He had remembered a procedure (to take the pill 30 minutes before eating), but he did not understand enough about how the pill worked to solve his problems. Without understanding, it can be difficult to solve unanticipated problems.

Our friend's dilemma illustrates important differences between understanding a situation and simply memorizing information about it. Strategies that improve memory without helping us to understand can create what Alfred North Whitehead[2] called "inert knowledge." He used the term to refer to information that a person is able to recall when explicitly asked to do so, but that he or she is not able to apply spontaneously to the solution of problems. A goal of this chapter is to show that comprehending new information—learning with understanding—is different from merely memorizing that information. *The strategies necessary to solve comprehension problems differ from those necessary for memorization.* We begin by showing how comprehension involves problem solving and how the goal of understanding differs from the goal of simply remembering.

■ Comprehension as Problem Solving

To illustrate how comprehension involves problem solving, read the passage below.[3]

> Sally let loose a team of gophers. The plan backfired when a dog chased them away. She then threw a party but the guests failed to bring their motorcycles. Furthermore, her stereo system was not loud enough. Sally spent the next day looking for a "Peeping Tom" but was unable to find one in the yellow pages. Obscene phone calls gave her some hope until the number was changed. It was the installation of blinking neon lights across the street that finally did the trick. Sally framed the ad from the classified section and now has it hanging on her wall.

Most people have difficulty comprehending this passage. They understand each word and each sentence alone, but something seems to be missing. They cannot find an explanation for why Sally is doing what she is doing and how one sentence in the story leads into the next one.

After identifying the existence of a comprehension problem, some readers may feel that the passage is gibberish and *define* their goal as not wasting time on such nonsense. Other readers may approach the problem differently. For instance, they may conjecture that the passage presupposes some information not available to them that might be available to someone more familiar with Sally. Consequently, they may *define* their goal as trying to find the presupposed information. These readers may then *explore* various strategies for solution. For example, they may think of possible reasons for Sally's activities (maybe she's in love with somebody), *anticipate* possible outcomes, and *act* on the strategy that seems most likely to help them understand the passage. Then they can *look* at the effects. If their initial hypothesis doesn't work, they can generate and test alternative hypotheses. They may move through the IDEAL cycle a number of times.

Now imagine that you are going to be tested on the Sally passage. Many students might assume that their goal is simply to remember the information in the passage, and they will explore strategies appropriate to that goal. You could undoubtedly memorize all the sentences by using one of the strategies discussed in the previous chapter (for example, interactive imagery). But consider what would happen if you were asked the following questions:

1. Where did Sally put the gophers?
2. Why did Sally want the guests to bring motorcycles?
3. Whose number was changed?
4. Who probably made the calls?
5. What did the advertisement say?

If you failed to understand the passage about Sally and simply memorized it, you would find it very difficult to answer such questions.

The passage becomes much more comprehensible when you can formulate an explanation for Sally's actions. Assume, therefore, that Sally is trying to get a neighbor to move. Given this information, read the passage again and try to answer the questions posed above.

The Sally passage illustrates two points. First, comprehension involves a problem- solving process. Second, understanding often requires more than the simple memorizing of information (see Figure 22). The ability to remember all the sentences in the Sally passage does not guarantee your ability to do other things with the information, such as make intelligent inferences. When we learn with understanding, we are able to apply information to a broader range of tasks than when information is simply memorized.

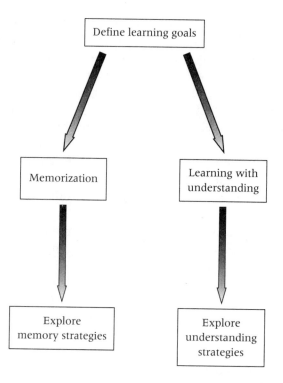

Figure 22

Comprehension and Inferences

The passage about Sally illustrates how comprehension can depend on additional knowledge. This seems to be the case in all instances of comprehension; people are often surprised to learn how much they make use of previously acquired knowledge in order to comprehend. Consider the following passage.[4]

> *A thirsty ant went to a river. He became carried away by the rush of the stream and was about to drown. A dove was sitting in a tree overhanging the water. The dove plucked a leaf and let it fall. The leaf fell into the stream close to the ant and the ant climbed onto it. The ant floated safely to the bank. Shortly afterward, a birdcatcher came and laid a trap in the tree. The ant saw his plan and stung him on the foot. In pain the birdcatcher threw down his trap. The noise made the bird fly away.*

A number of assumptions are necessary to understand this story. For example, readers usually assume that the ant walked to the river and the dove flew to the tree, although this information was never explicitly stated. Similarly, readers understand that the ant could drown because it requires oxygen (in contrast, you would not worry about a fish drowning in a river), that the dove probably plucked the leaf with its beak, and so forth. Basic information about doves and ants therefore plays an important role in the inferences that readers make.

Other inferences must also be made to understand this story. One involves the characters' goals. For example, most people assume that the dove plucked the leaf to save the ant, that the birdcatcher's plan was to trap the dove, and that the ant bit the birdcatcher to repay the dove for its previous favor. Note that none of this information is stated in the story; all of it is generated by the reader. Indeed, the story does not even state that the ant and the dove saw each other. The author of the passage did not need to state this information explicitly; it was assumed that readers would supply it. Communication would be cumbersome if speakers and writers had to provide all the information necessary for comprehension. If we lack the relevant background knowledge, however, we may be unable to make the assumptions necessary to understand what speakers and writers wish to communicate.[5]

Prerequisites to Understanding

In the previous discussion we noted that many of the inferences required for comprehension draw on relevant background knowledge. In some situations this background knowledge may involve many complex and interconnected concepts. Consider the following summary of a talk at a scientific meeting.

> Pete argued that data gathered from a NASA spaceship's voyage to Venus calls into question current theories about the formation of our solar system. Part of his talk emphasized the importance of mass spectrometers. He then discussed the isotopes of argon 36 and argon 38 and noted that they were of higher density than expected. He also cited the high values of neon found in the atmosphere. He has a paper that is already written, but he is aware of the need for further investigation as well.

Most people who are asked to read this passage could do little more than memorize it. They simply do not have the background knowledge necessary to understand with any depth. As a result, they are unable to make inferences such as

1. The extent to which high levels of isotopes of argon have anything to do with theories of the formation of the solar system
2. Whether and why high values of neon are significant
3. How these questions relate to the importance of mass spectrometers

Clearly, the only way to understand the summary of Pete's talk would be to learn the concepts that underlie the science of astronomy. But these concepts would have to be learned with understanding rather than merely memorized. In the next section we explore some of the processes involved in learning about a new domain.

■ Learning about New Areas of Knowledge

One of the best ways to understand the process of learning is to consider how expertise is acquired in various fields such as mathematics, physics, biology, and psychology. For example, assume that you know only a little about biology and that your goal is to learn more. Assume that the current lesson involves veins and arteries. You might read in a textbook that arteries are thick and elastic and that they carry blood rich in oxygen from the heart, blood that is pumped in spurts; veins are thinner and less elastic and carry blood rich in carbon dioxide back to the heart. For a novice, even this relatively simple set of facts can seem arbitrary and confusing. Was it veins or arteries that are thin? Was the thin one or the thick one elastic? Which one carries carbon dioxide from the heart (or was it *to* the heart)?

The problem of arbitrariness can be illustrated in simple sentences that are comprehensible to nearly everyone. Spend no more than a few seconds reading each of the following statements about a group of people.[6]

The fat one bought the padlock.
The strong one cleaned the paintbrush.
The cheerful one read the newspaper.
The skinny one purchased the scissors.
The funny one admired the ring.

The toothless one plugged in the cord.
The barefoot one climbed the steps.
The bald one cut out the coupon.
The sleepy one held the pitcher.
The blind one closed the bag.
The kind one opened the milk.
The poor one entered the museum.

Now try to answer the following questions without looking back at the preceding sentences.

Which one purchased the scissors?
Which one cut out the coupon?
Which one climbed the steps?
Which one closed the bag?
Which one read the newspaper?
Which one cleaned the paintbrush?
Which one admired the ring?
Which one held the pitcher?
Which one plugged in the cord?
Which one bought the padlock?
Which one entered the museum?
Which one opened the milk?

Most people have a difficult time remembering which person performed which activity. The major reason for this difficulty is that the relationship between the person and the action performed seems arbitrary; there is no clear reason that a particular person should perform that particular activity. Novices in the field of biology feel similarly about the properties of veins and arteries; relationships between these entities and their properties seem arbitrary. For example, why should arteries rather than veins be elastic or nonelastic, thick or thin?

Memory Strategies

There are several ways to approach the problem of mastering information that seems arbitrary at first. One is simply to repeat the facts until they are memorized (artery thick elastic; artery thick elastic). A more efficient approach is to use memory techniques similar to those discussed in Chapter 6.[7] The use of imagery is one technique. That arteries are thick could be remembered by forming an image of a thick, hollow tube flashing the word *artery*. That arteries are elastic could be remembered by imagining that the tube is suspended by a rubber band that stretches and contracts, causing the tube to move up and down. You could embellish the image by having red liquid (blood) and round (like an *o*) bubbles (oxygen) pouring out of the tube, and these could be moving away from an image of a Valentine's Day heart. This composite image could help you to remember that arteries are thick and elastic and carry blood rich in oxygen away from the heart. Another technique would be to use verbal elaborations; for example, "Art(ery) was *thick* around the middle so he wore pants with an elastic waistband."

Comprehension Strategies

We noted earlier that the ability to remember information is no guarantee that you will be able to make inferences and use it to solve new problems. Suppose you learn that arteries are elastic by imagining either a rubber band holding a tube or thick-waisted Art and his elastic waistband. What if you were confronted with the problem of designing an artificial artery? Would it have to be elastic? What would be the potential implications of hardening of the arteries? Would this have a serious impact on people's health? Having used the imaging techniques to remember that arteries are elastic, you would have little basis for answering these questions.

Memory techniques are useful for many purposes, but a very different approach is needed to develop an understanding of veins and arteries. Effective learners attend to facts, but they also try to understand their significance. For example, the passage stated that arteries are elastic. What is the significance of elasticity? How does this property relate to the functions that arteries perform? An effective learner might seek out information to clarify this relationship. The passage also stated that arteries carry blood from the heart, blood that is pumped in spurts. This provides one clue about the significance of elasticity—arteries may need to expand and contract to accommodate the pumping of blood. An effective learner might ask why veins do *not* need to be elastic. Perhaps because veins carry blood back to the heart, they have less need to accommodate the large changes in pressure resulting from the heart's pumping of blood in spurts.

Some learners could carry this process a step further, asking why blood does not flow back to the heart through the arteries. Since there are arteries in the neck and shoulder regions, arterial blood must flow up as well as down. The answer to this question might provide an additional clue about the significance of elasticity—the expansion and contraction of arteries might help blood move in a particular direction. Elasticity might therefore serve as a one-way valve that enables blood to flow forward but not back. An artificial artery might therefore be equipped with valves instead of being nonelastic. However, this solution might work only if the spurts of blood did not cause too much pressure on the artificial artery.

The passage does not provide information about pressure requirements, so a learner would have to look elsewhere for this information. Note, however, that he or she could *identify* the need to obtain this additional information. The effective learner's methods are not unlike those employed by good detectives or researchers confronting a new problem. Initial assumptions may ultimately be found to be incorrect, but the act of seeking clarification is fundamental to the development of expertise. In contrast, the person who simply concentrates on techniques for memorizing facts will never know whether there is something more to be understood.

Arbitrary Sentences Reconsidered

The importance of searching for information that can clarify the significance of facts and relationships can also be illustrated by the set of sentences about the people and their activities that was presented earlier. We noted earlier that memory strategies can help us retain important information. However, these techniques do not help us understand *why* each person performs a particular activity.

An alternative approach to the problem is to figure out how each person might be suited to a particular activity. This is analogous to asking why certain entities (such as veins or arteries) have the particular structures and functions they do. The following list of sentences is identical to the earlier list, except that each contains an elaboration that should help you explain why it might be appropriate for each person to perform the activity that he or she does. Read the sentences through once, and then attempt to answer the questions that follow.

The fat one bought the padlock to place on the refrigerator door.
The strong one cleaned the paintbrush used to paint the barbells.
The cheerful one read the newspaper announcing that he had won the lottery.
The skinny one purchased the scissors to use when taking in her pants.
The funny one admired the ring that squirted water.

The toothless one plugged in the cord to the food blender.
The barefoot one climbed the steps leading to the vat of grapes.
The bald one cut out the coupon for the hair tonic.
The sleepy one held the pitcher containing water for the coffee machine.
The blind one closed the bag after feeding her seeing-eye dog.
The kind one opened the milk to give to the hungry child.
The poor one entered the museum to find shelter from the snowstorm.

Here are the questions:

Which one purchased the scissors?
Which one cut out the coupon?
Which one climbed the steps?
Which one closed the bag?
Which one read the newspaper?
Which one cleaned the paintbrush?
Which one admired the ring?
Which one held the pitcher?
Which one plugged in the cord?
Which one bought the padlock?
Which one entered the museum?
Which one opened the milk?

Most people find it relatively easy to remember who did what given elaborations that clarify the reason for each activity. These elaborations must be relevant, however; they must help one understand why each person performs each activity. Elaborations that make sense and yet are irrelevant can actually impair memory rather than improve it. Examples of irrelevant elaborations in this case are the following:

The fat one bought the padlock to place on the garage door.
The strong one cleaned the paintbrush used to paint the chair.
The cheerful one read the newspaper bought at the newsstand.
The skinny one purchased the scissors to use when trimming her nails.
The funny one admired the ring in the jewelry store.

The Importance of Exploring Explanations While Learning

A series of studies that we conducted with several colleagues[8] illustrates some important differences in the ways students approach the task of learning new information. We created a passage about two imaginary robots and asked two different groups of fifth-grade students to study them until they felt that they had learned the information. Both groups of students could decode words adequately; however, one group was more successful academically than the other.

Here is one of the passages that we presented to the children. Imagine that your goal is to understand why each robot has the particular features that it does. Pay attention to the learning strategies you use to achieve this goal.

> Bill's father worked for a company that made robots. His company made robots for a business that washed outside windows. They needed two kinds of robots. One kind of robot was needed to wash windows in two-story houses. These windows were small. The other kind of robot was needed to wash the outside of windows of high-rise office buildings. These windows were big.

> Billy went to visit his father at work. He saw the new robots that his father had made. The robot used for houses was called an extendible robot. It could extend itself so it would be almost as tall as a two-story house. Billy saw that this robot had spikes instead of feet. It had legs that did not bend. Its stomach could extend in length to make it taller. The arms on the robot were short. Instead of hands, it had a small sponges. In its head was a nozzle attached to a hose. Billy also saw that the extendible robot was made of heavy steel. It had an electric cord that could be plugged in. The robot also had a ladder on its back.

> Billy then saw another robot called a nonextendible robot. This robot had suction cups instead of feet. It had legs that could bend. Its stomach was padded. The arms on the robot were long. Instead of hands, it had large sponges. In its head was a bucket. Billy also saw that the nonextendible robot was made of light aluminum. There was a battery inside the robot. The robot also had a parachute on its back.

Did you find yourself attempting to understand why each robot has its particular features? For example, did you try to explain why the window-climbing robot might have a battery and the extendible robot an electrical cord? If so, you approached this passage in a manner similar to that of the academically successful students who participated in our study. Here is one fifth grader's explanation for why each robot had particular properties:

> You would know that the robot that had to go up on tall buildings to wash the windows would need to be lighter and not use an extension cord because it would be too long and might make it fall. It had a parachute in case it did fall. It also had large sponges because the windows were big. You'd also know that the robot used to wash two-story houses was more heavy and had an extension cord 'cause there are plugs. It would rise up with its stomach and could spray with the hose that came through its head. You can't have a hose if you climb real high.

Michelene Chi and her colleagues[9] have also found that successful students are more likely to explore explanations during the learning process than are less academically successful students. They examined the learning strategies that college students used as they encountered problems in their physics texts. Chi and her colleagues found that successful students engaged in a process of explanation; they tried to figure out why each aspect of the solution was applicable, and they asked themselves about other problems to which the solution might also be applicable. As a result, they acquired an understanding that was more general than a mere memorization of the specific steps involved in a particular problem would afford.

Further Illustrations of Memory Versus Comprehension Strategies

It is useful to consider other examples of strategies for memorizing facts and relationships versus strategies for understanding the significance of those facts and relationships. Consider first the pairs of scissors shown in Figure 23.[10] Imagine that you study them until you can draw each pair of scissors from memory. This will provide no guarantee that you understand how the physical features of each pair of scissors are related to its function. Table 2 lists the primary function of each pair of scissors. Given this information, the particular structure of each pair becomes more meaningful. Clearly, the relationship between each pair's structure and function are not arbitrary; for example, the structure of the dressmaker's shears allows fabric to be cut on a flat surface. The ability to understand the significance of relationships such as these has a number of potential benefits. One is that people who understand them are in a better position to invent a new pair of scissors that would allow them to perform particular tasks more efficiently. They are certainly better equipped to create

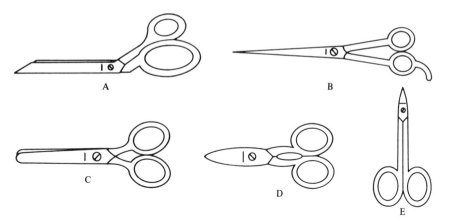

Figure 23

useful inventions than are those who merely memorize differences in appearance without understanding the related functions.

As another example of differences between memorization and comprehension strategies, imagine reading a text that contains these statements: "The Indians of the Northwest Coast lived in slant-roofed houses built of cedar plank. . . . Some California Indian tribes lived in simple earth-covered or brush shelters. . . . The Plains Indians lived mainly in tepees. . . ."[11] You could undoubtedly create some type of memory aid that would enable you to remember which Native American tribe had which type of house, but this is a far cry from understanding the significance of the information. To gain the latter, you would need to understand why different tribes chose different types of houses. For example, you would have to consider how the style of house was related to the geographic area in which the tribe lived (the style would undoubtedly be related to the climate and to the raw materials available for building). The house type would also be related to lifestyle. For example, tepees are relatively portable, whereas cedar-plank houses are not.

It is instructive that the preceding text was taken from a story written for elementary-school children. To children, the information presented seems arbitrary; no attempt was made to supply elaborations explaining why different tribes chose the houses they did. This problem occurs at all age levels, from elementary school to college.[12] One reason is that the writers of such texts are usually experts in their particular fields, whereas the readers are often novices. The texts do not seem

Table 2

SOME FUNCTIONS FOR THE SCISSORS ILLUSTRATED IN FIGURE 23

Structure	Function
A. Dressmaker's shears	
Heavy	Because of heavy use
One hole larger than other	Two or three fingers will fit in larger hole—allows greater steadiness as one cuts cloth on flat surface
Blades off-center and aligned with finger-hole edge	Blade can rest on table surface as cloth is cut—again, greater steadiness
B. Barber's shears	
Very sharp	To cut thin material; for example, hair
Pointed	Permits blades to snip close to scalp and to snip very small strands of hair
Hook on finger hole	A rest for one finger, which allows scissors to be supported when held at various angles—hence, greater maneuverability
C. Pocket or children's scissors	
Blunt ends	Scissors can be carried in pocket without cutting through cloth; children can handle without poking themselves or others
Short blades	Allow greater control by the gross motor movements of the child just learning to cut
D. Nail scissors	
Wide and thick at pivot point	To withstand pressure from cutting thick and rigid materials; that is, nails
Slightly curved blades	To cut slightly curved nails

Table 2

CONTINUED

Structure	Function
E. Cuticle scissors	
Very sharp blade	To cut semielastic materials; for example, skin of cuticles
Small curved blades	To allow maneuverability necessary to cut small curved area
Long extension from finger holes to joint	As compensation for short blades, necessary for holding

arbitrary to the writers because they can fill in the gaps. For example, they already know why arteries are elastic and why various Native Americans chose certain types of houses. In short, they not only know the facts, they also understand the significance of those facts. To the novice, however, the knowledge necessary to fill in the gaps is not available. They are therefore often forced to resort to memorizing information without really understanding it.

As you become better able to spot arbitrariness in texts, you will also be more likely to search other sources or ask questions that can help you understand what you learn. Remember, though, that the processes necessary to achieve understanding are frequently more complex than those necessary for memorizing. It is helpful to think again about the ultimate goal of learning: to develop conceptual tools that make it easier to solve important problems. Mere memorization of information rarely enables one to solve new problems later on.

Note-Taking Strategies That Support Understanding

As discussed in the preceding sections, the search for information that can clarify the significance of facts may take a considerable amount of time. It can therefore be important to preserve the material we are trying to master until we are able to explore it more carefully. This requires effective note taking.

The lack of note-taking skills can hinder learning in a number of ways. One is the loss of important information, often due to the erron-

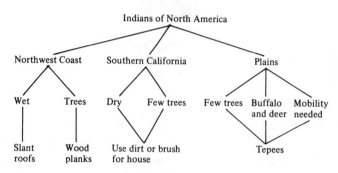

Figure 24   An illustration of lecture notes.

eous belief that the information is too important to forget. Another problem is that people write down cues that are too vague. For example, if you wrote down the phrase "Native American houses" but included nothing to remind you of its significance, you might have a difficult time remembering that a passage on this topic was used to illustrate the problem of arbitrary facts.

An obvious way to overcome these problems is to record all the information that you will use. Often, however, the exact wording is not important or there is not enough time to write down the information in full. In these situations it is necessary to use an abbreviated form of the information. When making such notes, most people focus on the main points and incorporate them into a list or outline. Ruth Day has conducted extensive research on note taking and has found that such notes may provide ineffective retrieval cues for reconstructing underlying relationships. For example, try using the following outline to reconstruct the joke to which it refers.[13] (See Appendix A for the joke.)

I. Theater joke
   A. Good news
      1. Balcony
      2. Flames reach in several minutes
   B. Bad news
      1. Theater fire
      2. Don't tell

One of the problems with this outline is that it does not remind us of the order of the parts of the joke or what the punch line is. The method of abbreviation used is not appropriate to the task. Many other forms of notes can be used to help us understand and remember information. For example, diagrams and graphs are often the most precise way to represent relationships among concepts. The treelike diagraam in Figure 24 represents the information contained in the paragraph about Native American houses. In some cases illustrations can also help us understand the significance of facts (see Figure 25).

The form of notes that works best obviously depends on the material to be learned and how it is to be used. The selection of a note-taking strategy should therefore begin with the identification of an information retrieval problem and a careful analysis of the use to which the information will be put in the future.

■ Anticipating Outcomes and Acting on Comprehension Strategies

Discussion in the preceding sections assumed that the existence of a learning problem had been identified and recognized as an opportunity to acquire new knowledge. We also assumed that the learning goal had

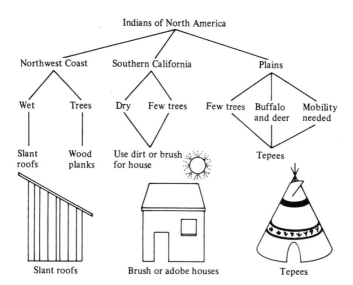

Figure 25 Some diagrams that may help people understand the significance of facts.

been *defined* as gaining understanding rather than just exercising memory. We emphasized that learning with understanding requires a set of strategies different from and often more complex than those required by mere memorization. As we *explore* various comprehension strategies it is important to *anticipate* their effects.

Many researchers have emphasized how important it is to monitor the effectiveness of learning strategies. Ann Brown[14] and John Flavell[15] were pioneers in the study of what has come to be called *metacognition*— the ability to monitor and regulate one's own learning.

Monitoring the outcome of our attempts to learn depends, to a great extent, on our ability to anticipate situations in which we will need to use the new information. Whether a mountain-climbing trip, a speech, or a test in school is involved, it is important to imagine how you will ultimately use the knowledge to decide if you have learned enough to handle the challenges that you will confront. The clearer your idea of what you will need to know, the better your ability to assess whether you are prepared. Some examples are provided below.

Levels of Understanding

Anticipating the effects of learning strategies by imagining future uses for the knowledge gained is especially important because there are many levels at which concepts and phenomena can be understood. Knowledge can be mastered at different levels of precision, and the precision necessary depends on the uses to which the knowledge will be put.

As an illustration of different levels of precision, assume that a group of people read a passage about veins and arteries, such as the one described earlier. Some may feel that they have learned enough when they understand that veins and arteries are parts of the body as opposed to, say, parts of a car engine. Others may not feel they have learned enough until they understand that veins and arteries carry blood rather than serve some other bodily function. Still others may study until they understand how veins and arteries are similar and different in structure and function. For example, they may feel it is important to know that arteries are more elastic than veins and to understand why.

Differences in the precision of one's knowledge may or may not be important for subsequent performance. Assume, for example, that you are asked the following multiple-choice question.

Arteries are
a. Good to eat
b. A type of insect
c. An important part of the body
d. Sold only at gas stations
e. A kind of tree

One needs to know very little about arteries to answer such a question. In contrast, consider the following:

Arteries
a. Are more elastic than veins
b. Carry blood that is pumped from the heart
c. Are less elastic than veins
d. Both a and b
e. Both b and c

This question requires a considerable amount of information about arteries. However, one may answer such a question correctly yet still fail to understand why arteries are elastic. As a result, additional questions might not be answered correctly.

For another illustration of levels of precision, think of how nearly all adults know the concept "gold," as in gold watch or valuable metal.[16] This understanding is precise enough for many purposes. For example, most of us can distinguish a gold ring from a silver ring, and we know what is being referred to when people talk about the price of gold. But what if you are presented with 100 large rocks. Of these, 99 are fool's gold and 1 is real gold. You may keep one rock. To solve this problem you need to have a geologist's technical understanding of gold. Our everyday idea of gold is precise enough for most purposes, but it is not sufficiently precise to solve a problem such as distinguishing real gold from fool's gold.

Finally, imagine a young child who knows only that airports are places where planes take off and land.[17] In contrast, adults know a great deal more about airports; for example, that they are places where tickets can be purchased and where metal detectors are used. Though limited, the child's knowledge is sufficient for many purposes. For example, the child should be able to comprehend the statement, "We are going to the airport because Aunt Jane is coming to visit." However, assume that the child hears the statement, "Ruth decided not to wear her matching silver earrings, necklace, and belt because she wanted to avoid delays at the airport." Most adults would assume that Ruth wants to avoid problems with metal detectors but since the child doesn't have this knowledge, he or she would have a difficult time understanding Ruth's decision.

Tests of Understanding

A powerful approach to gauging the adequacy of your current level of understanding is to devise tests that model or simulate the kinds of problems that you expect to confront in the future (designing an artificial artery or explaining the principles of astronomy). Such tests provide the opportunity to actively apply one's knowledge and, ideally, reveal any confusions, uncertainties, or gaps in one's understanding. They serve a function similar to the simulations and tests used by NASA to uncover possible problems that might be encountered by astronauts on space missions.

The importance of discovering gaps in our understanding can be illustrated by reading the paragraph below.

> This is a two-player game. Each player is given a deck of cards numbered 0 through 9. The cards are placed face down in front of each player. Each player turns over the top card of his or her deck. If the sum of the two cards that are face up equals 10, they are removed from the table. If they do not equal 10 the player takes back the card, places it back in the deck, and shuffles it. The winner is the one with no cards left.

We have presented this description to many students with instructions to either memorize the description or evaluate its usefulness in teaching addition to young children. We have also asked them to answer the following questions. Please do so now.

1. Would learning the rules improve your chances of winning?
2. If you played this game 50 times, how many games would you expect to win?
3. Estimate how long it would take to complete each game.

Despite the fact that most people believe they understand this game, their answers to these questions suggest otherwise. The correct answers are no, 0, and forever, respectively. Most people fail to detect inconsistencies in the rules of the game that would make it impossible to win or end. This is caused in part by the failure to actively apply the rules to a real game situation. If you still have not found the inconsistencies in the rules, try working through an actual game mentally, or try using real cards (answers appear in Appendix A).

This example illustrates that monitoring the effectiveness of a learning strategy can involve the active application of ideas to specific situations. If we know we are able to use a set of rules to play a game, solve a mathematical problem, or produce a concrete model, then we have acquired a better understanding of our own understanding. In the game description provided above, instructions that make the game impossible to win or end were deliberately inserted. In other learning tasks such inconsistencies are a clear signal either that our level of understanding is not adequate or that there is something deficient in the material we are trying to understand. In either case, the detection of inconsistencies serves as a signal to *identify* a new problem in our understanding and to reenter the IDEAL cycle.

In his autobiography, Charles Darwin describes a conversation with Sedgwick, a geology professor, that dramatically illustrates the importance of detecting inconsistencies. Darwin was in his early 20s at the time. One evening Darwin told Sedgwick about a laborer he had met who had discovered a large tropical shell in an old gravel pit in the midland counties. Sedgwick immediately responded, "It must have been thrown away by someone into the pit," adding, "If really embedded there it would be the greatest misfortune to geology, as it would overthrow all that we know about the superficial deposits of the Midland Counties." Sedgwick's remark had a profound effect on Darwin because it sensitized him to the relationship between theory and data. Because of his theoretical knowledge, Sedgwick was very sensitive to potential inconsistencies between theory and data and hence was able to identify potential problems of interpretation that Darwin had not noticed at all.[18]

Anticipating Problems of Access

Understanding how people process information can also help you to better anticipate the adequacy of your current level of learning. In Chapter 6 we noted that there are important differences between storing information and retrieving (accessing) it later on. It is therefore important when gauging your level of preparedness to consider the degree to which cues are available to help you retrieve the knowledge you will need. People often fail to solve problems not because they lack the relevant knowledge but because they are unable to gain access to it.

Here is a problem we have given to a number of college students enrolled in our courses on learning and memory.

> Professor X claims that students who have difficulty in school do so because they have a much higher forgetting rate than do more successful students. He supports his claim with the following study. A group of academically successful and less successful fifth graders read a story during school on Monday. The next day they are all asked to recall as much of the story as they can. On average, the successful students recall 80 percent of the story correctly; the corresponding score for the less successful students is 65 percent. Professor X argues that these data support his claims about forgetting rates. Can you find problems with his argument?

Many students come up with weak answers to this problem. Some say, "He studied only fifth graders; maybe it's not true for kids in other grades." Others state, "You can't prove much by only a single study." Although these statements have some validity, they miss the crucial flaw in Professor X's reasoning. He claims to have studied forgetting, yet he hasn't shown that the less successful students learned as much initially. Perhaps a lack of attention or of previously acquired knowledge prevented the less successful students from learning as much of the story in the first place. Without some knowledge of how much was learned (obtained, for example, by giving the children a test right after they hear the story), one cannot make claims about the rate at which forgetting occurred.

As we have noted, many college students fail to find the crucial flaw in Professor X's argument. The interesting point is that this failure is not necessarily caused by a lack of knowledge. We gave students this problem after they had studied forgetting; lectures had emphasized that forgetting presupposes that something has been learned in the first place (you cannot forget something you haven't learned). The students' failure therefore stemmed from a failure to *access* relevant information.

Additional evidence for this is provided by the second part of our experiment. Approximately 5 minutes after the students had first attempted to solve the problem, we gave it to them a second time. This time we said, "Remember our earlier discussion of the relationship between forgetting and previous learning." Given this hint, the majority of the students noticed the flaw in Professor X's experiment. Ideally, however, they should not have had to rely on such hints.

Here is a third example of overreliance on hints or clues.[19] A graduate student we know was studying for a test in statistics. The previous test had covered a number of chapters on probability theory; the instructor had provided study sheets for each chapter. The graduate student found that he could easily solve each of the problem sets provided by the course instructor, so he was convinced he was ready for the test. At this point one of us took out a pair of scissors, cut out the test questions from each problem sheet, and mixed them up. The graduate student could no longer solve the problems. He had unconsciously been using his knowledge of the chapter each problem came from to decide which formula to apply. When this information was no longer available, he discovered a problem with the way he had learned the material. He therefore changed his study strategy, paying much more attention to questions about when and why particular formulas should be used.[20]

■ Looking at the Effects and Leaning to Learn

No matter how carefully you try to anticipate the context in which information will be needed, you will not always be completely successful. As a result, you will find yourself unprepared for some emergency or unable to answer a question. This can have negative consequences, such as a lower grade in a course or embarrassment at a meeting. The most important thing to do in such situations is to try to identify the reason for your error and to establish a goal that will prevent the same mistake from happening again. People who program computers use the word *debugging* for figuring out why a program they have written won't run (they have to get the bugs out). It is important to develop debugging strategies for all our activities.

Many people adopt strategies that make debugging difficult, if not impossible. After receiving a relatively poor score on a test, for example, many students avoid looking at the test in any detail: They try to forget about an unpleasant experience. Although it is natural to want to avoid unpleasant situations, this is a surefire way to keep from learning from one's mistakes.

If you have difficulty with a topic despite having studied, several debugging strategies can help you define the nature of your problem more precisely. First, look at the types of questions you were able to answer versus those you could not. Did the ones you missed require a more precise level of understanding than you had acquired? You should also try to discover where the information necessary to answer the questions you missed is located. Was it in the text? In your notes? If it was, you must have overlooked it, perhaps because you failed to realize that it could be important for solving certain problems. If the relevant information was neither in your notes nor in the book, chances are that you need to work on effective note-taking skills.

Professors and other experts can provide feedback helpful in debugging your learning strategies. To use these sources effectively, however, you must first attempt to communicate what you have mastered. It is only then that the expert can evaluate your understanding of the subject and make suggestions that can be used to modify your learning strategies.

Imagine you meet someone who is an expert in a topic with which you are having difficulty. You could begin by explaining that you have been having trouble determining whether you have learned enough. Explain further that you have studied several topics that seem important and that you would like help in determining whether your knowledge is adequate. You can then ask the expert to question you about problems that beginners should be able to solve. This will allow you to discover quite quickly whether you are missing information that is crucial. If you do this for a number of topics, you will also develop an understanding of the expert's criteria for adequate understanding.

This approach to debugging takes commitment and preparation, and you must be brave enough to risk making mistakes in front of others. Nevertheless, it is an efficient and valuable way to learn. Furthermore, we are confident that most instructors and experts will respect your motivation and maturity. They know that it is harder to understand than to memorize, and they respect genuine attempts to understand.

■ The IDEAL Cycle and Lifelong Learning

The previous discussion emphasized the importance of looking back at our approach to learning so that we can identify potential problems in our learning strategies. Indeed, identifying problems in our approach to learning can create opportunities for improvement that can be applied throughout life. We can take advantage of these opportunities by re-entering the IDEAL cycle with the general goal of improving the effectiveness of how we learn. We might discover that we have not defined our learning goals clearly or that we have selected a level of understanding that was inappropriate for the task we had to perform. These observations will help us recognize the need to pay more attention to our goals and to how well we anticipate future uses of our knowledge.

Reentering the IDEAL cycle and attempting to debug our approaches to learning creates opportunities for what many researchers refer to as learning to learn. Lauren Resnick[21] emphasizes that everyone in society must learn to learn and solve a range of problems—not just a select few. One reason we need lifelong learning skills is that job requirements tend to change rapidly. For instance, consider the field of auto mechanics. It used to be that the knowledge and skills necessary for success in this area were relatively stable. But today's auto mechanics need to keep up with rapidly changing technologies, such as advances in computerized electronic controls. Indeed, the skills required for most professions will change rapidly as new technologies are integrated into the workplace. Those who are able to learn new concepts and procedures will have a better chance of maintaining their jobs or advancing their careers.

■ Summary

In this chapter we applied the IDEAL framework to the problem of learning with understanding. The goal of learning with understanding requires different strategies than simple memorization of information. It is therefore important to carefully *define* your goals (learning with understanding versus simply memorizing) once a learning problem or opportunity has been *identified.*

Novices who learn about a new area of knowledge frequently confront the problem of how to master facts and relationships that seem arbitrary. For example, there appears to be no reason that an artery should be elastic or nonelastic, thick or thin. One approach to the problem of learning arbitrary relationships is to use such memory techniques as interactive images. An alternative strategy is to *explore* why things are the way they are—to search for relationships between the structure and function of veins and arteries, between the features of robots and their intended function, between the shape and materials used in Native American houses and the environment, and between the shape of scissors and their function.

Strategies for learning with understanding are often more complex and difficult than those that help us to merely memorize information. Nevertheless, the extra effort is usually worthwhile because concepts that are understood can function as conceptual tools that allow us to solve subsequent problems. Thus, the person who understands why veins and arteries are constructed as they are is in a much better position to approach the problem of designing an artificial artery. The mere memorization of facts rarely results in useful conceptual tools.

It is also important to *anticipate* the outcome of using a particular learning strategy so that we can *act* on the most effective strategy. One reason for anticipating the challenges that will confront us is that anything can be learned at different levels of precision. For example, our understanding of such concepts as airports, gold, or veins and arteries can vary in precision, and the level of precision necessary will depend on the goals we have for using that knowledge. Thus, a child may have only a vague knowledge of airports and yet be able to use this knowledge to understand the statement, "Aunt Jane is coming so we need to go to the airport." However, a child who is going to travel alone on commercial airlines may need a more precise understanding of ticketing, baggage-checking procedures, and airport security regulations.

There are several ways to improve our ability to anticipate the effects of our learning strategies. One is to devise self-tests and simulations. Another is to be sure that our knowledge can be retrieved with limited external cues.

It is often impossible to accurately anticipate all the problems (test questions, questions following a talk, and so forth) that we will ultimately face. As a result, we will sometimes be unable to answer questions, and we will make mistakes. Effective learners try to *look* back at their attempts to learn and *learn* from their mistakes; they develop strategies that enable them to avoid making similar mistakes in the future. The development of these debugging skills is an important aspect of learning to learn.

■ Exercises

Use the IDEAL Problem Navigation Guide in Appendix C to work through a nonroutine learning problem that is important to you. Be sure to clarify whether your goal involves learning with understanding or just memorization.

Try to make the sentences below comprehensible.

1. The breakfast was delicious because the thread was sticky.
2. The stream of water stopped because it started raining.
3. The car moved because the coin was bent.
4. The clothes were ruined because the sign vanished.
5. The street was full of potholes because the turning stopped.
6. The home was small because the sun came out.
7. The notes were sour because the seam split.

Listed below are some words that would be relatively easy to memorize. However, it is more interesting to try to understand them. For example, the combination "you just me" can be interpreted as "just between you and me."

8. $\dfrac{\text{wear}}{\text{thermal}}$

9. sttheory

10. T
    O
    W
    N

11. /r/e/a/d/i/n/g/

12. wheather

13. He's/Himself

14. $\dfrac{\text{knee}}{\text{lights}}$

15. Read the following instructions for operating a pencil sharpener: "After selecting the proper size of guide hole, turn the handle clockwise." Evaluate the adequacy of these instructions for people who have never seen or used a pencil before. Rewrite the instructions to resolve the deficiencies.

16. Imagine that a child reads the following passage about camels. "They have special eyelids that can cover their eyes yet still let in some light. They can close their nose passages. They have thick hair around their ear openings." What might you do to help the child understand the significance or relevance of these facts rather than merely memorize them?

17. How might children's ability to understand the significance of these facts allow them to better understand other events they read about?

18. A spy wants to hide a roll of film he has reduced to ⅛ inch in diameter and 2¼ inches long. Looking at his bookshelf, he notices the two-volume desk-top encyclopedia illustrated below. Using a drill that is ¼ inch in diameter, the spy begins on page 1 of volume 1 and drills straight through to the last page of volume 2. Assume that the cover of each book is ¼ inch thick and that each book without its cover is 1 inch thick. Is the hole long enough to hold the roll of film? How long is the hole?

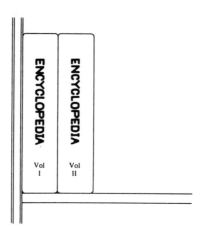

19. The term "sea breeze" is familiar to most people who sail. It usually refers to breezes that move from the sea to the land during the day and from the land to the sea at night. Most people who are unfamiliar with this term find that it is easy to be confused about which direction the breeze will move during the day or night. Explore strategies that will help you understand this information and compare them with strategies that will only help you to remember it.

■ Notes

1. A. N. Whitehead, *The Aims of Education & Other Essays*. New York: Macmillan, 1929.

2. See note 1.
3. This passage was adapted from one that was written originally by Nancy McCarrell.
4. This passage is from J. R. Mehan, Tale-spin, an interactive program that writes stories. *Proceedings from the Fifth International Joint Conference on Artificial Intelligence*, 1977, pp. 91–98.
5. Additional discussion of the importance of previously acquired knowledge for learning can be found in J. D. Bransford and M. K. Johnson, Contextual prerequisites for understanding: Some investigations of comprehension and recall. *Journal of Verbal Learning and Verbal Behavior* 11 (1972):717–726; J. D. Bransford, R. S. Sherwood, N. J. Vye, and J. Rieser. Teaching thinking and problem solving: Research foundations. *American Psychologist* 41 (1986):1078–1089; K. Nelson, R. Fivush, J. Hudson, and J. Lucariello, Scripts and the development of memory. In M. T. H. Chi (ed.), *Contributions to Human Development, Vol. 9, Trends in Memory Development Research*. New York: Kargar, 1983; R. C. Schank and R. P. Abelson, *Scripts, Plans, Goals and Understanding*. Hillsdale, N.J.: Lawrence Erlbaum Associates, 1977; R. Glaser, Education and thinking: The role of knowledge. *American Psychologist* 39 (1984):93–104.
6. Based on material developed by B. S. Stein and J. D. Bransford, Constraints on effective elaboration: Effects of precision and self-generation. *Journal of Verbal Learning and Verbal Behavior* 18 (1979):769–777. See also B. S. Stein, K. F. Brock, D. R. Ballard, and N. J. Vye, Constraints on verbal and pictorial elaboration. *Memory & Cognition* 15, no. 4 (1987): 281–290.
7. See C. E. Weinstein, Elaboration skills as a learning strategy. In H. F. O'Neil, Jr. (ed.), *Learning Strategies*. New York: Academic Press, 1978.
8. See J. J. Franks, N. J. Vye, P. M. Auble, K. J. Mezynski, G. A. Perfetto, J. D. Bransford, B. S. Stein, and J. Littlefield, Learning from explicit versus implicit texts. *Journal of Experimental Psychology: General* 111 (1982):414–422.
9. M. T. H. Chi, M. Bassok, M. W. Lewis, P. Reimann, and R. Glaser, Self-explanations: How students study and use examples in learning to solve problems. *Cognitive Science* 13 (1989):145–182.
10. From J. D. Bransford and N. S. McCarrell, A sketch of a cognitive approach to comprehension. In W. Weimer and D. Palermo (eds.),

Cognition and the Symbolic Processes. Hillsdale, N.J.: Lawrence Erlbaum Associates, 1974.

11. From J. D. Bransford, *Human Cognition: Learning, Understanding and Remembering.* Belmont, Calif.: Wadsworth, 1979.

12. See J. D. Bransford, Schema activation versus schema acquisition. In R. Anderson, J. Osborn, and R. Tierney (eds.), *Learning to Read in American Schools: Basal Readers and Content Texts.* Hillsdale, N.J.: Lawrence Erlbaum Associates, 1984.

13. From R. S. Day, Teaching from notes: Some cognitive conse-quences. In W. J. McKeachie (ed.), *New Directions for Teaching and Learning: Learning, Cognition and College Teaching.* San Francisco: Jossey-Bass, 1980.

14. A. L. Brown, Knowing when, where, and how to remember: A problem of metacognition. In R. Glaser (ed.), *Advances in Instruc-tional Psychology* (Vol. 1). Hillsdale, N.J.: Lawrence Erlbaum Asso-ciates, 1978.

15. J. H. Flavell and H. M. Wellman, Metamemory. In R. V. Kail, Jr., and J. W. Hagen (eds.), *Perspectives on the Development of Memory and Cognition.* Hillsdale, N.J.: Lawrence Erlbaum Associates, 1977.

16. This example is discussed by G. A. Miller, Addendum to "Lexical Meaning." In J. F. Kavanagh and W. Strange (eds.), *Speech and Lan-guage in the Laboratory, School and Clinic.* Cambridge, Mass.: MIT Press, 1978.

17. See note 11.

18. F. Darwin (ed.), *The Life and Letters of Charles Darwin,* New York: D. Appleton and Company, 1897, p. 48.

19. See note 10.

20. Additional examples of access failure are discussed in J. J. Franks, J. D. Bransford, K. Brailey, and S. Purdon, Understanding memory access. In R. Hoffman and D. Palermo (eds.), *Cognition and the Sym-bolic Processes: Applied and Ecological Perspectives.* Hillsdale, N.J.: Lawrence Erlbaum Associates, 1991, pp. 281–299; K. J. Holyoak and K. Koh, Surface and structural similarity in analogical transfer. *Memory & Cognition* 15 (1987): 332–340; R. S. Lockhart, M. Lamon, and M. L. Gick, Conceptual transfer in simple insight problems. *Memory & Cognition* 16 (1988): 36–44; B. S. Stein, Memory and creativity. In J. A. Glover, R. R. Ronning, and C. R. Reynolds, *Handbook of Creativity.* New York: Plenum Press, 1989.

21. L. Resnick, *Education and Learning to Think.* Washington, D.C.: National Academy Press, 1987.

▋ Suggested Readings

Theoretically Oriented Readings

Anderson, R. C. 1984. The role of reader's schema in comprehension, learning and memory. In R. Anderson, J. Osborn, and R. Tiemey (eds.), *Learning to Read in American Schools: Basal Readers and Content Texts*. Hillsdale, N.J.: Lawrence Erlbaum Associates.

Asher, J. 1981. Fear of foreign languages. *Psychology Today* (August).

Bransford, J. D., B. S. Stein, N. J. Vye, J. J. Franks, P. M. Auble, K. J. Mezynski, and G. A. Perfetto. 1982. Differences in approaches to learning: An overview, *Journal of Experimental Psychology: General* 11:390–398.

Bransford, J. D., N. J. Vye, L. T. Adams, and G. A. Perfetto. In press. Learning skills and the acquisition of knowledge. In R. Glaser and A. Lesgold (eds.), *Handbook of Psychology and Education*. Hillsdale, N.J.: Lawrence Erlbaum Associates.

Brown, A. L. 1992. Design experiments: Theoretical and methodological challenges in creating complex interventions in classroom settings. *Journal of the Learning Sciences 2*, no. 2:141–178.

Brown, A. L., J. D. Bransford, R. A. Ferrara, and J. C. Campione. 1983. Learning, remembering and understanding. In J. H. Flavell and E. M. Markman (eds.), *Carmichael's Manual of Child Psychology* (Vol. 1). New York: Wiley.

Brown, A. L., and J. S. DeLoache. 1978. Skills, plans and self-regulation. In R. S. Siegler (ed.), *Children's Thinking: What Develops?* Hillsdale, N.J.: Lawrence Erlbaum Associates.

Chase, W. G., and H. A. Simon. 1973. Perception in chess. *Cognitive Psychology* 4:55–81.

Glenberg, A. M., A. C. Wilkinson, and W. Epstein. 1982. The illusion of knowing: Failure in the self-assessment of comprehension. *Memory and Cognition* 10: 597 - 602.

Harris, R. J. 1977. Comprehension of pragmatic implications in advertising. *Journal of Applied Psychology* 62:603–608.

Just, M., and P. A. Carpenter. 1986. *The Psychology of Reading and Language Comprehension*. New York: Allyn and Bacon.

Markman, E. M. 1977. Realizing that you don't understand: A preliminary investigation. *Child Development* 48:986–992.

Ng, E., and Bereither, C. 1991. Three levels of goal orientation in learning. *Journal of the Learning Sciences* 1, no. 3 and 4:243–271.

Scardamalia, M., and C. Bereiter. 1991. Higher levels of agency for children in knowledge building: A challenge for the design of new knowledge media. *Journal of the Learning Sciences* 1, no. 1:37–68.

Spilich, G. J., G. T. Vesonder, H. L. Chiesi, and J. F. Voss. 1979. Text processing of domain-related information for individuals with high and low domain knowledge. *Journal of Verbal Learning and Behavior* 18:275–290.

CHAPTER 8

INSTRUCTION THAT FACILITATES PROBLEM SOLVING

Human history becomes more and more a race between education and catastrophe.

H. G. Wells

The two preceding chapters explored ways of using the IDEAL framework to improve our ability to master new information. We noted that successful learners try to identify potential learning problems and to define their goals so that they can select appropriate learning strategies. If our goal is to acquire conceptual tools that can help us solve problems in the future, it is also important to select strategies that facilitate understanding rather than just memorization. Much of our previous discussion focused on what the individual learner can do to improve learning. Indeed, it is important to look at learning from the perspective of the individual because much of what we learn is acquired through personal experience. But a great deal of learning also occurs in more formal educational contexts—contexts that can encourage people to pursue effective approaches to learning or discourage them from doing so. In this chapter we consider some reasons that many traditional approaches to instruction do not facilitate problem solving, and we discuss alternatives that hold more promise for helping students learn to think and learn on their own.

Why Problem Solving Needs to Be an Integral Part of Education

In a recent article, Alan Schoenfeld describes a study by Kurt Reusser that is both revealing and disturbing.[1] Reusser gave schoolchildren the following problem in the context of other mathematics problems:

> There are 26 sheep and 10 goats on a ship. How old is the captain?

Approximately three-quarters of the children in Reusser's study attempted to supply a numerical answer to this problem. Their approach was to add, multiply, or divide rather than check to see if the problem made sense.

Our reaction to Reusser's data was that this must have been a special group of students who had been taught poorly. We gave the problem to one of our own children who was in fifth grade. Much to our surprise and dismay, the answer given was 36. When we asked why, we were told, "Well, you need to add or subtract or multiply in problems like this, and this one seemed to work best if I add." Procedures such as addition and multiplication are often applied in very rote ways.

Findings like these are just one of many reasons that people have begun to seriously question the effectiveness of our educational system. The major concern is that schools are not doing enough to help people become proficient at solving problems and learning on their own. These concerns are justified on the basis of experimental studies like the one just described, poor scores of American students in science and math compared to those of students in other countries, and the complaints of business leaders that most graduates cannot learn effectively and think for themselves.

In a world that is changing at an increasingly rapid pace, people must be able to adapt to new situations that require creative and nonroutine thinking. For example, Susan Berryman[2] notes that economic factors have forced businesses to become more proficient at adapting to changing competitive markets. Businesses that rely only on the higher levels of management to generate new ideas and solve problems will not be successful. In today's business environment it is important for employees at all levels to become problem finders and problem solvers rather than simply people who follow orders. Indeed, the changes affecting business will also affect organizations such as schools, universities, and even families in a world in which change—especially technology-driven change—demands the ability to deal with nonroutine problems.

In this chapter we address three basic issues concerning instruction. First, we explore the problems of traditional approaches to instruction, focusing on their failure to promote effective thinking. Second, we discuss some new approaches to instruction that organize learning around the goal of solving authentic, meaningful problems. These approaches differ from traditional methods that first present the facts and principles and then present applications problems at the end of each lesson. Third, we consider assessment and its relationship to the IDEAL framework. The ability to look at the effects of our actions and learn from them is critical. If we want to improve our ability to think rather than memorize, we must be able to evaluate our thinking. Most assessments, however, test memory for specific facts and procedures. One of the major challenges in redefining instruction is to invent new ways of assessing creative thinking and problem solving.

■ Problems with Traditional Approaches to Instruction

An increasing number of educators believe that typical instructional practice fails to help students acquire knowledge in a form that facilitates thinking and problem solving. They argue that most instruction is based on an antiquated "transmission model" by which teachers and authors attempt to directly transmit their expertise to students. With the transmission model, instruction is usually decontextualized; that is, it takes place outside the context of problems that actually require the use of the knowledge gained.

Researchers have identified a number of problems with instruction that is based on the transmission model. For example, Charles Gragg[3] argues that the basic problem is that "wisdom can't be told." The ability to hear or read transmitted information and to remember it later is no guarantee that people can use that knowledge to identify, define, and solve problems. In Chapter 7 we discussed Alfred North Whitehead's point that our educational system was adept at producing inert knowledge—knowledge that people can recall but cannot apply to problems. This idea has been explored and expanded over the past 25 years. For example, Nobel laureate Herbert Simon has argued that a student's familiarity with basic facts and isolated skills is not sufficient to support effective problem solving. Such a familiarity provides no guarantee that people will know when, why, and how to apply their knowledge. He notes that "students may possess calculus skills without recognizing that they are applicable to a particular physics problem or without knowing exactly how to apply them."[4]

An Example of Inert Knowledge

A story related to us by a colleague, Ann Michael, illustrates the problem of inert knowledge.[5] She served for several years as a clinical supervisor of college students who were beginning a practicum in language therapy for language-delayed children. The students had all passed the required college course on theories of language and their implications for therapy, but there was almost no evidence that the students ever attempted to use this knowledge in the clinical therapy sessions. Michael concluded that the college course must have been very poorly taught.

Michael was later asked to teach that college course herself. She did what she thought was a highly competent job and was pleased with the general performance of the students on her tests. A year later, she encountered a number of her students again in the clinical practicum on language therapy. Much to her surprise and dismay, these students also showed almost no evidence of applying anything they had learned in their language course. Many could remember facts when explicitly asked about them, but they did not automatically draw on that knowledge to help them solve problems in the clinic.

Michael was reluctant to conclude that her college students performed poorly because of poor instruction. Instead she was motivated to explore problems with traditional approaches to instruction and to study ways to overcome them. Overall, Michael's experiences confirmed Whitehead's, Gragg's, and Simon's observations that much of the information acquired in school tends to remain inert.

Uses of Applications Problems to Teach Problem Solving

Of course, helping people to develop usable (that is, noninert) knowledge by having them solve problems is not new. A time-honored approach is to present students with applications problems such as those that appear following chapters in textbooks. The general approach is first to teach students relevant skills and knowledge and *then* to let them see how this knowledge can be applied. If you were teaching the concept of density, for example, you might first present the relevant facts and formulas (for example, that density equals mass divided by volume) and then present applications problems for solution (for example, "An object weighs 4 grams and has a volume of 8 cubic centimeters. What is its density?").

It seems clear that the effectiveness of the transmission model of instruction can be improved by using applications problems. However, traditional applications problems have severe shortcomings. Researchers in the Cognition and Technology Group at Vanderbilt University have discussed several of these shortcomings.[6] One is that they often fail to help students think about realistic situations. Instead of bringing real-world standards to their work, students tend to treat word problems mechanically, failing to consider constraints imposed by real-world factors. Ed Silver[7] provides an excellent example of a relatively mechanical approach to word problems. Students were asked to determine the number of buses needed to take a specific number of people on a field trip. Many of them divided the total number of students by the number that each bus would hold and came up with answers like 2⅓. The students failed to consider that one cannot use a third of a bus.

A second limitation of traditional applications problems is the habits of mind that they encourage. Applications problems can generally be solved by thinking back to information studied in the previous chapter or chapters. The goal is therefore to retrieve information rather than to develop a more intuitive and creative approach to problem solving. This can limit the development of people's ability to think for themselves. Furthermore, many applications problems provide only one correct answer to a problem. This can lead to misconceptions about the nature of problem solving and can inhibit creative thought.

A third limitation of traditional applications problems is that most of them explicitly define the problem to be solved rather than help students to identify the problem themselves and work through the process of clarifying their goals. Outside of school, people have to identify problems that others have ignored and deal with problems that are not clearly defined. For example, consider the problem of preventing people from getting injured in automobile crashes that was discussed earlier. Effective problem solvers will define their goals in a variety of ways (for example, to reduce injuries caused by people striking against hard objects inside the car, to create a system that absorbs the force of impact, or to prevent crashes from happening). Realistic problems can usually be approached from a number of different perspectives and usually have a number of potential solutions. It is therefore important to develop the skills necessary to define one's own goals and assumptions rather than always to have them defined for one in applications problems.

These arguments are not meant to imply that applications problems are useless. Indeed, we use them throughout this book to provide extra practice in when, why, and how to apply the concepts discussed. Our argument is that the general procedure of facts and principles first, followed by applications is not sufficient to develop powerful mental habits that support thinking and problem solving. Alternatives to this approach are discussed next.

■ Organizing Learning Around Problem Solving

In recent years, an increasing number of investigators have become interested in approaches to instruction that provide opportunities for students to acquire relevant knowledge *in the context of attempting to solve complex, authentic problems.* This is not a new idea. For example, theorists such as John Dewey and Norwood Hanson have noted that one reason experts can appreciate the potential value of new theories and concepts is that such information has implications for problems about which they are genuinely interested.[8] Consequently, experts are easily made aware of how new ideas produce changes in their own thinking. To novices, however, new theories often seem to be made up of arbitrary relationships and mechanical procedures that have to be memorized. Since novices have not been immersed in the phenomena being investigated, they cannot gauge how a new way of thinking may change the way problems are seen and understood. One of the major goals of situating or anchoring instruction in problem-solving environments is to help students appreciate the problems and opportunities that experts encounter and to experience the changes in thinking that result from new concepts and ideas.

John Seeley Brown, Alan Collins, and Paul Duguid[9] discuss other reasons for situating instruction in authentic problem-solving environments. They note that when students begin with authentic problems, they are more motivated to find solutions. In addition, this method helps students to identify issues and opportunities and to see the need for learning about new concepts and procedures relevant to solving problems. The importance of creating opportunities for students to become aware of the need for new concepts was also stressed by Alfred North Whitehead, who argued that the first thing we should do with a new idea is prove its worth by showing why it is particularly useful.

Poor Scholar's Soliloquy

A colleague sent us an article on education written in 1944 by Stephen Corey.[10] It provides an informative contrast between learning in formal settings and learning in the context of meaningful problems. Entitled "Poor Scholar's Soliloquy," the article is written from the perspective of an imaginary student (we'll call him Bob) who is not very good in school and has had to repeat the seventh grade. Many would write Bob off as having a low aptitude for learning. But when you look at what Bob is capable of achieving outside of school, you get a very different impression of his abilities.

Part of the soliloquy describes how teachers don't like Bob because he doesn't read the kind of books that they value. Bob's favorite books include *Popular Science*, the *Mechanical Encyclopedia*, and the Sear's and Ward's catalogs. Bob uses his books to pursue meaningful goals. He says, "I don't just sit down and read them through like they make us do in school. I use my books when I want to find something out, like whenever Mom buys anything second hand I look it up in Sear's or Ward's first and tell her if she's getting stung or not."

Later on, Bob explains the trouble he had memorizing the names of the presidents. He knew some of them, like Washington and Jefferson, but there were 30 altogether and he never did get them all straight. He seems to have a poor memory. Then he talks about the three trucks his uncle owns and how he knows the horsepower and number of forward and backward gears of 26 different American trucks, many of them diesels. Then he says, "It's funny how that Diesel works. I started to tell my teacher about it last Wednesday in science class when the pump we were using to make a vacuum in a bell jar got hot, but she said she didn't see what a Diesel engine had to do with our experiment on air pressure so I just kept still. The kids seemed interested, though."

Bob also discusses his inability to do the kinds of word problems found in his textbooks. Yet he helps his uncle make all kinds of complex plans when they travel together. He talks about the bills and letters he sends to the farmers whose livestock his uncle hauls and about how he made only three mistakes in his last 17 letters—all of them commas. Then he says, "I wish I could write school themes that way. The last one I had to write was on 'What a Daffodil Thinks of Spring,' and I just couldn't get going."

Bob ends his soliloquy by noting that, according to his dad, he can quit school at the age of 15, and he feels like he should. After all, he's not getting any younger and he has a lot to learn.

Bob's soliloquy is as relevant to the 1990s as it was to the 1940s. First, it provides a useful contrast between typical instructional practice and learning that occurs in the context of meaningful problem solving. Second, it highlights the fact that many students seem to learn effectively in the context of authentic, real-life activities, yet have great difficulty with the decontextualized type of instruction common in most schools.

Of course, not everyone is lucky enough to have an uncle like Bob's who, in effect, gives him an apprenticeship in everyday problem solving. A number of educators are exploring ways to recreate some of the advantages of apprenticeship learning by changing typical instructional practice. We discuss several examples below.

Case-Based Instruction

A number of professional schools such as law schools, medical schools, business schools, and schools of educational administration are using an approach called "case-based" or "problem-based" instruction. Susan Williams[11] provides an excellent review and analysis of case-based instruction in law schools and medical schools. The essence of the approach is to organize instruction around actual situations that students are likely to encounter later in their careers. In business, for example, a case might focus on a company that is in trouble and needs to be restructured. In medicine, a case might involve a patient with certain symptoms. Students work on cases over some fixed period of time, acquire any new information that is needed to solve the problem, and eventully discuss their ideas with classmates and with the professor. Ideally, students move from simple cases to more complex ones. In the process, they acquire relevant knowledge while learning to analyze problems, set learning goals, and present and discuss their ideas.

There are a wide variety of ideas about what makes a good case and what the best way is to use cases. Williams notes that the cases used in law schools tend to be quite different in structure from those used in medical schools. In addition, there are a variety of case formats within any particular area. For example, one format for a medical case is to provide data about a patient's symptoms and test results and then have students make a diagnosis. Another format is for a simulated patient to answer questions posed by students. This encourages questions from the students that are quite similar to those that practicing physicians will have to ask after they leave school.

Most variations on case-based and problem-based learning provide opportunities to develop effective problem-solving skills like those in the

IDEAL framework. For example, students learn to *identify* problems and opportunities in the context of the cases, to *define* goals (such as to acquire information relevant to a case), to *explore* strategies (such as where to look for information or what tests to perform), to *anticipate* the effectiveness of their current level of analysis, and eventually to *act* by presenting their ideas to the teacher and fellow classmates. This provides an opportunity for them to *look* at the effects of their actions and to *learn* something that will help them solve the next case.

Project-Based Instruction

Another way to organize instruction around problem solving is to create student projects. An excellent example is the Discover Rochester project discussed by Alan Collins, Jan Hawkins, and Sharon Carver.[12] In this project, eighth-grade students who were at risk of dropping out of school spent one day each week exploring aspects of their hometown—Rochester, New York—from a scientific, mathematical, historical, cultural, and literary perspective. Working in groups, the students conducted their own research on topics such as industry, weather, theater, and employment. On the basis of their research, they developed multimedia exhibits for the Rochester Museum and Science Center. The exhibits included text, audio, graphics, maps, and music. Students also studied the reactions of people to their projects and refined them based on the feedback they received.

Collins, Hawkins, and Carver used a variation of the IDEAL framework adapted to their project. They helped students *identify* problems and opportunities by encouraging them to pose interesting questions about their community. As students researched the answers to these questions, they were helped to further *define* their goals. They were then helped to *explore* a number of strategies for gathering and representing data, including strategies for using indexes, conducting interviews, and organizing and analyzing data. Students then attempted to *anticipate* the effects of their presentations (for example, by conducting tests with one another), and they eventually *acted* on their ideas by placing their multimedia products in the museum. Students were then encouraged to *look* at the effects of their products on the audience and to *learn* from the experience. Some students learned that their products were less interesting than they had thought; they therefore reentered the IDEAL cycle in order to improve the product the next time.

Many teachers in other fields have effectively used projects as anchors for instruction. For example, Lisa Glick and Michael Ross used the problem of establishing and maintaining a garden as an anchor for instruction in biology, botany, nutrition, and the scientific method.[13] Problems that typically confront the gardener, such as how to maximize growth and minimize the damage caused by pests and diseases, provide a meaningful framework for studying photosynthesis and the proper way to conduct scientific research. Teachers in business and economics have tried to anchor instruction in realistic problems such as establishing and maintaining a small business. Working on such problems makes it much easier for students to understand the need for accurate accounting procedures, principles of finance, and concepts of business management.

Other real-world problems that can serve as effective anchors for instruction may be narrower in scope than establishing and maintaining a new business. For example, we have explored with Bob Harwood such problems as determining what types of nails are hardest to remove from wood and what type of lubricant is best for a model race car.[14] These problems can serve as effective anchors for concepts in physics, chemistry, and the scientific method.

Some complex real-world problems, such as designing a better way to protect people from injury in automobile accidents, can be simplified and explored with the limited equipment and materials available in the classroom. For example, we have worked with teachers like Tony Petrosino, who asked his students to design an enclosure that would protect an egg from breaking after it was dropped from a second-story window. This problem has been used by many educators as an effective anchor for helping students learn about physics and the scientific method.

Debates as Anchors for Learning

Debates are often used in our society as a medium for communicating ideas and influencing attitudes, and they can also be used as effective anchors for learning. To effectively debate an issue, students must spend considerable time searching for and analyzing information about the underlying issues. The structure of a debate provides more clearly defined goals for this new information than students might otherwise have. For example, to prepare for a debate on the issue of national health insurance, it is important to understand both sides of the issue and to prepare an effective counterargument for each claim the opponent might make. Instead of being isolated facts, information about the cost and effectiveness of health care programs in other countries becomes significant and relevant to defending a particular position. The goals that the participants pursue in preparing for the debate help them to understand the potential value of new information and to place that new information under close scrutiny.

Debate topics can be formulated in almost any field. It is important to select a topic that students have some familiarity with but that can serve as an anchor for the sustained exploration of new concepts and ideas. For example, topics involving environmental issues such as recycling and incineration can provide a meaningful anchor for learning about chemical reactions, biological processes, and the ecosystem. The instructor can influence the topics explored in these debates by providing relevant readings or sources of information and by establishing criteria for evaluating the adequacy of arguments (for example, the presentation must include an adequate chemical analysis of the products of incineration).

Alternatives to Traditional Debates

One of the problems with traditional debates is that they usually take place during a short period of time. Even though the participants may have considerable time to prepare for the debate, they often have little time to communicate their positions and to prepare counterarguments against their opponents. The traditional debate format allows little opportunity for sustained exploration of topics once the debate is over.

We have experimented with alternative debate formats that permit more sustained exploration and give students input into the debate process. One format that seems particularly promising is the "challenge debate." This differs from the traditional debate in that each group of students presents its argument at different times. For example, one group may prepare its argument in response to a television program or current event. Its presentation is presented to the class and recorded, giving the other students a record of the presentations and a chance to carefully examine the argument. Successive groups of students then prepare arguments that challenge this presentation. The ongoing nature of these challenge debates gives each group of students the opportunity for sustained exploration of the issue as the debate progresses. An additional advantage of recording each presentation is that students can compare their arguments to those in other classes.

Video-Based Anchors or Macrocontexts

Another approach to problem-based instruction involves the use of video and computer technology to anchor or situate instruction within the context of meaningful problems. One example of a video-based anchor is the "Voyage of the Mimi" program developed at Bank Street College. It provides a series of exciting video stories about a group of students who go on a sailing trip to study whales. After watching the video, students (from the fifth grade and up) engage in paper-and-pencil and computer-based problem-solving activities that allow them to explore the usefulness of a variety of scientific and mathematical concepts.[15]

Another example of a video-based anchor for instruction is Vanderbilt University's Jasper Woodbury Problem Solving Series designed for students in the fifth grade and up. There are currently six adventures in the Jasper series. Two use stories that involve complex trip planning, two require the use of statistics to create and present a feasible business plan, and two use geometry to estimate heights and navigate. Each adventure in the series ends with an interesting, complex problem to solve; students generate the subgoals necessary to solve the problem and can then look back at the video to find relevant data embedded in the story. Each adventure also provides opportunities to integrate information from a variety of disciplines such as history, geography, literature, and science.

In the Jasper adventure "Rescue at Boone's Meadow," an ultralight airplane must be used to rescue a wounded eagle in a remote location. Students must help plan the rescue, and to do so they must search for relevant information that was presented earlier in the story. For example, they need data about the speed, fuel consumption, and fuel capacity of the ultralight; the location of the eagle; possible landing sites; areas where there are and are not roads; the weight of eagles; and needed supplies. In most classes, each Jasper problem takes from three to five class periods to solve. Students then work on "what if" problems that encourage them to expand their thinking about each adventure. For example, the original rescue was on a calm day, but what if there had been a 5-mile-per-hour headwind? As students work through this problem they discover the need to dramatically revise the original rescue plan.

The Jasper series is on videodisc rather than videotape, making it easier to search for relevant data. The Jasper series has been shown to enhance complex problem-solving skills and to improve attitudes toward mathematics.[16]

Simulations

Simulations provide another way to situate learning within the context of meaningful problems. Advances in microcomputer technology have made it much easier to simulate complex processes that would be difficult to study and explore in real life. For example, the computer program SimCity allows one to design and manage a model city. Users can control development (for example, commercial, residential, industrial, and transportation); set taxes; and monitor important indices such as public opinion, population growth, tax revenue, government expenditures, and property values. The simulation provides the opportunity to *identify* problems such as inadequate fire and police protection and to experience the effects of failing to deal with those problems. It allows users to *define* goals for their city (such as reliance on mass transportation versus the automobile, or controlled growth versus rapid expansion) and to *explore* a variety of strategies for achieving those goals. In addition, they can *anticipate* potential problems such as earthquakes and explore strategies that might mitigate their consequences (building redundancy into the electric power distribution network, for example). Simulations also allow people to *act* on their strategies and *look* back at the effects, something that can be difficult and costly to do in the real world.

SimCity can serve as an effective anchor for learning about the effects of tax rates on economic expansion and the design of effective transportation systems. Other simulations, such as SimEarth, can provide an anchor for learning about biology and earth sciences.[17]

A potential problem with simulations like SimCity is the degree to which they distort, simplify, or ignore variables that may have important effects in real life. For example, SimCity does not deal with waste disposal, an important problem in modern cities. It also does not permit users to select specific industries for development, which would encourage consideration of such important factors as their environmental impact and wage levels. In addition, the cost of developing new properties in the simulation is not realistic, and the mathematical models that underlie the simulated effects of tax rates on economic activity are oversimplified. Given the complexity of the problems that programs like SimCity and SimEarth are designed to explore, however, we cannot fault the developers for simplifying the underlying model.

To determine whether a simulation can serve as an effective anchor for instruction, it is necessary to carefully define the goals for problem-based learning and see if the simulation allows students to explore variables that are relevant to those goals. Ideally, the developers of simulation packages will work with educators to create programs that support a variety of educational goals.

■ General Issues Related to Problem-Based Learning

The effectiveness of problem-based instruction depends greatly on how the learning environment is structured and how the problem is approached. We have seen many attempts to use problem-based learning fail because insufficient consideration was given to key components of the instructional context. For instance, problem-based instruction can fail because the problems themselves are not interesting to students or because they are presented in a way that does not challenge or motivate students. We believe that almost any problem can be made into a challenging and motivating experience. Doing so requires many of the communication skills discussed in Chapter 5, especially those concerned with understanding the intended audience.

It is easy to present a problem that is insufficiently challenging, but it is also possible to present one that is too difficult for students to work with in a productive way. It is important to provide sufficient instructional support that students are not overwhelmed by a task. It is also a good idea to select problems that build upon knowledge acquired from previous learning experiences.

Problem-based instruction may also fail when the structure of the problem or the problem-solving environment is insufficient to permit the establishment of meaningful goals and the exploration of productive strategies. For example, earlier in this book we discussed the problem of long lines at grocery stores. We have found with this problem that it is important to impose realistic constraints on the solution (for example, that it must be cost effective and not cause the store to lose money). Without such constraints students are free to explore unproductive strategies (such as not admitting new customers or building another store nearby) that would not be feasible in real life. It is therefore important to impose constraints that encourage the use of relevant resources and the exploration of productive strategies. Of course, it is also possible to impose too many constraints on the problem-solving process, which can prevent people from exploring creative alternatives.

Finally, problem-based instruction can fail when students are not helped to take a systematic approach to problem solving and to carefully evaluate their actions. For many students, problem-based learning is a new experience, and they may be unprepared for a situation in which goals are not clearly defined and the strategies needed to solve problems are not readily apparent. We have found that prompting students to apply a model like the IDEAL framework can greatly facilitate the effectiveness of problem-based learning. An especially important consideration is the need to design opportunities for assessment. We discuss this issue later in the chapter.

Problem Selection

Anchoring instruction in realistic problem-solving tasks works best when these tasks are tailored to the needs, interests, and skills of students. Ideally, instructors interested in problem-based learning should find or develop their own anchors or find ways to help students design problems for themselves.

The process of developing effective problems can be facilitated by using the IDEAL framework. For example, one of our colleagues in the social sciences, Ada Haynes, identified a problem in her students' understanding of the concept of prejudice. Although many of them could recite a definition of the word, few could recognize many instances of prejudice in their environment. Rather than give a lecture on the topic, Haynes treated the problem as an opportunity to provide a learning experience that would promote greater understanding and recognition of prejudice. She *defined* her goal as teaching students to recognize prejudice in others through the irrational behavior that it promotes. She also wanted students to learn to recognize prejudice in themselves. To accomplish these goals, she *explored* realistic situations in which decisions could be based either on reason or on prejudice.

One task required students to decide who should be let into a special shelter during a nuclear war. Students were told that the 6 people chosen might be the only ones left on the planet and that they would have to choose these 6 out of a list of 12. They were given information about the 12 people that might be relevant to the goal of rebuilding society (for example, fertility, medical training, and agricultural training). In addition, some of the individuals were assigned characteristics that typically invoke prejudice (being Jewish, African-American, socialist, or Iraqi). She tried to *anticipate* the effectiveness of her strategy by finding out beforehand which cultural or ethnic groups elicited the strongest signs of prejudice.

Haynes *acted* on her instructional strategy by having students make and explain their decisions. She then was able to *look* back at the effectiveness of her strategy and to *learn* how to make improvements. These included modifying the descriptions to provide greater opportunities for exploring prejudice and involving class members in the identification of signs of prejudice.[18]

Cooperative Learning and Problem-Based Learning

The idea of having students work together to accomplish learning goals has a long history. Early advocates of cooperative learning include such theorists and practitioners as Francis Parker, John Dewey, Margaret Mead, and Morton Deutsch. Dewey argued that classroom life should embody the ideals of a democratic society. He felt that an important part of that ideal was that people work together to solve common problems.[19] More recently, educational researchers such as Elliot Aronson, David Johnson, Roger Johnson, and Robert Slavin have advocated the use of cooperative learning procedures.[20]

Much of the problem-based learning discussed earlier in this chapter can be used in conjunction with cooperative learning groups. Indeed, many of the problem-based methods we described work best when students work together in small learning groups. One advantage of combining cooperative learning with problem-based instruction is that it allows students to deal with more complex and time-consuming problems than they would be able to work with on their own. For example, a complex problem can be broken down into parts and the tasks divided among group members. Each student has his or her individual tasks to perform but also helps others when problems arise. Encouraging students to help one another reduces their dependence on the instructor and permits them to explore more creative approaches to problems. We have found that the IDEAL framework can facilitate cooperative learning during problem solving.

Unfortunately, we have also seen cases in which cooperative learning did not allow the majority of students to accomplish the learning goals we felt were important. Less able members of the group often let others do all the work (this is sometimes called "social loafing") or else those with the most ability did all the work. David Johnson and Roger Johnson[21] provide a variety of useful guidelines for developing cooperative learning environments that avoid these problems. For instance, they argue that it is important to create a learning environment in which students have a vested interest in promoting one another's success and each group member is understood to have a unique and indispensable contribution to make to the group's effort. In addition, it is important to ensure that each individual be accountable for the group's work as well as his or her own. These goals can be furthered by having each student's grade depend on his or her own performance and on the group's performance as a whole. We have also found it helpful for students to evaluate one another's performance.

The Importance of Opportunities for Assessment

Throughout this book we have emphasized the importance of the *look* and *learn* components of the IDEAL framework. For example, in Chapter 7 we discussed the importance of debugging learning strategies by looking at one's performance in various situations such as exams. If we fail to look at the effects of our actions (for example, of our study strategies) we cannot learn from them. Effective instruction requires frequent opportunities for students to analyze the effects of their actions and to learn from them.

Many years ago the noted psychologist Edward Thorndike performed a simple experiment that illustrates the importance of learning from the effects of one's actions.[22] He defined his goal as learning to draw a line while blindfolded that was exactly 4 inches long. He practiced hundreds of times—blindfolded—and never improved. Because of the blindfold he could never look at the effects of his actions, so he never knew the length of the line he had just drawn. Eventually Thorndike removed the blindfold and was able to see how close each line he drew came to 4 inches. He quickly mastered his goal. The purpose of the experiment was to demonstrate the role of feedback in learning. Removal of the blindfold allowed Thorndike to receive feedback; that is, to *look* at the effects of his actions and *learn* from them.

We noted in Chapter 7 that people often fail to analyze the effects of their activities. They act as if they were blindfolded—or if they do look it is not in enough detail. For example, we discussed the fact that many students note only their overall grade on an exam or paper, failing to identify the kinds of questions they missed and to understand why. Seeing only one's grade on a test is like being blindfolded, attempting to draw a line exactly 4 inches long, and then being told "right" or "wrong." This may help to some extent, but it is better to have more precise information about the effects of one's actions. The statement "It's ½ inch too long" is more helpful than "It's too long," which in turn is more helpful than "It's wrong."

In educational settings, both teachers and students can benefit by looking at the effects of their actions and learning from them. Students can learn to learn by analyzing the reasons for their performance on tests and other assignments such as papers and presentations. Teachers can learn to improve their own instruction by looking at its effects on student learning. If students are doing poorly, chances are that many elements of the instruction could be improved.

Tests Versus Opportunities for Self-Assessment

It is important to distinguish "testing" from "opportunities for self-assessment." Students are often tested in ways that do not help them learn to learn. On an essay exam or a paper, for example, students may receive a letter grade but never have an opportunity to explore with the instructor how their learning and writing strategies could be improved.

One reason instructors are more likely to give tests than opportunities for self-assessment is that their time is limited. It can be very difficult to find the time to work one-on-one—especially with large classes of students—but there are a variety of strategies that can be used to help students learn from essay exams and other written assignments.[23] Some of these provide opportunities for revising an exam or paper before the final grade is assigned. For example, we have found it very beneficial to have students provide detailed criticism and feedback (peer review) about one another's writing. Another strategy useful with college students is to provide anonymous examples of outstanding answers to each essay question when tests are returned. This lets each student compare an example of excellent performance to his or her own performance on the same question. We also attempt to help students analyze the elements that make up an excellent answer. A variation on this procedure is to provide students with anonymous examples of excellent, good, and average essay answers so that they have a larger set for comparison. In our experience, students can readily see the difference between excellent, good, and average performance; in the process, they develop better criteria for judging their own performance on future tests.

The Nature of Assessments

If our goal is to help students learn to solve problems and become independent learners, assessment is crucial. We have noted throughout this book that different learning goals require different learning strategies. If exams test only a few important learning goals, students will adapt their goals to the tests and learn only a few strategies for learning.

Educators and researchers like Joan Baron argue that schools will not be able to convert to a problem-solving curriculum until they change the nature of testing.[24] Most tests measure small pieces of knowledge such as definitions and procedures like addition or subtraction. These are important to know and to test, but if they are all that we test, we are not helping students to think and learn on their own. For example, imagine trying to implement one of the problem-based curricula discussed earlier by administering frequent tests of the facts in the curriculum. Effective learners would get better at memorizing facts, but this would be no guarantee that they would learn to find, define, and solve problems on their own.

A challenge facing all educators is to find ways of assessing learning that focus on authentic performances that are relevant to society and the workplace. Examples might include gathering data for a convincing business plan; working on a team to create interesting and informative educational products; presenting a coherent argument both in writing and orally and then answering questions; or designing a device that performs a useful function. The important point is that the overall goal requires that the student engage in a set of authentic performances rather than merely memorizing disconnected facts and procedures. As learning goals become more authentic, students begin to find and invent strategies that will be useful throughout their lives.

We want to emphasize, however, that more is involved in authentic assessment than a focus on authentic goals. We have seen many classroom implementations of problem-based curricula such as those discussed earlier in this chapter that do not provide opportunities for self-assessment as the project proceeds. Often the only assessment is at the end of the project, when students turn in their finished product. It is much more valuable for students to have opportunities for reflection and discussion at all stages of a project. For example, students can be helped to assess the reasonableness of all aspects of problem solving—their *identification* of interesting topics; their ability to *define* alternative goals, including learning goals; their *exploration* of strategies for achieving these goals; their ability to *anticipate* the effects of their actions; and their ability to *look* at the effects of those actions and *learn* from them.

▌Summary

In this chapter we discussed the importance of preparing people to think for themselves and solve problems so that they can adapt to a world that is changing at an increasingly rapid pace. There are several reasons that our educational system may not be preparing people for these goals. For instance, instruction often relies on the transmission model, according to which teachers and textbook authors attempt to directly transmit their expertise to students. The ability to remember transmitted information is often insufficient to ensure the ability to use that knowledge to identify, define, and solve problems.

A variety of instructional strategies might help people to develop usable (that is, noninert) knowledge and thinking skills. One traditional approach to achieving these goals are the applications problems that appear at the end of chapters in textbooks. Although the effectiveness of the transmission model can be improved by the use of applications problems, they have several shortcomings. One is that applications problems often fail to help students think about realistic situations and to develop the thinking skills that are important for solving realistic problems—skills such as identifying problems that others have ignored and working with problems that are not clearly defined.

Alternative approaches to instruction situate or anchor learning in more realistic problem-solving environments. These problem-based approaches include a variety of strategies for anchoring instruction in realistic problems. Some problem-based approaches involve the use of new technologies such as videodisc workstations to present real-life dramas. In contrast, other forms of problem-based learning involve little or no technology and instead use methods such as debates.

There are many problems that can serve as anchors for instruction, but selecting appropriate ones requires careful analysis of the desired goals for learning and the skills and interests of the students.

The use of problem-based instruction requires alternative ways of assessing student performance. If we are truly interested in developing more complex thinking skills, we cannot rely on tests that assess only the ability to remember facts and procedures. Many problem-based curricula do not provide opportunities for self-assessment as students progress through a project but instead focus only on the final product. Without systematic assessment, both learning and teaching are usually far less than ideal.

In this chapter we emphasized the importance of making learning a part of some larger goal-directed activity in which new information becomes a valuable tool or strategy. Even the best problem or new technology will have little effect on learning if students are forced to be passive recipients of information. Instead, students must be encouraged to actively participate in the process of solving problems, a process that includes identifying problems, defining relevant goals, and exploring new ideas and strategies that could help them achieve those goals. Effective instruction must also encourage students to anticipate the outcome of using particular strategies and then to act on the most promising ones. Students can then look back at the effects of their efforts and learn how to improve their approach to problem solving.

◼ Notes

1. A. H. Schoenfeld, Teaching mathematical thinking and problem solving. In L. B. Resnick and L. E. Klopfer (eds.), *Toward the Thinking Curriculum: Current Cognitive Research.* Alexandria, Va.: American Society for Curriculum Development, 1989, pp. 83–103; K. Reusser, Problem solving beyond the logic of things: Contextual effects on understanding and solving word problems. *Instructional Science* 17 (1988):309–338.

2. S. Berryman, Learning for the workplace: The state of play. *Review of Research in Education* (in press).

3. C. I. Gragg, Because wisdom can't be told. *Harvard Alumni Bulletin* (October 19, 1940):78–84.

4. H. A. Simon, Problem solving and education. In D. T. Tuma and R. Reif (eds.), *Problem Solving and Education: Issues in Teaching and Research.* Hillsdale, N.J.: Lawrence Erlbaum Associates, 1980, p. 82.

5. Ann Michael, personal communication with authors, Nashville, Tenn., 1991.

6. Cognition and Technology Group at Vanderbilt. The Jasper series: A generative approach to improving mathematical thinking. In *This Year in School Science.* Washington, D.C.: American Association for the Advancement of Science, in press.

7. E. A. Silver, Using conceptual and procedural knowledge: A focus on relationships. In J. Hiebert (ed.), *Conceptual and Procedural Knowledge: The Case of Mathematics.* Hillsdale, N.J.: Lawrence Erlbaum Associates, 1986, pp. 181–189.

8. J. Dewey, *How We Think.* Boston: D.C. Heath, 1910; N. R. Hanson, *Patterns of Discovery: An Inquiry Into the Conceptual Foundations of Science.* London: Cambridge University Press, 1961.

9. J. S. Brown, A. Collins, and P. Duguid, Situated cognition and the culture of learning. *Educational Researcher* 18, no. 1 (1989):32–41.

10. S. M. Corey, Poor scholar's soliloquy. *Childhood Education* 33 (1944):219–220.

11. S. M. Williams, Putting case-based instruction into context: Examples from legal, business, and medical education. *Journal of Learning Sciences* (in press).

12. A. Collins, J. Hawkins, and S. M. Carver, A cognitive apprenticeship for disadvantaged students. In B. Means, C. Chelemer, and M. S. Knapp (eds.), *Teaching Advanced Skills to At-Risk Students.* San Francisco: Jossey-Bass Publishers, 1991, pp. 216–243.

13. Information about the Life Lab Science Program and other project-based anchors for instruction can be found in *Educational Programs that Work* 18. Longmont, Colo.: Sopris West Inc., 1992.

14. *Explorations in Science and Problem Solving: The Trouble with Nails.* A production of WCTE public television and Tennessee Technological University, 1991.

15. Bank Street College of Education, *Voyage of the Mimi.* Scotts Valley, Calif.: Wings for Learning, Inc., Sunburst Co.

16. Cognition and Technology Group at Vanderbilt, The Jasper experiment: An exploration of issues in learning and instructional design. In M. Hannafin and S. Hooper (eds.), *Educational Technology Research and Development* 40, no. 1 (1992):65–80; Cognition and Technology Group at Vanderbilt, The Jasper series as an example of anchored instruction: Theory, program description and assessment data. In R. Lehrer (ed.), *Educational Psychologist*, in press.

17. SimCity and SimEarth are products of Maxis Software and are distributed by Broderbund Software.

18. Ada Haynes, personal communication with authors, Cookeville, Tenn., 1991.

19. J. Dewey, *School and Society.* Chicago: University of Chicago Press, 1899, and *Democracy and Education: An Introduction to the Philosophy of Education.* New York: Macmillan, 1937.

20. E. Aronson, N. Blaney, C. Stephan, J. Sikes, and M. Snapp, *The Jigsaw Classroom.* Beverly Hills, Calif.: Sage, 1978; D. W. Johnson and R. T. Johnson, *Learning Together and Learning Alone: Cooperative, Competitive, and Individualistic Instruction* (3d ed.). Englewood Cliffs, N.J.: Prentice-Hall, 1991; R. Slavin, An Introduction to cooperative learning research. In R. Slavin, S. Sharan, S. Kagan, R. Hertz-Lazarowitz, C. Webb, and R. Schumuck (eds.), *Learning to Cooperate, Cooperating to Learn.* New York: Plenum Press, 1985.

21. D. W. Johnson and R. T. Johnson, *Learning Together and Learning Alone: Cooperative, Competitive, and Individualistic Instruction* (3d ed.). Englewood Cliffs, N.J.: Prentice-Hall, 1991.

22. E. L. Thorndike, *The Psychology of Learning*. New York: Teachers College, 1931.
23. E. P. Maimon, *Writing in the Arts and Sciences*. Cambridge, Mass.: Winthrop, 1981.
24. J. Baron, Evaluating thinking skills in the classroom. In J. Baron and R. J. Sternberg (eds.), *Teaching Thinking Skills: Theory and Practice*. New York: W. H. Freeman, 1987, pp. 221–248.

■ Suggested Readings

Theoretically Oriented Readings

Baron, J. 1987. Evaluating thinking skills in the classroom. In J. Baron and R. J. Sternberg (eds.), *Teaching Thinking Skills: Theory and Practice*. New York: W. H. Freeman, pp. 221–248.

Barrow, H. S. 1985. *How to Design a Problem-Based Curriculum for the Preclinical Years*. New York: Springer Publishing Co.

Bransford, J. D., S. R. Goldman, and N. J. Vye. 1991. Making a difference in people's abilities to think: Reflections on a decade of work and some hopes for the future. In L. Okagaki and R. J. Sternberg (eds.), *Directors of Development: Influences on Children*. Hillsdale, N.J.: Lawrence Erlbaum Associates, pp. 147–180.

Bransford, J. D., R. S. Sherwood, N. J. Vye, and J. Rieser. 1986. Teaching thinking and problem solving: Research foundations. *American Psychologist* 41:1078–1089.

Brown, A. L., and A. M. Palincsar. 1989. Guided cooperative learning and individual knowledge acquisition. In L. B. Resnick (ed.), *Knowing, Learning, and Instruction: Essays in Honor of Robert Glaser*. Hillsdale, N.J.: Lawrence Erlbaum Associates.

Charles R., and E. A. Silver (eds.). 1988. *The Teaching and Assessing of Mathematical Problem Solving*. Hillsdale, N.J.: Lawrence Erlbaum Associates National Council for Teachers of Mathematics.

Nickerson, R. S., D. N. Perkins, and E. E. Smith. 1985. *The Teaching of Thinking*. Hillsdale, N.J.: Lawrence Erlbaum Associates.

Resnick, L. B., and D. P. Resnick. 1991. Assessing the thinking curriculum: New tools for educational reform. In B. Gifford and C. O'Connor (eds.), *New Approaches to Testing: Rethinking Aptitude, Achievement and Assessment*. New York: National Committee on Testing and Public Policy.

Riesbeck, C. K., and R. C. Schank. 1989. *Inside Case-Based Reasoning.* Hillsdale, N.J.: Lawrence Erlbaum Associates.

Schoenfeld, A. H. 1989. Teaching mathematical thinking and problem solving. In L. B. Resnick and L. E. Klopfer (eds.), *Toward the Thinking Curriculum: Current Cognitive Research.* Alexandria, Va.: American Society for Curriculum Development, pp. 83–103.

Simon, H. A. 1980. Problem solving and education. In D. T. Tuma and R. Reif (eds.), *Problem Solving and Education: Issues in Teaching and Research.* Hillsdale, N.J.: Lawrence Erlbaum Associates, pp. 81–96.

9

CONCLUDING REMARKS

We wrote this book because of our conviction that much of what we do in our lives involves problem solving and that everyone can learn to solve problems more successfully. To accomplish this goal, we must become more aware of the variety of problems we face in our everyday lives and of the processes we use in attempting to find creative solutions. This is why we discussed the IDEAL model of problem solving and illustrated how it is applicable to many types of problems.

Becoming more aware of the processes underlying problem solving does not necessarily mean *always* thinking in detail about these processes while attempting to solve problems. If you spend all your time analyzing your thinking processes, you will probably find that it interferes with your ability to solve problems (try to tie your shoe or drive a car while consciously analyzing each step). Awareness of the processes that underlie problem solving becomes most valuable when you are dealing with nonroutine problems. If you are observant, you can often catch yourself failing to (1) *identify* potential problems and opportunities, (2) *define* alternative goals, (3) *explore* a variety of possible approaches, (4) *anticipate* outcomes and *act* on your ideas, or (5) *look* at the effects of your actions and *learn*. By becoming aware of these components of problem solving, you will have a much better chance of approaching problems in optimal ways.

■ The Development of Problem-Solving Skills

One of our major themes has been that the improvement of problem-solving skills is an ongoing process. By using the IDEAL model you can become more aware of the processes involved in identifying opportunities and solving problems, which can improve your ability to notice possibilities for improvement. We have tried to show how the IDEAL model provides a framework for enhancing the way we think about a wide variety of problems. In the first part of the book we discussed how the IDEAL framework can help us use existing knowledge more effectively to solve problems, and in the second part we discussed how the IDEAL framework can help us learn new information. One of the most powerful ways to increase our ability to solve problems is to acquire new conceptual tools, which can often be very specialized. For instance, if you want to solve plumbing problems you should learn about the tools and concepts plumbers use to simplify their tasks. Similarly, improving your ability to solve other problems may require knowledge of biology, mathematics, or finance. It is particularly important to learn new information with understanding so that knowledge does not remain inert.

In many formal educational settings it is sometimes difficult to see how concepts and procedures can be used as problem-solving tools. Students are often exposed to concepts without having a good idea of the types of problems they were designed to solve. To be a successful learner, it is important to identify problems and define goals relevant to the knowledge you are attempting to master. An effective way to learn, therefore, is to become familiar with the activities pursued by those who work in the field you are studying; this can provide a context for more formal types of study, such as learning from lectures and books. For example, experience with the everyday problems faced by business executives can provide a context for understanding and evaluating books on management. If you have an idea of the kinds of problems faced by executives, you will be in a much better position to determine whether particular books provide the kinds of conceptual tools executives need.

■ Attitudes

We noted in the first chapter that one of the biggest stumbling blocks to improving problem solving can be negative attitudes about one's own abilities. It is easy to tell people to think positively about their ability to solve problems, but such a suggestion often has little effect on attitudes acquired over many years of experience. A lack of confidence in our ability to solve problems can manifest itself in a variety of ways, including lack of interest, fear of exploring new domains, and fear of criticism. These feelings can interfere with problem solving and can prevent us from engaging in activities that might improve our problem-solving skills. The IDEAL approach can be especially helpful in these situations because it provides a guide for debugging unsuccessful approaches. By identifying the attitudes that inhibit success and defining appropriate goals, we can begin to explore strategies that may stop us from repeating earlier failures. By actively using appropriate strategies, we can give ourselves the opportunity to experience success and so build our self-confidence.

The tendency to avoid new problems becomes especially strong when others are performing well and we are experiencing considerable difficulty. In such situations, we often explain our difficulty by assuming that we are inept or slow and others are talented. An alternative perspective is that *everyone* experiences difficulty when dealing with nonroutine problems or first learning about a new subject. We should not judge our ability to solve a nonroutine problem by comparing ourselves with those whose experience makes that same problem routine, or we may mistakenly underestimate our own abilities. As you continue to explore similar problems in the same area of inquiry, you will find that they become easier and easier to solve as they become more routine for you.

In Chapter 6 we asked you to remember what it was like when you were first learning to drive a car. If you are like most people, you felt extremely awkward. You probably had to think consciously about applying the brake, turning the wheel, using the turn signal, and so forth, and it was difficult to do something like carry on a conversation while driving. With practice, however, many aspects of driving became automatic, and simultaneously driving and carrying on a conversation became routine.

It is useful to keep the driving example in mind when you are trying to learn new tasks because the experience will almost undoubtedly be similar. At first, everything will seem overwhelming, and people who can already perform these tasks may seem almost superhuman. Later, you will perform them with little difficulty; they will become relatively routine and require much less conscious attention. Nevertheless, to reach this stage you must be prepared to go through a period of awkwardness. You must have the courage to risk making mistakes.

The problem of learning a second language provides an excellent illustration of the importance of risk-taking.[1] Researchers have found that an important difference between successful and less successful second-language learners is that the former will usually make a best guess about the meaning of an unfamiliar statement when they are not absolutely sure of the answer. In contrast, less successful students often avoid taking such risks. Similarly, one of the reasons young children learn so readily seems to be that they are less self-conscious about making errors.[2] Of course, young children often do not realize that they have made an error (for example, in interpreting a statement), whereas adults are more likely to do so. Nevertheless, to be effective problem solvers we must be willing to take the chance that we may not always be correct. The IDEAL problem solver realizes that problem solving is a self-correcting activity that allows for improvement only if we are willing to act on our best ideas.

▋ Notes

1. I. Rubin, What the "good language learner" can teach us. *Teachers of English to Speakers of Other Languages Quarterly* 9 (1975):41–51.
2. J. D. Bransford and K. Heldmeyer, Learning from children learning. In G. L. Bisanz and R. Kail (eds.), *Learning in Children*. New York: Springer-Verlag, 1983.

ANSWERS TO PROBLEMS
IN TEXT

Chapter 1

Answer to letter puzzles:
Scrambled eggs   Backward glance   Banana split

Answer to the bird and train problem:
Since the two train stations are 50 miles apart and the trains are traveling toward each other, each will travel 25 miles before they meet. Both trains are traveling at the rate of 25 miles per hour, so the time it takes for them to meet is 1 hour. Since the bird flies at a rate of 100 miles per hour, it will fly 100 miles before the two trains meet.

Chapter 2

Answer to the boxes problem:
There are 33 boxes (3 large, 6 medium, and 24 small).

Answer to the four chains problem:
The most common tendency is to work only with the end links of each chain. The solution requires that you open all the links in one of the chains (for a total of three links open at 2 cents apiece, or 6 cents). You can then use three open links to join the remaining three chains together (for a total of three links closed at 3 cents apiece, or 9 cents).

Answer to the trip to Chicago problem:
You need to take the 6 P.M. dinner flight, which will allow you to arrive at 6 A.M. If you did not arrive until 7:30, you would be late for your meeting, since you need 20 minutes to get your luggage and 20 minutes more for

a taxi ride. If you take the 6 P.M. flight, you will not need to buy dinner, since it is supplied on the plane.

Answer to racquetball tournament problem:
If you assume that only two people will be in the tournament, you will need only one score card for that match. If three people enter, you will need two score cards (one for the first match and one for the winner of that match versus the third participant). If four people enter, you will need three cards (one for each of the two initial matches and one more for the match between the winners of the two initial matches). If we let N stand for the number of people who play in the tournament, the general pattern for the number of cards needed is $N - 1$.

Alternative cookbook holder

Thick Lucite pieces fit into solid oak base with 5 notches, move to accommodate any size book

Figure A.1   A book holder that also guards against stains.

Answer to the cannonball problem:
There are a number of different ways to solve this problem. Here is one. On the first weighing, try four balls on each side. If the scales balance, you know that the oddball is one of the four not on the scale. If they do not balance, you know that the oddball is one of the eight balls on the scale.

Assume that the scales do not balance. You can now remove four balls from one side and replace them with the four that have not been weighed. Since you know that this new set of four does not contain the oddball, you can use it as a standard for weight.

For example, assume that you weigh this standard against four balls and the scales balance. You now know that the oddball is one of the four you just removed from the scale. If you also note whether these four balls are heavier or lighter in the second weighing, you will know whether the oddball is heavier or lighter than the other balls.

Assume that you have now reduced the options to four balls. For the third weighing, you can weigh two of these balls against two of the balls of standard weight. If the scales balance you know that the oddball is one of only two remaining balls. You can then use the fourth weighing to balance one of these two against one of the standards. If the scales balance you know that the one remaining ball is the oddball. If they do not balance, you know that the oddball is the one not on the scale (and not the standard you have been using). This problem can also be solved using just three weighings.

Chapter 3

Answer to the Einstein problem:
The clock would appear to be going backwards.

Answer to the bird in the room problem:
The instructor turned out all the lights in the seminar room. The bird immediately headed toward the light from the window and escaped from the room through the window.

Chapter 4

Answer to the typing and grades problem:
The relationship between typed papers and higher grades is correlational. Although it is possible that students get higher grades *because* they type their papers, it is equally possible that students who are more serious about their education are more likely to learn to type, that students who are more motivated are more likely to take the time to type their papers, and so on.

Answer to the gas-saving device problem:
You would need to know whether the gas mileage of the two cars was comparable *before* the gas-saving device was used. In addition, you would

want to be sure that the device was effective for other makes of cars, especially your own.

Answer to the rebate problem:
You need to know how many people of each income category purchased products that had the $1 rebate form. For example, there are probably fewer people in the higher income category than in the lower and middle income categories. Furthermore, assume that only 4100 people in the higher income category purchased the product. If 4000 of them sent for the rebate, this very high percentage could indicate that people with high incomes are *more* likely to send in rebate forms.

Answers to the "If it is a triangle, then it is red" problem (If A, then B):
The first problem (if the shape is not a triangle, is it not red?) can be expressed as "If A, then B; not A, therefore not B." To reason in this manner would be to commit the fallacy of denying the antecedent. The argument is not valid.

  The second problem (if the shape is not red, is it not a triangle?) can be expressed as "If A, then B; not B, therefore not A." This is a valid argument.

Answer to the mop problem:
Sally used a dirty mop.

Answer to the "John is able to come to the party tonight" problem:
John was originally going to leave town in his car and hence would have had to miss the party. However, since his car broke down, he could now attend.

Answer to the wrinkled dress problem:
Jill does not know how to iron.

Answer to the murder problem:
The woman cannot be prosecuted because she is a Siamese twin and the law prohibits an innocent person from being jailed.

Chapter 6

Answer to credits and debits problem:
One strategy is to remember that the word *credits* has an *r* in it, so credits go on the right.

Answer to the poisonous snakes problem:
One possibility is to create a rhyme, such as "Red and black venom lack; red and yellow kill a fellow."

Answer to port and starboard problem:
One strategy is to remember, "Left is shorter than right, and port is shorter than starboard."Another is "Port [a type of wine] should be *left* standing before drinking it."

Chapter 7

Answer to the theater joke:
The joke, which was told by Dick Cavett, goes as follows: "I have some good news and some bad news for people in the balcony. I am not going to tell you the bad news, but the good news is that the flames won't reach you for several minutes."

Answer to the card game problem:
If both players remove cards from the table at the same time, neither one can run out of cards first. Furthermore, what card can be added to the card with a 0 on it to add up to 10?

APPENDIX B

ANSWERS TO EXERCISES

Chapter 2

1. Most people produce the answer 2, which is wrong. The correct answer is 0. If you answered 2, you probably failed to identify a problem with the problem; namely, that it asks about Adam rather than Noah.

2. This is another example of how people fail to identify of a problem with their own interpretation. Did you notice the two *the*'s in the first and third phrases and the two *a*'s in the second phrase?

3. The inventors of the talking scale seem to have identified some real problems that people face. For example, an advertisement for a talking scale we saw asks

> Can't see over your tummy?
>
> Can't read the numbers way down there?
>
> Can't remember whether you lost weight?

However, there may be some situations in which you would not want to use this scale. For example, many people would not want their weight revealed in places where others might hear it.

4. The inventors of the sound-activated light switch also identified some problems that this device can help people solve. In particular, it can

> Hear you coming and switch on, so you won't come home to a dark house or garage.
>
> Surprise burglars who enter your house.

However, the device may not be appropriate for all situations. For example, the switch will turn off the lights after a short period of time if it does not continue to detect noise. This would probably not be appreciated in a reading room.

5. The description of the solar watch cap reads, "Warms head nicely. . . . Collector must face south for optimum heating effect, so rotation of hat or wearer may be necessary in extreme cold." This item is from a collection of humorous gadgets in A. Gingold, *Items from our Catalog,* New York: Avon Books, 1982.

6. This shovel is supposed to help relieve back strain. The advertisement states that the bend in the shovel reduces the amount of bending you will have to do. We are not sure how this bend affects the durability and performance of the shovel.

7. These are flip-down makeup glasses. They consist of magnifying glasses on hinges that can be flipped down on one side when the wearer wants to apply makeup or put on a contact lens, allowing her to see through the other eye.

8. This is a new kind of chair designed to allow your body to relax in a position of natural balance. The goal is to help relieve pain in the back, neck, hip joints, and upper legs.

9. Punctuation marks are designed to solve a general problem with written language, which is that it loses pauses and tones of voice that convey questions, exclamations, and so forth. Punctuation marks supply this information in written form.

10. The important role played by punctuation marks can be ap-

preciated by comparing your comprehension of the string of words in the text to the following:

> That that is is not that that is not.
> Is that it? It is!

11. Part of the difficulty with this problem results from incorrect definition of the problem. Notice that the problem is not to find the exact spot or time at which the event will occur. Instead, the problem is to show that there is a spot that will be occupied at the same time of day on both trips. The precise day the trips are made is not especially relevant. One helpful strategy is to imagine that there are actually two monks making this trip on the same day; one monk is walking up the trail, and one monk is walking down the trail. There must be one spot on the trail where the monks meet.

12. This problem requires a careful scheme for representing all the information given. Try designing a table in which each person is represented at the top and side. Then fill in the table to keep track of which people shook hands with each other. You can start off by arbitrarily assigning a number to each person. After each such assignment, look back and see if any specific conclusions can be drawn. Let H = husband and W = wife.

   a. Let H1 be the person who shook hands with eight people.
   b. The person who shook hands with zero people had to be his spouse (W1).
   c. Let H2 be the person who shook hands with seven people.
   d. Since everyone else shook hands at least twice, W2 had to be the person who shook hands once.
   e. Let H3 be the person who shook hands with six people.
   f. W3 has to be the person who shook hands with two people.
   g. Let H4 be the person who shook hands with five people.
   h. W4 has to be the person who shook hands with three people.
   i. Let H5 be the person who shook hands with four people.
   j. W5 had to shake hands with four people also.

Since each person the psychologist asked gave a different answer, the only couple both halves of which could have shaken hands four times each would be the psychologist and his wife (he was the only one about whom we did not have data). Therefore, his wife shook hands four times.

| | Couple 1 | | Couple 2 | | Couple 3 | | Couple 4 | | Couple 5 | |
	H1	W1	H2	W2	H3	W3	H4	W4	H5	W5
H1	0	0	X	X	X	X	X	X	X	X
W1	0	0	0	0	0	0	0	0	0	0
H2	X	0	0	0	X	X	X	X	X	X
W2	X	0	0	0	0	0	0	0	0	0
H3	X	0	X	0	0	0	X	X	X	X
W3	X	0	X	0	0	0	0	0	0	0
H4	X	0	X	0	X	0	0	0	X	X
W4	X	0	X	0	X	0	0	0	0	0
H5	X	0	X	0	X	0	X	0	0	0
W5	X	0	X	0	X	0	X	0	0	0

13. This problem can be solved easily by examining specific cases. Try working out the problem with specific numbers and various combinations of colored beads, and you will discover that the answer is yes.

	Red-bead jar	Blue-bead jar
Assume 50 beads in jar	$5OR - 5R = 45R$	$50B + 5R$
Assume 1 red bead is moved back	$45R + (1R + 4B)$	$(50B + 5R) - (1R + 4B)$
Result	$46R + 4B$	$46JB + 4R$

14. Most people have a difficult time solving this problem. The usual response is that the paper will extend 1 or 2 feet after

50 folds. However, a systematic analysis of each step plus some mathematical tools shows that these answers are way off the mark.

Consider the following calculations. If the paper is originally 0.001 inch thick, it is 2 times thicker after folding it once (2 × 0.001). When the paper is folded a second time, it again becomes twice as thick, which is 4 times the original thickness; that is, 2 × 2(0.001) inch thick, or $2^2(0.001)$. When it is folded a third time it becomes 8 times as thick as the original, or $2^3(0.001)$—this is double the thickness after the second fold. Similarly, the fourth fold is $2^4(0.001)$ times as thick as the original. Thus, 50 folds of the tissue paper would equal 2^{50} (0.001), which is about 17,770,000 miles. This is considerably larger than the 2 or 3 feet of thickness most people estimate. Indeed, it is more than one-quarter the distance from Venus to Earth.

15. This problem also requires a systematic analysis of each step (fish 1 eats two 2s for a total of two 2s, each 2 eats two 3s for a total of four 3s, each 3 eats two 4s for a total of eight 4s, and so on. This shows us the beginning of a geometric progression (2, 4, 8, etc.). Mathematical tools make it much easier to solve this problem. The formula is 2^6, for a total of 64 size 7 fish that must be eaten each day.

Incidentally, it is this progression in the food chain that results in "biological magnification." Even a small percentage of toxins in a lake can become much more concentrated in larger fish because they eat a large number of small fish each day.

16. When the robot is seen in context, some of its design flaws become more apparent. For example, its sponges are too big to be dipped into its head (the bucket). Furthermore, since the arms do not bend, the robot will push itself off the building if it lowers its arms much farther.

Gleaning information from observing things in context is analogous to acting on the basis of some idea or invention and then looking at the effects. If we ignore the *act* and *look* components of problem solving, we will often fail to spot flaws in our ideas. Ideally, we should spot flows by means of imagination or the use of prototypes so that they can be corrected as soon as possible and with the least expense.

17. The common answer to this problem is 5. However, if you imagine making and smoking the cigars and then look at the effects, you will see that the correct answer is 6. The man can
make one additional cigar from the butts of the other 5.
18. This is a problem that can be worked backward very easily. If
the greenhouse is completely full on day 29, on the day
before that (day 28) it will be half full.
19. Many people assume that the hospital is for people. In this
case the problem concerns an animal hospital.
20. This problem is often solved incorrectly because people fail to
look back and carefully evaluate their strategy. In fact, an incorrect answer to this problem was published in *Parade*

Magazine. The author of the column "Ask Marilyn" acknow-ledged the mistake after a reader pointed it out in a letter. Many people think that the problem states that a hen and a half produce an egg and a half every day. They then figure that it will take one hen to produce six eggs in six days. The problem really states that it will take a day and a half for a hen and a half to produce an egg and a half. Thus, one and a half hens should lay the equivalent of one egg every day, or six eggs in six days.

21. This is a problem that can be solved by working backward. On the last move of the game you want to be able to pick up 1 to 5 coins to win. To do that you have to leave your op-ponent 6 coins on the preceding turn. To be able to leave 6 coins on the previous turn you must leave 12 coins on the turn before that. The only way you can be certain of leaving 12 coins for your opponent is to make the first move and remove 3 coins. Of course, if you are playing someone who is not aware of this strategy, it will be possible to win even if your opponent goes first, as long as he or she does not remove 3 coins on the first turn. While this particular version of Nim is played with 15 coins, other versions can be played with any number of coins, matches, or other small objects. The objects are grouped into any number of piles and players can remove all or part of a pile on each turn. See if you can find a strategy to win this more general version of Nim.[1]

22. This problem can be solved by working out or testing specific cases. For example, if both people are truthtellers, do the answers coincide with what they would say? In this case, yes. Note that if the first person was a liar, the second person could not be a truthteller, because he or she told you that the first person was a truthteller. Similarly, if the first person was a liar, the second person could not be a liar because he or she told the truth that the first person said he or she was a truth-teller.

23. This problem can be solved by working backward. The man paid his last dollar to get out of the third casino. That means that after he lost half his money at the third casino, he had $1. He must have had $2 before he lost. Since he paid $1 to get in, we know that he had $3 after he left the second casino. Since he had to pay $1 to leave the second casino we

know he had a total of $4 after he lost half of his money there. This means he must have started with $8. Since he paid $1 to get into the second casino, we know he had $9 after he left the first casino. He paid $1 to leave the first casino, which means he had $10 after he lost half of his money. He must have started with $20 plus the $1 he paid to get into the first casino. The man started with $21.

Chapter 3

1. Most people generate such inventions as a magnifying glass, an underwater sound amplifier, or an underwater light. These are all fine answers, but it is useful to ask whether they are constrained by any assumptions. For example, these inventions are designed to help people enjoy live fish in an aquarium. However, the problem of helping people enjoy the sight of tropical fish in their own homes could also be solved by an aquarium videotape. In fact, such tapes are on the market and can be bought in many video stores.

2. The simplest solution is to pour the water from the next to last glass on the left into the next-to-last glass on the right. Many people fail to generate this solution because they assume that the water cannot be poured from one glass into another.

3. Most people generate such reasons as

> Wants the exercise.
> Needs the exercise.
> Wants to surprise you.
> Wants to visit someone on the way.
> The elevator is broken.

All of these involve assume that the cousin is essentially normal. An alternative possibility is that the cousin is so short that he cannot reach the higher buttons. He therefore punches the highest button he can reach and walks from there.

4. The most obvious solution to this problem is the one least often generated. Simply throw the ball straight up in the air. It will eventually stop and reverse direction.

5. The most common error made with this problem is to assume that you must stay within the imaginary lines that form the square. The solution illustrated below is based on going outside these lines.

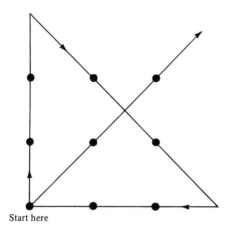

Start here

6. This problem is similar to the classic nine-dot problem in that people tend to make assumptions that are not necessarily true and that make a solution impossible. In this case most people assume that the tire tracks were produced by a car. The only reason the sheriff knew which man he wanted was that the tire tracks were produced by a wheelchair, and the man sitting in the middle of the porch was in a wheelchair.[2]

7. A seeming inconsistency in the passage is that the man took off his overcoat, yet the passage says it was cold and dark. But assume that the car had fallen into a lake ("his submerged car came to a halt"). Now the apparent inconsistency between the low temperature and the act of removing the coat is resolved.

8. People have difficulty solving this problem when they assume that the eggs came from a chicken. In this case they were duck eggs.

9. People have difficulty solving this problem when they assume that the end of the rope is anchored to something. In this case it is not.

10. People have difficulty solving this problem when they assume

that the fall occurred outside the building. In this case it happened inside.

11. People have difficulty solving this problem when they assume that the boys must crawl through the pipe at the same time. The problem does not state that they must crawl through the pipe at the same time. It is easy if you assume that Jim crawls through the pipe first in one direction and then Tom crawls through the pipe in the opposite direction.

12. They stand back-to-back.

15. He was bald.

16. The new baby was Bill.

Chapter 4

1. This statement encourages the reader to make many inferences, but what it actually means may be quite different from those invited inferences. For example, it could mean that nine out of ten doctors surveyed have at one time or another recommended this product to at least one person (not necessarily a patient and not necessarily to the exclusion of other similar products). It does not necessarily mean that the doctors prefer this product or advise patients to use it more than they do any other product. Try to think of some unusual products or substances that could legitimately fit this claim.

2. An advertising claim similar to this was used by the Chrysler Corporation to promote one of its luxury cars. They compared their car to vehicles manufactured by more recognized luxury-car makers like Mercedes Benz and BMW. The invited inference is that the Chrysler product is as good as or better than the other well-known luxury models, but the factual evidence does not support such a conclusion. For example, it would be possible for the Chrysler vehicle to outperform at least one vehicle on each of the tests and still rank last in overall performance.

3. Many people who hear this advertisment might conclude that the Dodge is rated better than cars made by other manufacturers. Actually, people were comparing the new Dodge to their own old cars. It is not surprising that many people would prefer a new car in place of their old car. People who hear this ad might also conclude that 70 percent of Toyota

and Honda owners prefer a Dodge. Actually, the facts presented do not specify whether 70 percent of the owners of each competitor's vehicle preferred a new Dodge or whether 100 percent of the owners of two of the competitors' vehicles preferred a new Dodge and 40 percent of the owners of the other two competitors' vehicles preferred a new Dodge.[3]

4. Assuming that all the children were of a comparable age and received comparable achievement tests, we would still want to have additional information, especially about the sample of students tested. Was the average score for American children lowest because all American children are required to go to school, even those who are not interested, whereas such children were not included in the sample from other countries? Data relevant to this question would include whether the best American students (the top one-third) did as well as the best in other countries. This would indicate whether the average scores say more about sampling than about the quality of instruction students receive.

5. This is an amazing advertisement.[4] If you read the print carefully you will see that this is an ordinary pair of rabbit ears with a decorative dish on it. The claims are factually accurate and consistent. Why would anyone purchase one of these devices?

6. There are a number of problems with this statement. One possible reason for higher incomes is that the first school may teach courses (like business) whose majors usually receive higher salaries than those who major in courses (like education) taught by the second school. A second possible reason may be that the first university has been in operation much longer, and therefore its graduates have had time to earn higher salaries because of seniority. A third possible reason may be that the first university attracts better students in the first place. They may graduate and earn more only because they began at a higher level, not because the instructional program is inherently better.

7. The relationship between grades and computers is correlational. Computers at home could contribute to better grades, but it is also possible that students who get better grades are more likely to take an interest in computers, or that parents who take an active role in their children's intellectual development

influence their children to perform better in school and are more likely to buy computers to improve the learning environment at home. If the school board wanted to know if computers at home actually influenced performance in school, it would need to conduct a controlled experiment.

8. This finding is part of a series of investigations known as the Hawthorne studies, which were conducted at the Western Electric Hawthorne plant. The findings are indicative of what some have labeled the Hawthorne effect. In these investigations worker productivity at times improved and at other times remained unchanged regardless of the illumination level in which workers operated. For example, in one experiment the lighting was *reduced* to the intensity of ordinary moonlight and subjects still maintained their production level. In another study, when light bulbs were replaced with bulbs of the same intensity, subjects reported that they liked the increased illumination. Although it is difficult to draw clear conclusions from the Hawthorne studies, the findings suggest that people's performance can be affected when they think management is interested in their problems.[5]

9. No. None of the men who love strawberry pie live on Gorky Street. See the diagram below.

Figure B.4

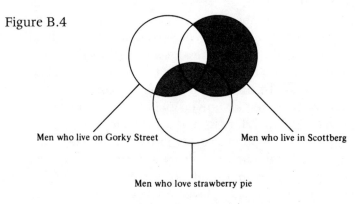

Men who live on Gorky Street   Men who live in Scottberg

Men who love strawberry pie

(Shaded areas denote no members)

10. No. It is possible that some xenos are not red. See the diagram below.

Figure B.5

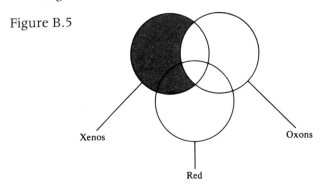

(Shaded areas denote no members)

11. Yes. See the diagram below.

Figure B.6

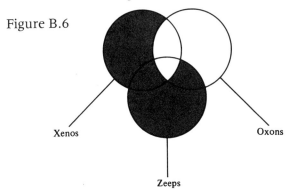

(Shaded areas denote no members.)

12. No. It is possible that some pennies are not silver. See the diagram below.

Figure B.7

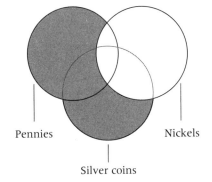

13. No. I may have skipped the party yet still failed to do my homework. The form of reasoning being used here is "If A (go to party), then B (cannot do my homework)." If one were to reason "B, therefore A," one would be committing the fallacy of affirming the consequent.

14. No. There may be other reasons interest rates were raised. The form of reasoning being used here is "If A (the annual inflation rate rises above 7 percent), then B (the Federal Reserve Bank will raise interest rates)." If one were to reason "Not A, therefore not B," one would be committing the fallacy of denying the antecedent.

15. No. The form of reasoning being used here is "If A (we put more money into public education) then B (we will not necessarily improve education)." If one were to reason "Not A (we do not put more money into education), therefore not B (we will necessarily improve education)" we would be committing the fallacy of denying the antecedent.

16. Although the form of logical reasoning that leads to such a conclusion is valid, this is a clear case in which not only a theory but also additional assumptions that relate that theory to observable data are being tested. For example, it is possible that the theory is correct and yet injections of RNA will have no immediate effect on memory. It is also possible that the site of the injection could be an important determinant of the effect observed, that the injection must be given several days in advance, and so forth.

17. It is most likely that the evidence used to support this conclusion came from correlational data. It would be unethical to conduct an experiment in which depression (or any other variable thought to be responsible for a person's well-being) was manipulated. In a correlational study it is difficult to draw conclusions about causality. In this case, it seems possible that the severity of a patient's illness might be causing the depression.

18. This game will have no winner, because players will quickly encounter a situation in which neither player can advance without breaking the rule of never occupying the same square simultaneously.

19. The first step is to define the problem. What information is being requested? Is the problem to differentiate the liar from

the one who is truthful or simply to obtain correct directions? In the first problem the task is to obtain correct directions. Since only one question can be asked, the problem really becomes "What question will the liar and the one who is truthful both answer correctly?" Lying is negating the truth, so one might think about situations in which negation or negatives can be eliminated. For example, in grammar a double negative is really a positive and in mathematics multiplying two negative numbers results in a positive number. To use a similar strategy in this problem, we would need to ask a question that required the liar to lie twice. One way to do this is to ask a question such as "If I asked you if this was the correct path would you say yes?"

20. In the second problem the task is really to differentiate the liar from the brother who tells the truth or to formulate a question that each will answer differently. This problem is related to the previous example in that it involves a double negative—the liar lies but is always misinformed—so that the answer is correct. When will the two brothers answer questions differently? Since both the truthful brother and the liar will give an answer that is usually correct, all we need to do is ask either of them about themselves or the other brother. For example, if asked, "Are you a liar?" the truthful brother would say no. The liar would think he wasn't a liar but would lie about it and say yes. A question such as "Is your brother a liar?" will produce similar results.

Chapter 6

1. How many stops did the bus make? Most people are not prepared for this question. They anticipated a different question; namely, how many people were left on the bus? Different strategies are necessary to prepare for these different questions. This is a good illustration of how a strategy may or may not be the most appropriate depending on the memory problem one is attempting to solve.

   What was the name of the bus driver? Most people have a difficult time answering this question from memory because they cannot remember being told anyone's name. If you look back at the first sentence of the passage, you will see that the answer is quite familiar to you.

2. An acrostic for remembering the cranial nerves that has been around for some time is "On old Olympus' towering tops a Finn and German vend some hops."

3. A helpful acrostic for remembering whether to set one's clock forward or back an hour is "Spring forward and fall back."

4. You could combine the rhyming peg-word system (one is a bun, two is a shoe, and so on) and an acrostic in the following manner. Think of the acrostic "You must wear two shoes to get in the door and stand in line." From the peg-word system you know that "two is a shoe" (so two shoes equals 22). Similarly, you know from the peg-word system that "four is a door" (so door helps you remember the number 4) and that "nine is a line" (so line helps you remember 9).

5. You could use acrostics such as "Fir is smooth" and "A rough hem stands out." For the latter, think of "hem" as short for hemlock and think of "standing out" as a rough twig.

6. For "across," an example using acrostics is "You only cross the gate to heaven once." Let "across" remind you of "cross" and let "once" remind you of the number of *c*'s.

7. For "facilitate," you might say to yourself that "the face of a penny has one picture of Lincoln." Let facilitate remind you of "face" and let the thought of one picture of Lincoln (which begins with an *l*) remind you that the word contains only one *l*.

8. For "development," you might think, "When you want to develop film, people should not enter the darkroom while the process is going on." Let "development" remind you of develop (as in developing the film) and let "do not enter" remind you of "no *e*" after the word *develop*.

9. You might imagine someone climbing a big hill (for the first part of his last name) and use the sound of the last part of his name to signify Everest.

10. One possibility is to let the *bert* part of Hubert remind you of dirt and to let *Booth* remind you of boots. Dirt left by boots needs to be removed, preferably by a vacuum cleaner.

11. You could let John remind you of Johnny Appleseed, and let Appleseed remind you of the Apple in Apple Computer Corporation. Let the *Scull* in Sculley remind you of a skull, the place where human intelligence is located. You can remem-

ber the *computer* in Apple Computer Corporation by thinking of where artificial intelligence is found.

12. For Harriet Eisely you might let her flowing hair remind you of Harriet and her distinctive eyes remind you of Eiseley.

13. For Lynn Foreman you might let his big chin remind you of Lynn (they rhyme) and let his big forehead remind you of Foreman.

14. For Rose Lipman you could let her round face remind you of something like "ring around the rosey" and her thin lips remind you of Lipman.

15. You can imagine the first letter in *dromedary* and *Bactrian*, capitalized and lying on its side. The D has one hump and the B has two humps.

16. You might look at the ending of each word. If you can remember to eliminate the *r*, one ending sounds like the woman's name, *Jenny (gyny)*, and the other sounds like the man's name Andy.

17. Some examples of macros we have found easy to remember are

CTRL U	underline function
CTRL B	boldface type
CTRL C	center text
CTRL +	superscript text
CTRL −	subscript text

Chapter 7

Possible answers include

1. Spider web
2. Lawn sprinkler
3. Parking meter
4. Wet paint
5. Cement mixer
6. Igloo
7. Bagpipes

Some possible answers are

8. Thermal underwear
9. The inside story
10. Downtown

11. Reading between the lines
12. A terrible spell of weather
13. He's beside himself
14. Neon lights
15. As noted in the text, people need to make inferences in order to comprehend. If they lack the background knowledge, it must be supplied. The instructions could be improved if they clarified the need to insert the pencil in the hole, how much pressure to apply to the pencil, how long to continue cranking, and what to use as a reference in determining the clockwise direction. For people who have never used a pencil, it might also be necessary to clarify the purpose of the pencil sharpener, the time it will take to perform the operation, which end of the pencil to insert, and what the finished product will look like.
16. One way to help children understand the significance of the previous facts about camels is to help them see how these features permit camels to survive in deserts. One characteristic of deserts is sudden, severe sandstorms that can have adverse effects on the eyes, nose, and ears. Camels' eyelids, nasal passages, and ear openings have evolved to protect against sandstorms.
17. Children who understand the significance of these characteristics of camels should be better able to understand other facts, such as why people traveling across a desert wear veils over their faces despite the heat.
18. Many people miss this problem because they fail to gain access to knowledge that is potentially available to them. The most common mistake is to assume that the spy begins drilling inside the *left cover of the book on the left* and that he continues drilling until he reaches the *right cover of the book on the right*. People who make this mistake have usually failed to imagine picking up the first book, opening it, and starting to read on the first page. *The first page is on the right of the first book.* Similarly, the last page of the second book is on its left. The hole drilled by the spy therefore goes through only two book covers (each ¼ inch thick), for a total of ½ inch.

    This example illustrates a common problem. We often fail to gain access to relevant information (such as where the first and last pages in a book are found). Once we are prompted to use this information, our errors seem obvious. The IDEAL problem solver constantly works to minimize such access errors.

19. Most people can develop effective techniques for remembering this confusing relationship. For example, we have found that the phrase "During the day, I see light," can be used to help us remember that during the day the breeze moves from sea to land. At night, the breeze will move in the opposite direction. Because these memory strategies do not help us understand the concept, however, using them will not prepare us to apply that knowledge to problems. For example, people who simply memorize the information will probably not know whether a sea breeze like the one described above will occur when the sky is very cloudy. In contrast, learning strategies that enhance our understanding of phenomena will

Figure B.8

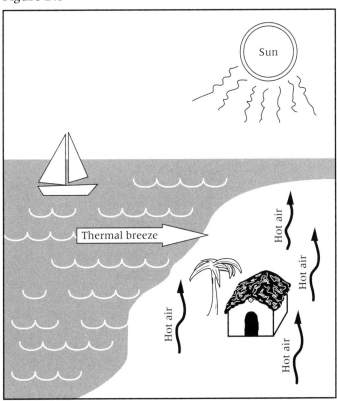

prepare us to solve problems. For example, a sea breeze or thermal breeze is caused in part by air being heated. During the day, the sun heats the surface of the land faster than the water. The air above the land, in turn, is heated and rises like a hot-air balloon. Cooler air above the water moves in to fill the void, creating a breeze from the sea to the land. See if you can explain why and when the breeze will move from the land to the sea at night.

■ Notes

1. Nim is described in F. V. Grunfeld, *Games of the World: How to Make Them—How to Play Them—How They Came to Be.* New York: Plenary Publications and Swiss Committee for Unicef, 1975. Grunfeld notes that the game of Nim was enjoyed for centuries until the mathematician Charles Leonard Bouton described a formula, in 1901, that ensured victory to any player acquainted with it.
2. Joe Hatcher, personal communication with the authors, 1982.
3. A discussion of this advertisement appeared in the column "Selling It," *Consumer Reports,* August 1992., p. 551.
4. Copyright 1989, R. B. M. Limited, 1200 Shames Drive, Westbury, New York.
5. Many scholars have raised questions about the conclusions that can be drawn from the Hawthorne studies. See R. Gillespie, *Manufacturing Knowledge: A History of the Hawthorne Experiments.* New York: Cambridge University Press, 1991; S. R. G. Jones, Was there a Hawthorne effect? *American Journal of Sociology* 98(1992):451–468.

IDEAL PROBLEM
NAVIGATION GUIDE

Identify the problem and explain how it can be an opportunity.

_____

_____

_____

Define at least three different goals for your problem-solving task.

Goal 1:

_____

Goal 2:

_____

Goal 3:

_____

Explore possible strategies and new information that could help you accomplish each of the important goals listed above.

Strategies and information to accomplish **Goal 1**

_____

Strategies and information to accomplish **Goal 2**

_____

Strategies and information to accomplish **Goal 3**

_____

Anticipate the outcomes of different strategies to help you decide which ones you will **act** on.

Strategy _____

Possible Positive Outcomes	Possible Negative Outcomes

Strategy _____

Possible Positive Outcomes	Possible Negative Outcomes

Strategy _____

Possible Positive Outcomes	Possible Negative Outcomes

Strategy _____

Possible Positive Outcomes	Possible Negative Outcomes

Strategy _____

Possible Positive Outcomes	Possible Negative Outcomes

Strategy _____

Possible Positive Outcomes	Possible Negative Outcomes

Look back and **Learn.**

After acting on your strategies, what did you notice about the problem you identified?

_____

_____

_____

After acting on your strategies, what did you notice about the goals you defined?

_____

_____

_____

After acting on your strategies, what did you notice about the strategies you explored?

_____

_____

_____

After acting on your strategies, what did you notice about your ability to anticipate their effects?

_____

_____

_____

AUTHOR INDEX

SUBJECT INDEX

ISBN 0-7167-2204-6

EAN

9 780716 722045

90000 >